CHARLES RENNIE MACKINTOSH'S ITALY

GEORGE RAWSON

Stenlake Publishing Ltd

St. Peter's, Rome

First published in the United Kingdom, 2020
Stenlake Publishing Ltd
54-58 Mill Square, Catrine, KA5 6RD
Telephone 01290 551122
email: enquiries@stenlake.co.uk
www.stenlake.co.uk

Copyright © George Rawson

The moral right of the author has been asserted.
All rights reserved.
Without limiting the rights under copyright reserved above, no part of this publication may be reproduced, stored in or introduced into a retrieval system. or transmitted in any form or by any means (electronic, mechanical, photocopying, recording or otherwise) without the prior written permission of the copyright owner and the above publisher of this book.

Designed by Ashley Rawson

Printed by Claro Print

ISBN 9781840338782

Palazzo Vecchio, Venice

Contents

- Glasgow School of Art — 4
- Acknowledgements & Picture Credits — 5
- The Author — 6
- Map of Italy — 8
- The Italian Tour — 9
- Chapter 1: Background to the Tour — 10
- Chapter 2: Naples and Palermo — 18
- Chapter 3: Rome — 30
- Chapter 4: Orvieto, Siena and Florence — 40
- Chapter 5: Pisa to Ferrara — 50
- Chapter 6: Venice to Como — 56
- Chapter 7: Milan and Pavia — 68
- Chapter 8: Influence of the Tour — 76
- Appendix 1: Catalogue of drawings — 89
- Appendix 2: 1892 Lecture illustrations — 121
- Appendix 3: Student reference books — 121
- Bibliography — 122
- Index — 124

Glasgow School of Art

The Glasgow School of Art building was Mackintosh's masterwork as an architect. Designed and built in two stages, 1896-99 and 1907-09, the School housed a collection of artworks of international significance produced by Mackintosh and his contemporaries which covered the whole of his career, from his admission as a student in 1883 until his death in 1928. Despite two devastating fires which the building suffered in 2014 and 2018, a large part of this collection survives as an indispensible source for researchers.

The School's Archives include an extensive range of photographs, correspondence and documentation relating to Mackintosh's time as a student and the subsequent development of the Mackintosh building.

The Collections include almost 300 works designed or made by Mackintosh, providing outstanding and often unique examples of his achievements as an architect, designer and artist. These comprise original designs for a number of his most important private buildings, an extensive range of items for the celebrated Glasgow tea rooms, a series of architectural drawings for the Mackintosh building, plus symbolist watercolours, still life compositions and late French landscapes. These demonstrate the full range of Mackintosh's work throughout his career.

For more information, visit www.gsa.ac.uk/archives.

West wing, Glasgow School of Art

Acknowledgements

Acknowledgements

The research for this book began with an analysis of the contents of Mackintosh's North Italian Sketchbook in the Glasgow School of Art's Archives and Collections. The idea came from Elaine Grogan who had published a book based on the National Library of Ireland's sketchbook which covers southern and central Italy. It quickly became apparent that my study should cover all of Mackintosh's Italian drawings and watercolours, many of which were in public and private collections and had featured in exhibitions and sales. The majority of these were well-documented having been included in exhibitions in Toronto, curated by Professor Thomas Howarth. When Howarth sold the bulk of his collection, it was catalogued by Roger Billcliffe, to whom I am grateful for help and advice. I am also indebted to Professor Pamela Robertson of the Hunterian Art Gallery at the University of Glasgow and Stuart Robertson, director of the Charles Rennie Mackintosh Society, for their encouragement and support.

I must also thank the Glasgow Institute of Architects for access to the Alexander Thomson Memorial Minute book.

The research involved four trips to Italy, two of which were supported by Glasgow School of Art's Architecture and Fine Art departments.

Ann, my travelling companion, gave invaluable help in locating and identifying the sources of the drawings. Special thanks are due to my colleague in the library of the Glasgow School of Art, David Buri, who researched Mackintosh's tour between Bologna and Ferrara and on Lake Como and checked my text in its early stages, and to Clare McGrade, Susannah Waters and Peter Trowles, past and present Archivists and Curator of Glasgow School of Art's Mackintosh Collection. Thanks to Anne Lindsay for checking the text and producing the index.

Picture Credits

T. & R. Annan, Glasgow: Front cover, p.15 above
Roger Billcliffe: pp.26, 61
Bridgeman Images: pp.25, 27, 34, 41, 46, 47
Eric Eunson Collection: p.10
Glasgow School of Art: pp.6-7
Glasgow School of Art Archives and Collections: pp.63, 65, 66 right, 70, 71 right, 72, 78 right, 81 below, 83 above left, below left, 84, 103, 104, 105
Glasgow School of Art Library: pp.11, 13 below, 14 above, 21, 33, 45, 59 left, 64, 75, 81 right, 95, 111
Hunterian Art Gallery, University of Glasgow: pp.42, 53, 85, 107 left
Mitchell Library, Glasgow: pp.79 above, below left, 81 left, 82 above, below, 83 above right
National Library of Ireland: pp.15 below, 23 left, 93, 98
Private Collection: pp.44, 110
Ashley Rawson: pp.12, 23 right
George Rawson: pp.6, 37, 43, 52 above, below, 54, 57, 66 left, 71 left, 74, 78 left, 79 below right, 83 below right, 84 below, 91
Giorgio Sommer: p.22
Richard Stenlake Collection: pp.2-3, 4, 13 above, 17, 18, 19, 20, 28, 30, 32, 36, 40, 49, 50, 55, 56, 68, 76, 86, 87, 88, 93, 98, 102, 105, 107, 110, 113, 117, 120
University of Strathclyde Archives: 107 right
Christine S. Wright: 59 right

The publishers are grateful to those listed above for permission to reproduce images. Every effort has been taken to trace copyright holders. Any we have been unable to identify are invited to contact the publishers.

CHARLES RENNIE MACKINTOSH'S ITALY

The Author

George Rawson is an art historian with a particular interest in 19th-century Britain who became acquainted with the work of Charles Rennie Mackintosh in 1968 and was a member of the library staff at the Glasgow School of Art from 1977 until 2006 where he was instrumental in helping to establish its Archives. In 1996 he completed a Ph.D. on Mackintosh's mentor, the painter and art educationalist Fra H. Newbery. He has curated two exhibitions on Newbery's work. In 2009 he contributed to a book and exhibition, *The Flower and the Green Leaf*, on Glasgow School of Art in the time of Charles Rennie Mackintosh. He also produced the website on Mackintosh's North Italian Sketchbook and worked on sketchbooks produced by Mackintosh in the British Isles in the collection of the Hunterian Art Gallery at the University of Glasgow. His interest in Italy goes back to 1960 when he first visited Rome and Venice.

Right: George Rawson working in The Glasgow School of Art Library in the 1980s

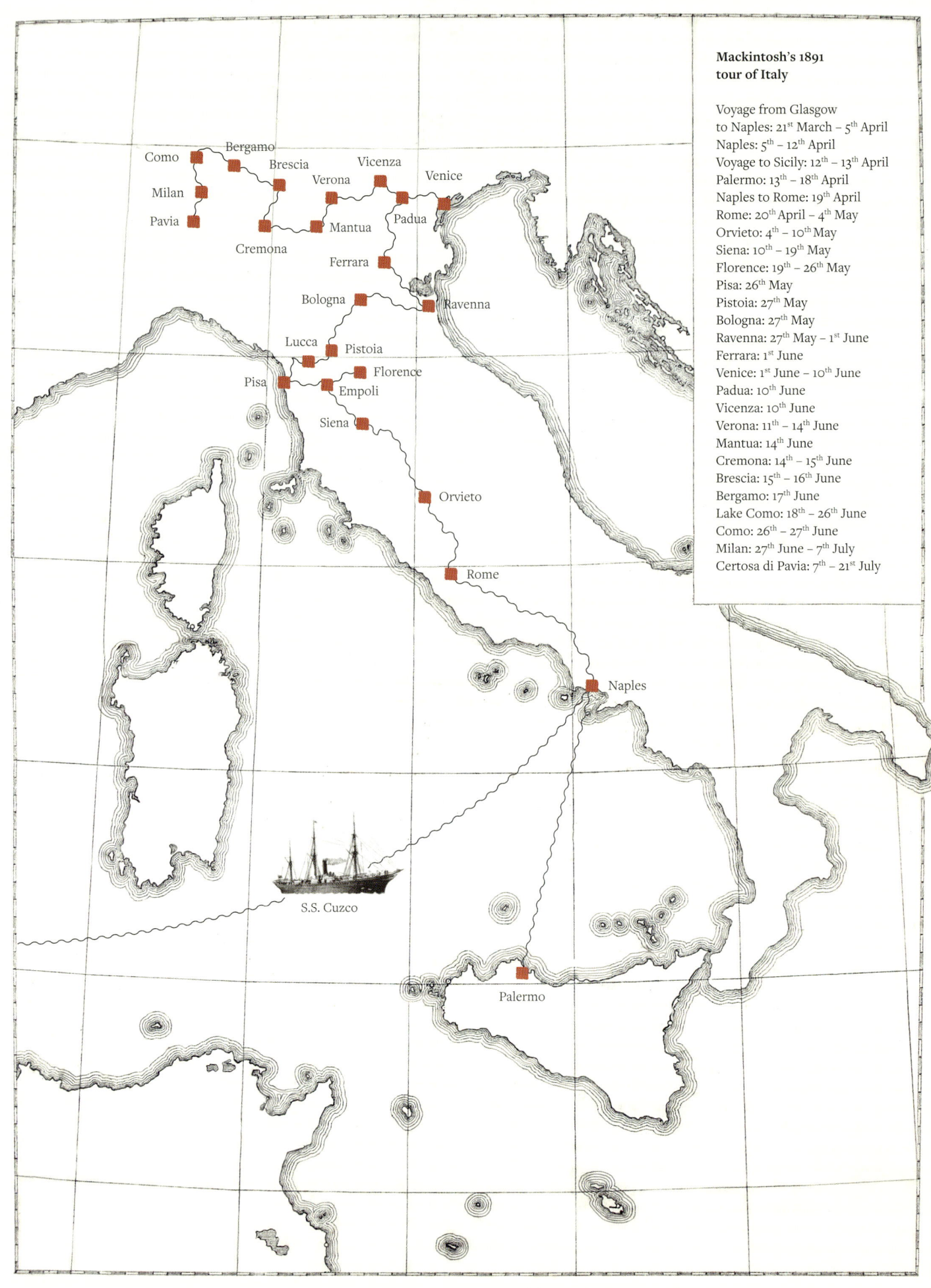

The Italian Tour

Charles Rennie Mackintosh's 1891 Italian tour is the best-documented aspect of his whole career in terms of primary sources. For most of his trip the young architect kept a diary; after his return he gave a lecture; and during and after his journey he corresponded with the secretary of the Alexander Thomson Trustees, the body which had awarded him the scholarship that enabled him to make his visit. All of these sources are available.[1] Additionally, most of the 200-plus sketches, drawings and watercolours produced on the tour still exist. Despite all this, the tour has received scant attention from scholars, almost certainly because it came at the very beginning of Mackintosh's career as an architect and designer. Aged 22, he had only just joined the firm of John Honeyman and Keppie as a draughtsman, and he would be a student at the Glasgow School of Art for another three years, the emergence of the Glasgow Style was still two years away,[2] and his work on the Glasgow School of Art building, the commission which saw him mature as an architect, was five years in the future.

Mackintosh's Italian drawings themselves are studies of historical buildings and ornament – many of them made in museums – and can easily be dismissed as mere student work of little interest to those who value him most as a precursor of Modernism. Thomas Howarth, Mackintosh's most important biographer, regarded the drawings as of little artistic merit,[3] and Mackintosh's engagement with Italy has been seen as having very little impact on his subsequent work.[4] Such an assessment can only be upheld, however, if Mackintosh's work between 1891 and 1896 is ignored. During that time he would be a prolific contributor to national student competitions and collaborated on the design of several buildings for Honeyman and Keppie. These schemes saw Mackintosh drawing on the resources amassed during his Italian tour. This is the first full attempt to look at the 1891 journey based on all the available sources. Mackintosh's tour has been followed on the ground, identifying most of the subjects for his drawings, occasionally correcting the artist's own attributions. The privilege of touring one of the world's most culturally exciting countries with such a perceptive companion who sees so much that many would pass by, and is ever ready to express an opinion even when it differs from the established canon, is to see Italy in a new and different way.

The quotations from Mackintosh's paper, held by the Hunterian Art Gallery, throughout the book, retain his punctuation but have corrected his idiosyncratic spelling.

Notes

[1] Pamela Robertson, editor, *Charles Rennie Mackintosh: the Architectural Papers* ((Oxford: White Cockade in association with the Hunterian Art Gallery, 1990)

[2] The earliest Glasgow Style work was publicity material produced by the Macdonald sisters for the 1893 Glasgow School of Art Club Exhibition. The Style came to prominence in the 1894 Exhibition. Distortion of the human figure, a feature of the Style, was already in evidence on the finger-plates designed by Mackintosh for the Glasgow Art Club in 1892-93

[3] Timothy Neat and Gillian McDermot, *Closing the Circle: Thomas Howarth, Mackintosh and the Modern Movement: a Biography* (Aberdour: iynx, 2002), p.117

[4] Alan Crawford, *Charles Rennie Mackintosh* (London: Thames and Hudson, 1995), p.18

ONE

Alexander Thomson, Queen's Park United Presbyterian Church, Glasgow, 1869

Background to the Tour

The Alexander Thomson Travelling Studentship Competition

On 18th September 1890, the 22 year-old Charles Rennie Mackintosh was named as the winner of the Alexander Thomson Travelling Studentship, set up in 1883 with the purpose of enabling aspiring British architects between the ages of 18 and 25, 'of approved moral character' to make a three-month sketching tour to study 'Ancient Classic architecture'. The term 'Ancient' was further defined as the period 'prior to the commencement of the third century of the Christian era'. Additionally, the tour should be undertaken 'with special reference to the principles illustrated in the work of the late Alexander Thomson'.[1]

Thomson (1817-75) had developed an inventively eclectic Classicism, using elements derived from Ancient Greece, Egypt and India to express a sense of permanence and grandeur in his architecture.[2] The Studentship competition brief had, appropriately, asked for a public hall in 'the Early Classic style', to be situated on an isolated site, to accommodate 1,000 persons seated, and committee rooms. Additionally, because a knowledge of the canons of Classical ornament was essential for any architect who wished to design a good Classical building, the competitors were required to send in a study, or studies, of details of ornament or sculpture drawn from a building or cast.[3] Mackintosh, like other young architects of his generation, was well-versed in the language of Classical architecture, a knowledge acquired, in his case, in classes at the Glasgow School of Art, where in 1885 he commenced studying architectural design. A major element of the course was a series of lectures designed to inculcate 'a knowledge of the five orders of Classic architecture, with their mouldings, and a general knowledge of the leading features of Ancient Architecture'.[4] This led to a four-hour 'elementary architecture' examination in 1887

Above: William James Anderson, Alexander Thomson, Queen's Park Church; Anderson, *Architectural Studies in Italy*, frontispiece; the drawing formed part of Anderson's winning entry for the 1887 Alexander Thomson Travelling Studentship.

C. R. Mackintosh, Ionic capital, Wylie Hill Department Store, 1889

for which Mackintosh obtained the award 'excellent' and a prize. This had required him to draw the Greek and Roman orders to scale, together with their mouldings and ornaments from memory, and to answer questions on their development, from archaic forms to the use made of them by Renaissance architects. Reading for the course included most of the more useful books then available [Appendix 3]. The importance of the study of ornament was underlined and students were advised to make scale drawings from actual buildings or from casts, to develop their knowledge of architectural styles.[5]

Mackintosh's architectural studies were further reinforced by an independent course in ornamental design, which required a thorough knowledge of historical ornament and for which he gained a 1st class prize in 1890.[6] This was an important part of Mackintosh's course as he continued to make drawings from the School's large collection of ornamental casts throughout his student career, carrying off several prizes in the process.[7] Mackintosh's training, however, went beyond the need to acquaint himself with Classical architecture. His knowledge of the Renaissance and Gothic styles was endorsed when, in May 1889, he obtained a '1st class, excellent' prize for an architectural design examination. This was a gruelling six-hour session in which it was stipulated that 'candidates should be prepared to work in some style of Renaissance or Gothic and correctness in the use of the style will be considered of more importance than originality'.[8]

Mackintosh, however, was already showing evidence of a developing skill as a designer of original ornament, of the individuality that would characterise his future career. This was acknowledged by his employer, the architect John Hutchison, where he served his apprenticeship from 1884 to 1889 and for whom his design for a plaster Ionic capital in the Free Renaissance style was used in the practice's scheme in the Wylie Hill department store on Glasgow's Buchanan Street.[9]

On completing his articles under Hutchison, Mackintosh obtained a position as a draughtsman in the firm of John Honeyman and Keppie. John Keppie, who had entered into partnership with Honeyman in 1888, had been an assistant in the leading Glasgow firm of Campbell Douglas & Sellars who had continued and developed Thomson's monumental Classicist tradition. It was a Sellars' design, Glasgow's St. Andrew's Halls (1873-77) with its giant Ionic order and copious use of figure sculpture, that Mackintosh used as a major inspiration for his winning entry for the Studentship.[10]

Mackintosh only just managed to achieve first place. The five sets of entries – four from Scotland and one from London – were submitted anonymously on 30th August 1890, and were hung in Glasgow's Corporation Galleries from 4th to 20th September. The first meeting of seven trustees on 11th September failed to come to a decision. At the second, with eight members present, Mackintosh's entry, inscribed with a griffin, achieved four votes, one more than the runner-up, to be declared the winner.[11]

Under the conditions of the Studentship, Mackintosh was to receive £60, half of which was to fund a three-month long tour, once he had submitted an approved itinerary. The other half would be awarded when a satisfactory memoir of the tour, together with sketches and drawings, had been endorsed by the Thomson Trustees on his return. At a meeting with the Trustees, however, where Mackintosh submitted his route – set out on a map of Italy – he informed them that he intended remaining on the Continent for nine months, and asked if he could receive the remainder of the prize money after the allotted time without returning home. This was agreed on condition that he sent satisfactory sketches to Glasgow after the three months had expired.[12]

Italy was still very much the centre of Western culture, and a major source for those who wished to study architecture. Mackintosh would be able to examine examples of the ancient Classical architecture stipulated by the Trustees, but he would also have the opportunity of acquiring a

Upper: James Sellars, St. Andrew's Halls, Glasgow, 1873-77
Lower: C. R. Mackintosh, Design for a Public Hall: elevation, *British Architect*, vol. 34, 21st November 1890; Mackintosh's winning entry for the Alexander Thomson Travelling Studentship

first-hand knowledge of more recent buildings. Italy, from at least the 16th century, had been the finishing school of any gentleman who wished to study Roman civilisation or to acquaint himself with some of the best modern Classical edifices. Since the 1840s, however, largely through the critic John Ruskin's influence, English Gothic Revival architects had been crossing the Alps to study Lombardic Romanesque and Italian Gothic. Later, there had been a renewed interest in Renaissance architecture amongst the English as an adjunct to the Free Classic styles they were evolving out of revived Gothic. The Renaissance, however, had continued to recommend itself to Scottish architects as a means of extending their preferred Classical vocabulary. During the 1890s, practitioners on both sides of the border would also begin to turn towards a re-engagement with the Baroque, a style which had been out of favour, and with which Mackintosh was probably far less acquainted.

The familiarity of historical Italian architecture to Mackintosh would have been enhanced by first-hand accounts from friends, employers and other members of the Glasgow architectural profession who had visited the country; and he probably consulted with at least some of these when deciding on his route. John Honeyman was a scholar architect, well-versed in archaeology, who had designed the Scottish church in Genoa. Honeyman's partner, John Keppie, had toured the northern provinces at least as far as Tuscany in 1886. George McKenzie, a friend of both Keppie and Mackintosh and a fellow student at Glasgow School of Art, had recently returned from a rapid tour in September 1889, covering 11 major towns, from Milan and Venice in the north to Naples in the south.[13] The meetings of the Glasgow Architectural Association featured several lectures on Italian architecture: one timely address was given on 23rd September in the School of Art, only a few days after Mackintosh won the Studentship, by William Leiper, an architect governor of the School, on 'Ravenna and some other Italian cities', describing a tour of northern Italy but focusing on Byzantine buildings and mosaic decoration.[14]

Arguably, however, it was William James Anderson, a young Glasgow architect and architectural historian, who was of most importance in preparing Mackintosh for his tour. Anderson had visited Italy in 1888 as the first recipient of the Studentship. Despite the requirements of the scholarship, Anderson, who was to become an expert on the history of Italian Renaissance architecture, had chosen 'with the counsel and consent of the Trustees',

Upper: William James Anderson, *Building News*, 14th September 1890
Lower: William James Anderson, Study of mosaic fragment from Campo Santo, Pisa; Anderson, *Architectural Studies in Italy*, pl. 5b

Upper: Charles Rennie Mackintosh, photograph by James Craig Annan, c.1893
Lower: C. R. Mackintosh, Study from Anderson's drawing of a mosaic fragment from Campo Santo, Pisa, c.1890

to focus on 'the Classical Renaissance' as his '*chief subject*, [italics mine] not however, neglecting opportunities of directly studying the Antique'.[15] Without any evidence that Mackintosh consulted with the Trustees on what the focus of his tour should be, it might be assumed that his 'chief subject' would have been Ancient architecture. Yet, his drawings testify that Mackintosh took the broad view that the Studentship had been granted to him so that he could build up his architectural knowledge from *any* historical source that might recommend itself as useful to his future career. Anderson's studies clearly informed Mackintosh's journey. He had lectured to the Glasgow Architectural Association in July 1889 on 'The three periods of Italian Renaissance Architecture', and was its President in 1891, when Mackintosh himself gave a paper on 'Scotch Baronial Architecture'.[16] The previous year Anderson had published a volume of drawings, *Architectural Studies in Italy*.[17] Mackintosh's familiarity with Anderson's book prior to his own tour is suggested by a rough copy he made of the latter's drawing of an early mediaeval mosaic fragment in the Campo Santo in Pisa, which appears in a sketchbook Mackintosh had been using from at least 1888.[18] His interest in Anderson's work is further seen in the way he was to seek out and draw from several of his predecessor's sources, some of them quite specific.[19] Anderson's later book, *The Architecture of the Renaissance in Italy*,[20] based on lectures given in 1894 at the Glasgow School of Art, provided far greater coverage of the early Renaissance outside Florence than previous writers. Mackintosh's own interest in this area was excited by familiarity with Anderson's approach and outlook which had probably already been outlined in his 1889 lecture.

Mackintosh was a keen student of the works of John Ruskin and in 1889 he chose Ruskin's influential *The Seven Lamps of Architecture* along with his *Frondes Agrestes* as an art school prize,[21] and would agree to some extent with that writer's view that the revival of Classicism which had followed in the wake of 'the foul torrent of the Renaissance' had had a corrupting influence on architecture, in that the reintroduction of that style and its canons had substituted obedience to rules for originality of thought.[22] A little later in his career, Mackintosh would argue against the building of modern churches in the form of ancient Classical temples because the culture that produced them was radically different – an architect must design buildings that grew out of his own culture and responded to the needs of his times.[23] Yet this was not to say that he shared Ruskin's hatred of Renaissance architecture *per se*. One of Anderson's major arguments was that, far from received opinion, the Renaissance was not a mere reversion to Classical styles characterised by imitation, but that it had been a response to the needs of its time by a group of highly inventive architects. Renaissance Classicism had grown organically from mediaeval forms, Romanesque and Gothic, and it was only in its later phase that it 'degenerated into formal copyism and died in affectation'.[24] Thus in studying Italian architecture in all its phases up to the High Renaissance, Mackintosh would be engaging with an evolving genre, created at the hands of individuals. Another of Anderson's concerns was the exercise of a high level of craftsmanship in the ornamentation of buildings and a responsiveness to materials. Throughout his tour, Mackintosh would show a similar interest, noting, particularly in his sketches, the materials used on specific buildings and the colours employed.

Anderson had enjoyed the aid of an assistant in making a large number of measured drawings, but Mackintosh's single-handed work, although he did employ some measurement and probably intended producing similar drawings from measurements and notes on his return, would be mostly freehand. In this, he was claiming a position for himself as an artist who found his main expression as an architect. His Italian drawings would be a useful instrument in enabling him to develop his facility as a draughtsman as well as his ability as a designer, dictated by the discipline of arranging his studies in the two-dimensional format of the sketchbook page.

Notes for Chapter 1

[1] Alexander Thomson Memorial Minute Book (Glasgow Institute of Architects), pp.91-92; the competition had been advertised in the autumn of 1889, e.g. *Glasgow Herald* (15th November 1889).

[2] Miles Glendinning, Ranald MacInnes and Angus MacKechnie, *A History of Scottish Architecture from the Renaissance to the Present Day* (Edinburgh: Edinburgh University Press, 1996), p.253.

[3] Alexander Thomson Memorial Minute Book, pp.113-117; also *British Architect*, 34 (1890), pp.386-387.

[4] Glasgow School of Art, *Syllabus of Lectures, Session 1888-89*, (University of Strathclyde Archives), p.7.

[5] Glasgow School of Art, *Annual Report* (1888), p.18 (Glasgow School of Art Archives and Collections, GSAA/GOV/1/2); and Department of Science and Art, *Directory* (London: H.M.S.O., 1889), p.67.

[6] Department of Science and Art, op.cit., p.68; and Glasgow School of Art, *Annual Report* (1891), p.18 (Glasgow School of Art Archives and Collections, GSAA/GOV/1/2).

[7] One of these was for a detail of the Erecheum frieze, Glasgow School of Art, *Annual Report* (1888), (Session 1886-87), p.27 (Glasgow School of Art Archives and Collections, (GSAA/GOV/1/2); another was a sepia drawing of a detail of a frieze from the Forum of Trajan, (Hunterian Art Gallery, University of Glasgow).

[8] Glasgow School of Art, *Annual Report* (1890), p.18 (Glasgow School of Art Archives and Collections, (GSAA/GOV/1/2); and Department of Science and Art, op.cit., p.253.

[9] Thomas Howarth, *Charles Rennie Mackintosh and the Modern Movement*, 2nd edition (London: Routledge & Kegan Paul, 1977), pp.3-4; the building (1888-89) is at 20 Buchanan Street.

[10] David Walker, 'The Glasgow Years', Wendy Kaplan, editor, *Charles Rennie Mackintosh* (New York: Abbeville Press in association with Glasgow Museums, 1996), pp.118 and 123.

[11] Alexander Thomson Memorial Minute Book, pp.121- 125. The other entrants were Ambrose Macdonald Poynter (1867-1923), London; Robert James Gildard, Glasgow; George Smith Hill (1868-1944), Glasgow; John Daniel Swanston (1868-1956), Dollar. The members attending the first meeting were: John Gordon, William Leiper, Alexander Petrie, William Forrest Salmon, Alexander Skirving, Malcolm Stark Jnr., and John Shields. Leiper did not attend the second meeting in which the new members were James Chalmers and T. L. Watson. There was some unspecified discontent amongst the Trustees expressed at the first meeting "on account of the general character of the competition", the term "character" being substituted in the minutes for the stronger phrase "unsatisfactory nature". It is not clear whether the drawings or the conditions were seen to be at fault. The ballot taken at the second meeting was anonymous but when the runner-up, Ambrose Macdonald Poynter, failed to win the vote, Salmon and Stark moved that he, rather than Mackintosh, should receive the prize, whilst Gordon and Shields moved for Mackintosh. The latter motion was carried.

[12] Ibid., pp.126-127; meeting dated 27th February 1891.

[13] Aylwin Clark, *The McKenzie Sisters* (Duns: Black Ace Books, 1996), pp.26-30.

[14] *British Architect*, 34 (3rd October 1890), p.258.

[15] William James Anderson, *Architectural Studies in Italy* (Glasgow: Maclure, Macdonald & Co., 1890), preface.

[16] *The Architect* (20th February 1891), p.113.

[17] Anderson, op. cit.

[18] Elaine Grogan, *Beginnings: Charles Rennie Mackintosh's Early Sketchbooks* (Oxford: Architectural Press in association with the National Library of Ireland, Dublin, 2002), p.50.

[19] Mackintosh drew the same chimney piece in the Doge's Palace in

Venice as Anderson when a large number of other examples were available to him.

[20] William James Anderson, *The Architecture of the Renaissance in Italy: a general view for the use of students and others* (London: B. T. Batsford, 1901).

[21] Glasgow School of Art, Correspondence to Department of Science and Art, 1882-89. (The Glasgow School of Art Archives and Collections, GSAA/SEC/3).

[22] John Ruskin, *The Stones of Venice*, Vol. 3: *The Fall* (The Works of John Ruskin, Vol. 11), edited by E. T. Cook and Alexander Wedderburn (London: George Allen, 1904), pp.16 et seq. and *The Seven Lamps of Architecture* (The Works of John Ruskin, Vol. 8), edited by E. T. Cook and Alexander Wedderburn (London: George Allen, 1903), p.98.

[23] Mackintosh, 'Architecture (1893)' in Robertson (1990), p.207.

[24] Anderson, *The Architecture of the Renaissance in Italy*, pp.4-6. To be fair to Ruskin he praised the early Renaissance architects for their originality in seeking to discard Gothic architecture which had become decadent, but regretted their reintroduction of Classicism.

The Glasgow Bridge, Glasgow

TWO

Naples

Naples and Palermo

'I would advise you to go there as I did by sea, as it sets you up splendidly for the hard work before you'[1]

Glasgow to Naples: 21st March – 5th April 1891
Mackintosh's £30 was worth something over £2,000 today, yet it seems barely adequate to have financed a three-month tour. He commenced his journey by leaving Glasgow on 21st March for a week in London[2], but did not record how he spent his time there and possibly used it to finalise his travel arrangements and set up a bank account with Thomas Cook, as he later made withdrawals in Naples and Rome where the firm had branches. He also probably bought circular rail tickets (*viagi circolari*) which allowed him to travel at a 45 per cent saving,[3] as he never mentioned the price of his train fares in his diary but almost always recorded the cost of his hotels. That is except for the Hôtel du Vésuve in Naples, probably having booked it in advance. Unlike Keppie, McKenzie and Anderson, Mackintosh did not travel to Italy by rail through France and Switzerland. Instead, perhaps because of the time of year, he made the decision to approach by sea, landing at Naples. This would take advantage of the mild climate – a practice common to many British expatriates making long stays in Italy, who wintered in the south, moving north as the weather grew warmer.

Starting in Naples required an expensive outlay for the journey. Mackintosh embarked on the *S.S. Cuzco* at Tilbury on the Thames on Friday 27th March. The *Cuzco*'s owners, the Orient Steam Navigation Company, ran a service to Sydney in Australia via the Suez Canal and Ceylon; and Naples had been added as a port-of-call the previous year. The *Cuzco* was a 384 ft, Clyde-built, passenger cargo vessel of 3,898 tons.[4] For 17 guineas, the ship offered a nine-day voyage via Plymouth and Gibraltar with a 'high class cuisine, electric lighting, hot and cold baths, good ventilation and every comfort'.[5]

Below: *S.S.Cuzco*

Lounge, *S.S.Cuzco*

Naples: Sunday 5th – Sunday 12th April
When the *Cuzco* finally dropped anchor in the blue waters of the Bay of Naples on the morning of 5th April, Mackintosh awoke to the idyllic sight of a great sunlit city rising up before him. After taking breakfast on board, the distant vision with all its tantalising promise was to become a jarringly disappointing reality. Mackintosh did not enjoy Naples. With permission to disembark, the passengers were taken with their luggage on board a small tender which conveyed them to the *Dogana*, the customs house, where their bags were examined. Here Mackintosh's tobacco was confiscated as he was unwilling to pay the 10 francs[6] duty (more than it had cost him). Smarting from this first encounter with his Italian hosts, his luggage was placed on a carriage which conveyed him to his hotel.

Naples was the most populous city in the country with over 530,000 inhabitants and had been capital of the Kingdom of Naples until its absorption into the Kingdom of Italy in 1860. The Hôtel du Vésuve was one of the best in the city, recently patronised by Queen Sophia of Sweden and the haunt of such luminaries as Oscar Wilde. At 12 francs per night it was also the most expensive hotel that Mackintosh was to patronise for any length of time. Like most other hotels used by foreigners, it lay in the smarter part of town close to the gardens of the Villa Nazionale, the site of the daily *passeggiatta*[7] of the fashionable world. Mackintosh's route from the port took him past some of the city's most impressive sights: along the quayside, then inland past the great Angevin Castel Nuovo with its magnificent marble Renaissance entrance; skirting the largely 16th-century Royal Palace of the Bourbon kings; through the Piazza del Plebiscito dominated by the domed and colonnaded Neo-Classical church of San Francesco di Paola, modelled on Rome's Pantheon; on to the Via Partenope with its smart hotels overlooking the Castello dell'Ovo and affording views across the bay to Vesuvius and the Sorrentine Peninsula.

The Baedeker guidebook informed Mackintosh that Naples, despite 'occupying one of the most beautiful situations in the world' was singularly deficient in objects of real artistic or architectural significance.[8] The only reason for the student to visit the city was to study the Ancient Classical heritage of the surrounding area. In the hinterland of Naples there were the extensive remains of the Roman sites of Pompeii and Herculaneum which had been buried by the eruption of Vesuvius in A.D. 79 and systematically excavated after their rediscovery in the early 18th century. Further afield was the Ancient Greek colony of Paestum with its well-preserved temples, while close at hand were the archaeological riches contained in the Museo Nazionale (now the Museo Archeologico Nazionale) drawn principally from Pompeii, Herculaneum and other sites devastated in A.D. 79. This was undoubtedly Mackintosh's purpose, as it afforded a better opportunity than practically any other Italian location, except perhaps Rome itself, of fulfilling the conditions of his scholarship. Mackintosh's broader agenda, however, was to take in as much of Naples as he could and after a wash and shave, he was ready to begin exploring.

Almost immediately, however, he ran into and joined a group of friends from the ship who had embarked on a sightseeing tour and were en route for the Central Station with the object of visiting Pompeii. The train (at 2.5 p.m.) took them as far as Torre Annunziata where they hired a carriage for the 20-minute drive to the excavations. Mackintosh did not record what he saw in Pompeii apart from the museum which stood by the main entrance at the Porta Maritima and consisted of three rooms where he encountered plaster casts of victims of the eruption and was impressed by the different forms of its collection of amphorae. Returning from Torre Annunziata to Naples at 6.14 p.m., he and his friends visited the Galleria Umberto Primo, a smart shopping arcade completed in the previous year as part of an urban renewal scheme following a devastating cholera epidemic in 1884.[9] Mackintosh was full of praise for this cruciform glass-covered gallery with its central dome rising to 187 feet, describing it as a 'most magnificent building, really good architecture'.[10] His day ended with a visit to an 'Italian restaurant', where the group 'tried macaroni but couldn't manage to turn it round the fork in the most magnificent manner of the Italians'. After seeing the 'Cuzcoits' off at about 9 p.m., he returned to his hotel for a smoke – he must have restocked his tobacco pouch during the day – and was in bed by about 10.30 p.m.

Monday 6th April was Mackintosh's first day of serious study. He rose at 7.30 a.m., had a breakfast of bread, butter and coffee and went for a walk in the gardens of the Villa Nazionale. He then took a horse car to the bank where he drew out £10 and 'got tips about the town'. His next visit, an equally essential one, was to the British Consulate at Monte di Dio 4 where he acquired his *permesso* allowing him, as a student, to sketch in Pompeii and the Museo Nazionale. He then went straight to the museum, the first of three visits, to begin work.

The museum lies at the top of the busy Via Toledo, a straight thoroughfare laid out in 1540 on the orders of the Spanish Viceroy, Don Pedro de Toledo, as a link between the newly-developed western districts and the old city, and forming part of a route which ran from the Piazza del Plebiscito in the south to the Palazzo Reale di Capodimonte in the north. With its handsome mansions of the wealthy, it had once been considered the most beautiful street in Europe. The museum's buildings were erected in 1586 as a cavalry barracks, then transferred to the University of Naples in 1615. From 1790 they had been adapted to receive the royal collection of antiquities and pictures which included the extensive Farnese collections, with their major Roman antiquities in addition to the excavated treasures from Herculaneum, Pompeii, Stabiae and Cumae. So rich are the collections that Mackintosh was only exaggerating slightly when he observed that 'there is more of Pompeii here than there is at the excavations of the town itself'.[11] The three sheets of drawings which survive from his visits indicate Mackintosh's primary interest in ornament and three-dimensional objects, as opposed to two-dimensional works such as frescos and paintings. They comprise a sheet of studies from the large collection of ancient Greco-Italian vases,[12] a drawing of one of a pair of Roman marble candelabra, from a room containing antique reliefs near the north-western corner of the ground floor;[13] and a Renaissance bronze tabernacle,[14] executed by the 16th-

Street of Tombs, Pompeii. Rosengarten, *A Handbook of Architectural Styles*, fig. 223

century sculptor Jacopo Siciliano, an assistant of Michelangelo, from a design attributed to that master. The candelabrum reflected the interest of Glasgow's architects, particularly the late James Sellars, in incorporating this form into his buildings, a motif that Mackintosh had borrowed for his Thomson competition entry. The day was rounded off with dinner at the hotel followed by a visit to the Opera San Carlo with the Swords, a family with whom Mackintosh had become friendly on the *Cuzco*. The young traveller 'got home about 1 o'clock & went to bed immediately'.

Armed with his *permesso*, Mackintosh would make two subsequent trips, on Tuesday and Thursday to Pompeii. The whole of Tuesday was spent there, arriving about 11 a.m. He again began in the museum, covering a sheet with drawings of some of the amphorae he had admired on his first visit, together with depictions of a terracotta frieze and rain spouts. After lunch he visited the Temple of Mercury (more correctly the Temple of Vespasian) in the Forum, the only Pompeiian sketching site he mentioned in his diary. In the absence of any extant drawings, it is reasonable to assume that he made a sketch of the small marble altar that it contains before catching the train back to Naples at 6 p.m. On his Thursday visit he made drawings in the Street of Tombs by the Porta Ercolano at the north-western corner of the town, taking a study of a marble frieze and of the altar tomb of Naevoleia Tyche.

Porta Capuana, Naples

His decision to study this particular monument might have been prompted by an existing familiarity with it, as it was the only Roman tomb illustrated in Rosengarten's *Architectural Styles*,[14] a book which Mackintosh had won as an art school prize. His other Pompeiian drawings were of architectural details mostly from the houses of private citizens: a Corinthian capital, a water trough, a pedestal, a well head, an ornamental street sign and a superb table leg, depicting griffins, from the House of Cornelius Rufus.

Although much of his time in Naples was spent in the study of Roman antiquities, Mackintosh did not neglect its more recent monuments. On Wednesday 8th April, after a trip to the post office on the Strada Monte Oliveto, he set out to reconnoitre the city's churches. His tour took him away from the more modern quarter of the town, on the west of the Via Toledo, into the narrow streets of the old city: 'a more noisy, filthy place I'm sure you couldn't find anywhere. The streets are narrow, the people lazy & filthy, in fact every thing about seems to do its levelest to make the place disagreeable and increase the pestilential smell which pervades the whole town'.[16] Added to these discomforts and the necessity of running the gauntlet of numerous beggars and street vendors, Mackintosh was subjected to the intermittent frustration of finding some of the churches closed: 'One thing in Naples which is a constant incentive to bad language is that some of the churches are open from 10-12 & others from 3-5. To find out which is open when is a puzzle.'[17]

Not far from the post office is the Piazza Gesù Nuovo with its marble Rococo obelisk, the Guglia dell'Immacolata, erected in the mid-18th century by the Jesuits to honour the Virgin.[18] Mackintosh, who seemed to enjoy awarding marks, gave this a 'fairly good'. His comment 'not much outside' in reference to the exterior of the adjacent church of Santa Trinità Maggiore (Gesù Nuovo) was prompted by the plainness of its diamond-embossed front (adapted from the Renaissance palace of the Princes of Salerno) when contrasted with its Baroque interior. This he praised as 'really magnificent' remarking that the 'decoration surpassed anything' he had 'seen before'. He sketched the only highly-ornamented part of the exterior, its central doorway of 1685, his work in blue colour-washes making it the earliest surviving watercolour of his tour.[19] The neighbouring church of Santa Chiara was closed, and he had mixed success gaining access to several others, before finding himself at the Duomo (Cathedral) which, under restoration, was covered in scaffolding. The Angevin Gothic interior, swamped by many later accretions, Mackintosh 'unhesitatingly pronounced as bad'.[20]

He was more impressed by the Porta Capuana, 'about the best bit of work' he had seen in Naples. The marble triumphal arch, adorned with carvings of trophies and images of the winged goddess of victory, with its twin round flanking towers forming the principal eastern entrance to the city, was the work of the Florentine sculptor and architect Giuliano da Maiano.[21] Mackintosh's taste for 15th-century Florentine Renaissance architectural sculpture becomes increasingly apparent in his diary as the tour progresses. In his 1892 lecture about the tour, Mackintosh named this as one of two 'very good' gates in Naples, without identifying the other, but seeming to imply that the other was also a city gate. None of these, however, has the aesthetic pretensions or appeal of the Porta Capuana, so it is far more likely that he was referring to the triumphal arch of Alfonso of Aragon which forms the entrance to the Castel Nuovo.[22] He revisited the Porta Capuana early the next morning to make a sketch before catching the train to Pompeii.

C. R. Mackintosh, Campanile, Santa Maria del Carmine, Naples, 1891

Allan Dreghorn and Mungo Nasmith, St. Andrew's in the Square, Glasgow, 1739-59

He was also taken with the campanile of the church of Santa Maria del Carmine, which overlooks the Piazza Mercato close to the docks: a brick and stone structure commenced in the 15th century with a spire completed as late as 1631.[23] The tower, of which he made two drawings, might well have impressed him because of its similarity to the steeples of 18th-century Glasgow, particularly that of St. Andrew's in the Square.

Further churches were visited on the Friday and Saturday afternoons after Mackintosh had finished his work in the museum. His taste for Renaissance marble sculpture, revealed in his admiration for the Porta Capuana, was further excited by the tombs he discovered in San Domenico Maggiore and Sant'Anna dei Lombardi. Although these were the best he had yet seen he would later reflect that they did 'not come up to those in Florence and Venice'.[24] Gothic tombs, on the other hand do not seem to have attracted his notice, despite the fact that several of the churches contain impressive monuments. And if he believed that Naples only possessed second-rate Renaissance tombs, perhaps he would have revised his opinion if he had seen the monument to Cardinal Rinaldo Brancaccio in the little church of Sant'Angelo a Nilo, a masterpiece by the Florentine sculptors Donatello and Michelozzo. He would admire Donatello's work later in Siena and Florence.

Mackintosh was, though, delighted by his visit to the Certosa di San Martino which dominates the city from its height on the hill of the Vomero. This suppressed Carthusian monastery, begun in 1325, but radically modified by the Baroque architect and sculptor Cosimo Fanzago from 1623, was converted into a museum in 1866. Mackintosh thought it one of the most interesting places in Naples, admiring the wood panelling in the Conversation Hall and Chapter House, the fine design and craftsmanship of the intarsia work in the choir stalls and the baluster around the high altar. He drew the 'very nice well' in the Great Cloister and enjoyed the view of Naples from the Belvedere. After admiring collections of glass and porcelain in the museum, he viewed the other large building complex on the Vomero, the Castel Sant'Elmo, a 16th-century star fort. His remark that there was 'not much to see', possibly meant that he was only able to examine the exterior of what was then a military prison.

Despite being impressed by the Certosa and Santa Trinità Maggiore, opulent interiors were not always guaranteed to sway the young Mackintosh. The Palazzo Reale (Royal Palace) which he visited on the Sunday, his last day in Naples, was 'as wild an exhibition of extravagant vulgarity as' he 'ever wish[ed] to see'.[25] This was the verdict he gave in his lecture a year later. At the time he was slightly more complimentary, describing it as 'grand and handsome but can't be put down as the best work. Some very fine tapestry and pictures. Grand staircase best part of interior'.[26] The weather had gradually worsened during the week. On the Thursday he had to abandon a plan to use watercolour at Pompeii because of bad light. He had intended to go to Paestum on the Friday, to visit its ancient Greek temples. As he rose at 6.30 a.m., heavy rain made him decide to go back to bed for an hour before spending the day mostly indoors, although he visited the museum and some churches. It was still raining the next day and he put off his trip again. Continuing poor weather on the Sunday finally persuaded him to abandon his plans and leave for Sicily.

The Voyage to Sicily: Sunday 12th – Monday 13th April
Naples was usually the furthest south that architectural visitors ventured. None of Mackintosh's friends or colleagues are known to have gone to Sicily which was not particularly well covered in architectural textbooks. His main source of information on Sicilian architecture was James Fergusson's *History of Architecture* which was full of praise for the work around Palermo produced under the Norman kings during the 11th and 12th centuries.[27]

On Sunday morning, Mackintosh went to the offices of the Navigazione Generale Italiana to buy a ticket for that evening's sailing (leaving at 5 p.m.).[28] After lunch in his hotel, he made the stressful journey with his baggage to the quayside. After being 'fleeced on every hand by these beggarly Italians' he boarded the ship which to his consternation was full of 'Italians'. Dinner was the 'most disgraceful repast' – which most of the passengers were unable to eat. Only two remained at table and 'They were Italians', and 'able to eat anything', but the weather cannot have helped. Mackintosh thought he had acquired his sea legs on the *Cuzco*, but soon the steamer was 'rolling and tossing about in the most reckless manner' although

'it wasn't actually rough but the boat was about as bad as could be, just like a Clyde tug boat'. He was not far wrong as the *Leone* was a Greenock-built vessel.[29] Perhaps the sea was rougher than Mackintosh maintained, as before they had been out two hours, he 'was as sick (in company with most of the passengers) as a dog'. After a miserable night, the *Leone* arrived at Palermo at about 9.15 a.m. where Mackintosh went through the *Dogana*, this time without any trouble.

He had probably intended staying at the Hôtel de France close to the harbour, noted in his diary as the 'best hotel in Palermo', but instead decided on the Albergo Trinacria, a similarly priced hotel close by on the Via Butera. Omnibuses belonging to the various hotels waited for prospective customers on the quayside; after his recent experience in Naples, he was probably not ready to hire a cab for the mile-long journey to the town.

Palermo: Monday 13th – Saturday 18th April
Palermo, the capital of Sicily, had some 273,000 inhabitants. It sits in the fertile plane of the Conca d'Oro, beyond which rises an amphitheatre of imposing mountains, with the beautiful Monte Pellegrino to the north and Monte Catalfano to the east. The town had acquired the designation '*la felice*' because of its magnificent situation and superb climate. It was, and is, divided into four quarters by its two main streets: the Corso Vittorio Emanuele running from the coast, in a south-easterly direction to the Porta Nuova; and the Via Macqueda which bisects it, running roughly from south to north.

Palermo had its own Museo Nazionale which contained artefacts dating from Sicily's colonisation by the Ancient Greeks and its subsequent incorporation into the Roman Empire, but Mackintosh more likely came here because of its Norman churches praised by Fergusson for their unique mixed-Sicilian style, which Arab and Greek artists built and ornamented on the plan of a Roman basilica for their western Roman Catholic masters. He was 'much charmed' with the city in which 'good things' were 'turning up everywhere', immediately deciding that it was a 'very much finer town than Naples'.

Having checked into his 'rather expensive' hotel, Mackintosh went straight to the British Consulate to enquire about sketching. As it was raining heavily, he went quickly to the Cathedral, externally predominantly in the Arab-Norman style with Catalan Gothic additions,

C. R. Mackintosh, Porch, Palermo Cathedral, 1891

crowned by a late 18th-century cupola. The weather allowed him little leisure to do more than gain a general impression, and he quickly went inside where, to his extreme disgust, he was faced with an interior which was 'all most miserable classic'.[30] All he could find to admire were two Renaissance holy water stoups. When he set out to leave, as it was still raining, he took refuge in the Catalan Gothic porch (1453), and while there, noticed a small hotel opposite. On enquiring and discovering not only that it was 'very respectable' but that it supplied full board for only 6 francs per day, half as much as the Trinacria, he booked a room for the remainder of his stay.

The entrance to the Hotel Rebecchino afforded him a fine view of the Cathedral porch, which he knew from an illustration in Fergusson.[31] Having completed his booking he took out his sketchbook and began to draw it. As it was very cold as well as wet, he soon abandoned his attempt in favour of a visit to the Palazzo Reale to examine its chapel, founded in 1130 by the Norman king, Roger II. The Capella Palatina was Mackintosh's first encounter with an interior in the Arab-Norman style: the floors paved with mosaics, the lower part of the walls panelled with slabs of marble framed with mosaic ornament; the upper part filled with mosaic pictures on a gold ground; and the gilded and painted wooden ceilings, an early example of the Arabic stalactite style. He was so entranced that he recorded in his diary that he had 'almost fainted on the spot'. Two other churches mentioned in Fergusson were San Giovanni degli Eremiti (1132) and La Martorana (1143), and Mackintosh visited them next. San Giovanni, built for Roger II, is a ruined monastery whose cubic forms surmounted by red domes speak strongly of their Arab origins. La Martorana (Santa Maria dell'Ammiraglio) built by Roger II's Greek admiral, Georgios Antiochenos, but serving in 1891 as the headquarters of the Conservazione dei Monumenti di Sicilia, was closed when Mackintosh arrived. He was only able to admire its 'fine old Norman tower', while ignoring its Baroque façade. The last church he visited was San Francesco d'Assisi, which was probably also closed as he only recorded his favourable impression of its 'very good Norman work in front'.[32] His final visit of the day was to the Museo Nazionale, where 'there was not very much to be seen'. Perhaps his comment betrays his real lack of interest in Ancient Classical remains, but in his lecture given a year later to an audience which would have

C. R. Mackintosh, Cloisters, Monreale Cathedral, 1891

included some of the Thomson Trustees, he praised it as 'a fine collection'.[33]

His move to the Hotel Rebecchino on the following day allowed him to continue sketching the Cathedral, but as it was still raining and there were no shadows to add interest to his drawing, he put it on one side and despite the weather, set out for Monreale, some five kilometres distant from Palermo. This was reached by an electric tramcar which he probably boarded at the nearby Piazza dell'Independenza for the half-hour journey to Rocca, followed by a walk of another half an hour 'up a steep and rugged mountain path' to the town.

Monreale grew up around its Cathedral and adjoining Benedictine monastery, founded and largely built by the Norman king, William II. Mackintosh's first view of the church would have been its plain façade and front with its unassuming, square Romanesque towers and chaste 18th-century arcaded porch. This did not prepare him for the shock that awaited him inside: 'Church not much outside but golly what an interior. Fairly took away my breath, most magnificently decorated in mosaics. This church quite surpassed anything I had yet seen'. The ornamentation of the interior, the swansong and culmination of Arab-Norman architecture, had gained Fergusson's highest praise, ranking it 'among the finest Mediaeval churches' its 'ornaments in colour and gold making up a decoration unrivalled in its class by anything – except, perhaps, St. Mark's – the middle ages have produced'.[34]

Mackintosh made only one drawing of the interior, a sketch of one of the salvaged Roman capitals which support the nave arcade, but he was to find even more to his taste in the cloister which runs along the south side of the Cathedral. This is probably early 13th century and consists of twinned pillars supporting pointed stilted arches. He counted 112 of these (there are in fact 114 pairs) and remarked on their 'beautifully carved caps… nearly all different. Some of them wonderfully good'. The pillars themselves display a variety of ornamental treatment: some of the shafts are plain; some adorned with Islamic mosaic patterns; others intricately carved, whilst the capitals are loaded with Christian iconography.

He had to abandon any further drawings, as it was raining heavily and was dark and cold, but he returned for a whole day on the Thursday when there was some sunlight, amongst showers, and it was then that he probably made a watercolour of the south-western tower of the Cathedral. To produce this he sat in the south-eastern corner of the cloister's ambulatory to capture the profile of one of its arches and columns. From here, however, he would not have been able to see the whole of the tower, which he must have sketched from a position beneath the arcade itself. He also made a sensitive pencil drawing of the exquisite well at the cloister's south-western corner.

He would later recall that:

> The fine old monastery of Monreale gave me quite as much pleasure & delight as anything I saw in Italy, every bit – the exterior which is very old with its plain square tower and beautiful bronze doors, the interior which like the Capello [sic] Palazzo Reale is covered with mosaic representing sacred history, the cloisters, the garden, everything in fact, is fine. But there this beautiful work stands – unheeded and uncared for – left to the tender mercies of two or three custodians.[35]

The intervening day, Wednesday, had also been dull and wet and was spent in Palermo. After a fairly late breakfast at 9 o'clock, Mackintosh set out to attempt to make a watercolour of the campanile of La Martorana that he had admired on his first day. This was to prove an almost impossible task, not because of the weather, but because of the curiosity of the local population:

> Went to sketch Campanile Martorano [sic]. Gathered such a crowd. About 50 people looking at me as if I was a wild beast. Got very angry. then thought I would try the effect of laughing Laughed at the crowd. They just looked at me as if I was mad. Standing right round me couldn't see Campanile so had to stop Took up my board & went away. Came back in 5 minutes, found the remnants of the crowd still there went home and finished sketch in hotel.

The banded stonework on Mackintosh's watercolour was probably completed in the hotel as it is more highly-coloured than that on the tower itself. The remainder of the daylight hours were occupied in finishing his drawing of the Cathedral porch: 'Very fine doorway but very difficult to sketch'; and the evening in taking the first of two Italian lessons with Emile, the son of the hotel proprietor.

C. R. Mackintosh, Campanile, La Martorana, Palermo

The Friday and Saturday were spent making sketches of the Cathedral - where he once more attracted an audience – and revisiting the museum. He drew the Cathedral tower and it was probably also then that he filled a sheet with sketches of the Catalan Gothic window and door on the adjacent Archiepiscopal Palace, and a rough jotting of the 16th-century Porta Nuova[36] some hundred yards from his hotel. During his stay, he also filled a page with jottings[37] of Santa Maria della Catena, an early 16th-century church near the harbour, sketching its Renaissance west and north doorways and one of its Catalan Gothic windows. Unaccountably, he captioned this as 'S. Antonio', a church nearer the centre of town.[38]

On Saturday evening, it was time to face the return voyage which began at 4.30 p.m. His week in Palermo seems to have disposed him more favourably to Italians as he spent some of his time on board talking to a boy via a mixture of French and English. Once more, having spent a miserable night, in which the boat behaved 'as if it was drunk' and most of the passengers were sick, he arrived back at Naples.

Below: Palermo

Notes for Chapter 2

[1] Mackintosh, 'A Tour in Italy (1892)' in Robertson, *Charles Rennie Mackintosh: the Architectural Papers*, (1990), p.109.
[2] Mackintosh, 'Memoir of an Italian Tour (1891)' in Robertson (1990), p.235.
[3] Karl Baedeker, *Italy: Handbook for Travellers: second part: Central Italy and Rome*, 10th revised edition (Leipsic: Karl Baedeker, 1890), p.xix; these tickets were available from Cook's and the principal London Southern Railway stations.
[4] Built by John Elder and Co., Greenock in 1871.
[5] *Glasgow Herald* (20th March 1891), p.12, col. 9.
[6] Karl Baedeker, ibid., p.xiii; the French monetary system was in use in Italy; 10 francs was equivalent to 10 lire, a term which was also in use.
[7] A leisurely walk undertaken in the evening for the purpose of socialising.
[8] Karl Baedeker, *Italy: Handbook for Travellers: third part: Southern Italy and Sicily*, 13th revised edition (Leipsic: Karl Baedeker, 1900), p.30.
[9] Designed by Emanuele Rocco (1852-1922), built 1887-90.
[10] Mackintosh, 'Diary of an Italian Tour (1891)' in Robertson (1990), p.106; all Mackintosh's comments unless otherwise specified are taken from his diary.
[11] Mackintosh, 'A Tour in Italy (1892)' in Robertson (1990), p.110.
[12] Mackintosh unaccountably captioned this drawing: 'Egyptian pottery'.
[13] These are now in the principal room on the first floor, used in Mackintosh's day as the library.
[14] A receptacle for eucharistic elements.
[15] Albert Rosengarten, *A Handbook of Architectural Styles* (London: Chatto and Windus, 1878), fig. 222.
[16] Mackintosh, 'A Tour in Italy (1892)' in Robertson (1990), p.110.
[17] Ibid.
[18] Known as the Guglia dell'Immacolata it was built between 1747 and 1750 by Giuseppe Genuino (fl. 18th century).
[19] The façade dates from, c.1470; the interior of 1603-31 is enriched with coloured marbles and frescos in the Baroque style by Belisario Corenzio (c.1560-1640), Massimo Stanzione (1585-1656) and Giuseppe Ribera (1591-1652); the diary entry for Mackintosh's visit is dated 8th April: the drawing is dated '9th April'.
[20] Mackintosh, 'A Tour in Italy (1892)' in Robertson (1990), p.110.
[21] The gate was commenced in 1485 and dedicated in 1494; Mackintosh's drawing dates it to 1535, when the coat of arms of the Emperor Charles V was added to the attic storey.
[22] Begun 1453, designed by the Dalmatian architect Onoforio di Giordano and executed by several sculptors from Italy and Catalonia.
[23] The campanile was completed to the design of Fra. Nuvolo (Giuseppe Donzelli, d. 1637).
[24] Mackintosh, 'A Tour in Italy (1892)' in Robertson (1990), p.110.
[25] Ibid.
[26] The Royal Palace was commenced in 1598 by Domenico Fontana (1543-1607); its state wing was added in 1759 by Ferdinando Fuga (1699-1781), but the Palace was not completed until 1837 when Gaetano Genovese (1795-1860) built the Belvedere overlooking the sea; the Grand Staircase (1651) was the work of Francesco Antonio Picchiatti (1617-94).
[27] James Fergusson, *A History of Architecture in all Countries from the Earliest Times to the Present Day*, vol. 2 (London: John Murray, 1874), pp.397-406.
[28] There was a steamer each night between Naples and Palermo; Mackintosh was unhappy with the high fare, which the Baedeker (1900) quotes as 34F, 20c.
[29] Built by Scott and Co., Greenock in 1864: a steamship of 639 tons.
[30] The Neo-Classical interior, together with the cupola (1771), were designed by Ferdinando Fuga (1699-1781) one of the architects of the Royal Palace at Naples; the interior dates from 1809.
[31] James Fergusson, *A History of Architecture in all Countries from the Earliest Times to the Present Day*, vol. 2, p.401.
[32] In his diary entry Mackintosh confused the two churches, praising San Francesco's Norman tower – its much later tower is difficult to see – and La Martorana's Norman front; this is Baroque whilst San Francesco's Romanesque front dates from the 13th century.
[33] Mackintosh, 'A Tour in Italy (1892)' in Robertson (1990), p.111.
[34] Fergusson, op. cit., p.401.
[35] Mackintosh, 'A Tour in Italy (1892)' in Robertson (1990), pp.111-112.
[36] Built in 1583 to commemorate the Emperor Charles V's arrival in Palermo in 1535; it was later completely rebuilt in 1669 by Gaspare Guercio (1611-79).
[37] 'Jottings' was a term frequently used to refer to sketches.
[38] Sant'Antonio is an early 13th-century church restored and freely modernised after an earthquake in 1823.

THREE

The Vatican from the River Tiber, Rome

Rome

Naples to Rome: Sunday 19th April 1891
Mackintosh's haste to leave the town where he had had such bad experiences a week earlier is almost palpable from his terse diary entry: 'Got into Naples at 8 o'clock. Drove to Station left luggage went to breakfast got ticket got into train and started for Rome at 10 minutes to 9.'

The 11-hour journey gave Mackintosh his first real experience of the agricultural landscape of the Italian mainland: 'Country rather nice. After we were out from Naples passed a great many vine fields miles and miles corn planted on ground trees growing about 10 feet to 15 feet apart in long avenues and vines growing up and from tree to tree. Leaves just coming out.' But then he grew bored with the sameness of it all: 'Vine fields got tiresome. Not much to see till we came on a bit. Towns or villages nestling in a most extraordinary manner half way up on the mountainside.' Monte Cassino with its monastery was a point of interest as were the snow-capped hills, but the train was 'disgustingly slow' and Mackintosh must have been glad at around 8 p.m. to reach Rome and the Hôtel Europa where, after dinner, he 'went to bed immediately. Quite tired out'.

The Europa, situated in the centre of the tourist district at Piazza di Spagna 35, was of a similar standard and price (12 francs per day) to the Hôtel du Vésuve and the Albergo Trinacria. It is possible that Mackintosh had booked it before leaving Britain, but he would soon seek out cheaper accommodation.

Rome: Monday 20th April – Monday 4th May 1891
Rome at that time with an excess of 345,000 inhabitants, after Naples the largest population centre in the country, had only been the capital of Italy since 1870. Previous to that it had been the centre of the temporal domains of the Papacy. The 'Eternal City' on its seven hills, still mostly confined within its 3rd-century walls of Aurelian had been the capital of the vast Roman empire until the 4th century, after which it became the centre of the western church. The Imperial era had left the city strewn with the ruins of palaces, temples and stadia, enduring monuments to its past glory, but also a quarry for materials used from the 5th to the 18th centuries to build the churches and palaces of popes and cardinals. Through its patronage of the visual arts, the magnificence of its urban planning, its great processional streets and grandiose squares, its displays of public sculpture, its magnificent fountains, the Papacy had turned the city, by the 18th century, into the centre of western European art. Here a young architect or artist could study the highest quality works of two millennia. Mackintosh stayed for two weeks -- his longest sojourn of the whole tour.

He spent his first day familiarising himself with the city. After rising at 8 a.m. and breakfasting, he found his way to the Corso, Rome's main thoroughfare, occupied by shops and the site of the evening *passegiata* and the annual Roman carnival. His route led him north to the Piazza del Popolo, with its set-piece twin churches of Santa Maria dei Miracoli and Santa Maria in Montesanto,[1] its Egyptian obelisk and Neoclassical lion fountain.[2] None of this can have been to his taste as he commented 'Not much to see'. He would evince no interest in Papal town planning with its great promenades, monumental piazzas, and impressive vistas.

This was followed by official business along the Corso: a trip to the bank to draw out £10; to the British Consulate at Piazza San Claudio 96 for permission to sketch; followed by a visit to the post offic at Piazza di San Silvestro in Capite along the Via della Vite, where he picked up copies of newspapers sent from home. Lastly, he went to the 'director of arts' for further permissions. This might be a reference to a visit to the Vatican which, then as now, was under the jurisdiction of the Papal Curia. His search

Forum Romanum, Rome

for cheaper accommodation led him to a *pensione* run by Madame Michel, not far from the Europa, up the Spanish Steps at Via Sistina 72.[3] He seems to have felt at home here, describing it as a 'very nice hotel & very nice people'.

The most interesting part of his day was a trip to the Roman Forum as he recalled the impression it made on him in his lecture:

> ...the road from the Forum to the Colosseum taking in the Campo Vaccino bears a very striking resemblance to some parts of the east end of Glasgow assuming about two thirds of the population to be dead of cholera. It is as grimy, as filthy, as tumblesome as forlorn, and is as unpleasantly redolent of old clothes, and old women who were washerwomen once upon a time, but who have long since forsworn soap, either for their own or for others' use.[4]

Mackintosh would prove himself an assiduous student of Classical architecture during the following fortnight, spending at least seven days examining Roman remains or studying sculpture and ornament in the museums.

His second day in the city was taken up by a visit to the Vatican, equally divided between an examination of St. Peter's and a tour of the museums. Like many 19th-century British visitors before him, his reactions to the great basilica were not entirely positive. Carlo Maderno's front,[5] he unhesitatingly pronounced as 'very very poor', whilst the church's interior initially struck him as 'much better', but, on reflection, he decided that its main attraction was its immense size:

> The interior, well, it's vast – vast – I try to get away from the word 'vast', but it won't work. I know there is lots of beautiful marble, real and imitation, lots; lots of silver and bronze; lots of jewels & precious stones; lots of fine frescos & an abundance of gold paint; but the whole of this vast structure, all this conglomeration of marble, plaster, stone, gold, silver, bronze & paint, did not give me a fraction of the pleasure I derived from any one of the mosaics at Monreale.[6]

In the 1890s, access to the Vatican Museums was via the left side of the Basilica's colonnade, around the whole of the exterior of St. Peter's following a route between the Vatican gardens and the Palace to reach the entrance near its north-western corner. Having paid his 1 franc entrance fee he admired the Egyptian section, the architectural collections, the vast array of statuary, and the Raphael Stanze – rooms decorated with frescos for Pope Julius II: 'most exquisite compositions and painting colouring something grand'.[7] In the picture galleries he was most impressed by Raphael's *Transfiguration*,[8] but the collection closed at 3 p.m., far too early for Mackintosh, who pronounced it 'a fraud'. Having only seen half of the exhibits, he determined on another visit.

His main objective on Wednesday morning was the Pantheon. He probably approached it along the Corso and the Via di Pietra, passing the Exchange known from its former role as a customs house as the *Dogana di Terra*, and noted its façade of Corinthian columns from an ancient temple built by the Emperor Antoninus Pius.[9] He reserved his encomiums for the Pantheon:[10]

> There is one old building in Rome more impressive than any other, not only because of its better state of preservation but because of the dignity with which it has been designed, the perfection with which it has been constructed, and the effectiveness of the mode of lighting. [by an oculus in the dome] You can't conceive of the grandeur of the old Pantheon when first you enter, it is so vast and grand.[11]

That morning he also walked along part of the Corso Vittorio Emanuele, visiting the huge church of Sant'Andrea della Valle,[12] the noisy vegetable market in the Campo dei Fiori and the Palazzo della Cancelleria nearby, remarking on the 'good tombs' in Sant'Andrea. These must have impressed him far more than those that he had earlier admired in Naples as he made a drawing of one of the most monumental, that of Pope Pius III placed high on the south wall of the nave opposite the almost identical tomb of Pius II.[13] The Palazzo della Cancelleria (1495-1505) was one of the earliest Renaissance palaces in Rome, noted for its Classical purity, but when he came to make a drawing of it, Mackintosh did not choose the façade dominating the Piazza Cancelleria, nor its colonnaded courtyard: instead he attempted the difficult feat of sketching a first-floor window facing onto the narrow Via del Pellegrino. This was the same window and balcony which had interested William James Anderson, and is an example of Mackintosh's interest in the research of the first Alexander Thomson travelling student. Along with contemporary opinion, Anderson considered the Palace to be by Bramante who had previously worked in northern Italy. Seeing parallels between the design of this window and

Alessandro Galilei, Front, San Giovanni in Laterano, Fergusson, *Modern Styles of Architecture*, p.73

Lombard work in terracotta, Anderson noted that its detailing, which would have been impossible to realise in Roman travertine or tufa, had been carried out in marble.[14] Other Roman examples, which betray an interest in materials and which also might have owed something to discussions with Anderson are Mackintosh's two drawings of the entrance to the Palazzo di Venezia,[15] the earliest Renaissance palace in the city. He made a quick sketch of this portal as well as a more considered drawing. The sketch, however, is more revealing by including a detail of the architrave which Anderson had singled out for comment as an example of the modification of architectural forms by jewellery design and goldsmiths' work: 'The architrave is studded with the semblance of jewels, relieved with delicate carving while the light and graceful scrolls connecting the little window with the door cornice suggest bands of beaten metal' – a comment that early-Renaissance architects were also artists and craftsmen, as young contemporary architects, influenced by the ideology of the Arts and Crafts movement, aspired to be.[16]

C. R. Mackintosh, Arch of Titus, Rome, 1891

After his morning's excursion, Mackintosh returned to his *pensione* for lunch, a leisurely routine which he would follow throughout his time in Rome. The afternoon was taken up with a return visit to the Forum where he made a watercolour drawing of the Arch of Titus[17] before visiting the Colosseum[18] and the adjacent *Domus Aurea* -- the Golden House of Nero – where he admired the 'very nice fresco decorations'. Strangely, he had not bothered to comment on the copious, better-preserved, paintings in Pompeii and the Naples Museum, but these examples from Nero's palace had been the source of the hugely influential arabesques executed by Raphael and his school for the Vatican *Loggie* which, throughout the second half of the 19th century, were held up to British art students as examples of fine design.

Thursday 23rd April was to be unusual: just after 7 a.m. the city was awoken by a huge explosion: 'Good gracious what's that? Most terrific noise then the house starts shaking and all around females are screaming. Got out of bed, windows are rattling and breaking on all sides.' The powder magazine at Fort Monteverde, outside the Porta Portese three kilometres south of Rome, had exploded, killing two people and injuring an estimated 150 more. It demolished several houses and a school, and shattered thousands of the city's windows including many in important churches.[19]

Making his way along the glass-strewn streets, thinking that the occurrence would make the glaziers 'leap for joy', Mackintosh arrived at his morning's objective, the Arch of Constantine[20] next to the Colosseum. He had decided to make a watercolour of it, a fitting companion to the one he had done of the Arch of Titus the day before, but he was unable to complete it when the sky became overcast. Further frustrations occurred when, on the return journey, he left his paints on the bus. He had to wait an hour and a half for it to return, to find his materials safe in the hands of the conductor, whom he rewarded with the princely sum of 4 francs. Perhaps unsettled by the near loss of his colours and inconvenienced by the commotion caused by the explosion, Mackintosh spent the remainder of the day visiting the post office to collect letters and newspapers from home.

Friday saw him concentrating on Rome's Post-Imperial heritage. His first objective, with a detour via the Porta Pia, was Santa Maria Maggiore. He had probably decided to examine the Porta Pia as it had been designed by Michelangelo; his last architectural work, but he was unimpressed, describing it as 'not much to look at'. Santa Maria Maggiore fared much better, being awarded one of his higher accolades: 'very good both outside and in'. Mackintosh's catholicity of taste is apparent here as the apsidal eastern façade is a 16th-century work by the Baroque architects Carlo Fontana and Flaminio Ponzio, whilst the west front was designed by Ferdinando Fuga in the mid-18th century (Fuga was the architect of the interior of Palermo Cathedral which had so disgusted Mackintosh over a week before). He must also have been impressed by the fine 12th-century Cosmatesque pavement as he would use similar motifs in one of his own schemes.[21] He remarked on the 'good monuments' he found here and drew one of them, the tomb of the French Cardinal Philippe de Levis and his brother Archbishop Eustache (1489), placed by Innocent VIII high on the west wall of the north aisle above the Porta Santa. He also sketched the 14th-century campanile, 'different from the rest of the church' from the Piazza di Santa Maria Maggiore.

As it had started to rain, Mackintosh sheltered in the nearby 9th-century church of Santa Prassede. Noting its antiquity and its early mosaics, he was particularly charmed by the 'very funny old doorway' to the Chapel of San Zeno. On his way home along the Via Urbana he admired the exterior of Santa Pudenziana, an even older church dating from the 4th century, its recently restored front sitting well below street level at the bottom of a flight of steps.

The wet afternoon was spent in a walk along the Via Sistina to the church of Trinità dei Monti. At some point in his stay Mackintosh made a quick drawing of its 16th-century façade with its twin bell-towers[22] from the top of the Spanish Steps, but he found little to interest him in the interior. Proceeding along past the Villa Medici, the headquarters of the French Academy which was closed, he found himself once again in the Piazza del Popolo. His drawing of the Porta del Popolo may date from this visit and it is perhaps instructive that he drew its exterior face (1561) by Nanni di Baccio Bigio, who had used a design adapted from Michelangelo, rather than the interior façade of 1655 by Bernini whose work in general terms seems to have been of little interest to him. Mackintosh's main attention was concentrated on the adjacent church, Santa Maria del Popolo where he sketched its 'very nice' chaste early-Renaissance façade.[23] In the interior, paying no attention to Raphael's Chigi chapel, or the fine paintings by Pinturicchio and Caravaggio, he was most impressed by the superlative quality and quantity of the monumental work, chiefly by Andrea Bregno and his school, drawing two tombs, an altar and a baptismal font.[24] Like almost all of the tombs he would sketch throughout his tour, these were early Renaissance works. Mackintosh was concentrating on the design of the monuments and their ornamentation rather than figure sculpture which only interested him as an element in the design. He tended to choose works in marble by sculptors who, like many in their profession during this period, were also architects. Like Mackintosh's own age, the early Renaissance was a period of transition, of inquiry and experimentation, and it was perhaps the spirit of this work as much as, if not more than, its form that interested him.

Mackintosh's age was also marked by its eclecticism. He spent Saturday morning revisiting Santa Prassede to draw its 'funny old doorway', an example of that same tendency from the 9th century. The doorway, which dates from the 820s, is composed of disparate ancient fragments, two porphyry columns with Ionic capitals supporting a 1st-century architrave from a pagan temple placed there by Pope Paschal I. After beginning a sketch of another tomb monument,[25] Mackintosh went home by a circuitous route passing the Porta Pinciana, a late Roman gate erected in 403.

Saturday afternoon saw Mackintosh in the south-east of the city, at the Basilica of San Giovanni in Laterano. Like Santa Maria Maggiore, this great church, the Pope's seat as Bishop of Rome, had been constantly added to and refurbished throughout its history, from its inauguration by the Emperor Constantine in the 4th century, through its radical restoration by Francesco Borromini in the 17th, to the completion of its entrance façade in the 18th. Being no historical purist, Mackintosh could respond to the building as a holistic piece of architectural design. He declared himself to be 'very much pleased with this church' which he pronounced to be 'quite as good as St. Peter's' with the added advantage over the latter that it had a 'very good front'; an early Neo-Classical work of 1734-36 by the Florentine architect Alessandro Galilei.[26] Mackintosh also responded positively to the 13th-century cloister, a masterpiece of Cosmatesque art,[27] the finest cloister he had seen since Monreale, but which the keeper, despite Mackintosh's attempt to bribe him, would not allow him to sketch. A major reason for his visit was the adjacent

Arch of Constantine, Rome

Lateran Palace which then housed the Museo Lateranese, an important collection of Ancient Roman sculpture. No drawings from the collection have been identified but Mackintosh sketched Domenico Fontana's Palace façade and its principal doorway from the Piazza San Giovanni in Laterano.[28]

From the Lateran, Mackintosh traced his steps to another major Roman church, Santa Croce in Gerusalemme, founded by St. Helena, mother of the Emperor Constantine, some time after 326 to enshrine a relic of the True Cross. Most of the church dates from its reconstruction in 1743-44, by Domenico Gregorini and Pietro Passalacqua. Mackintosh considered this late example of the Roman Baroque with its elliptical vestibule 'very poor'. His last visit of the day was to San Martino ai Monti, in the Via delle Sette Sale, a 4th-century foundation largely remodelled around 1650 by Filippo Gagliardi. He was unable to see much of the interior as it was undergoing alterations but perhaps it was the sight of the 24 Ancient Corinthian columns employed in the nave that caused him to speculate that it might be 'rather a good thing'.

Mackintosh decided to have a rest on the Sunday and only bothered to see 'two or three unimportant churches' before going to hear Professor Blackie preach at the Presbyterian Church on Via Venti Settembre 7, an experience which he 'enjoyed immensely'.[29] The Scottish church had two Sunday services: one at 10 a.m., the other at 3 p.m. and it was probably the morning service which he attended as he spent the afternoon writing letters. Perhaps the time allowed to him before the service would have seen him exploring the two adjacent Baroque churches of San Carlo alle Quattro Fontane and Santa Maria della Vittoria; the former a riotous masterpiece of concave and convex curves on an elliptical plan by Francesco Borromini; the latter, the location of Bernini's theatrical sculptural work, *The Ecstasy of St. Teresa*.[30] Such essays were not at this time considered as worthy of study: the Baedeker guide gave them very brief notice and Fergusson considered the 17th century as 'probably the worst period of Roman art'.[31] The next day, duly refreshed, on a 'splendid morning',

Mackintosh finished his drawing of the monument at Santa Prassede, going home via San Pietro in Vincoli (St. Peter in Chains). Although this is an ancient church with an early Renaissance façade of 1475, its main attraction was Michelangelo's tomb of Julius II with its powerful figure of Moses. Mackintosh also seems to have been fascinated by the church's most notable relic, the chains in which St. Peter, according to legend, had been fettered whilst awaiting execution in Rome. The afternoon was occupied with more sketching, the completion of the watercolour of the Arch of Constantine[32] that he had begun on the previous Thursday. He then strolled through the Forum on his way home.

Tuesday morning saw Mackintosh following up his findings of the previous day, revisiting Michelangelo's Moses before descending the Esquiline hill to San Pietro in Carcere, the site of St. Peter's incarceration in the Mamertine prison: 'a most interesting spot just overflowing with exciting and awful tradition'. The church is on two levels, the lower one a cistern, which in ancient times had been converted into a prison. On the way, he visited Sant'Adriano in the Forum, Ancient Rome's Senate House, where he found 'nothing to see' before ascending the Capitoline Hill to examine Santa Maria in Aracoeli. He liked this church with its approach up a steep and impressive flight of steps, remarking on its 'good tombs and pictures'[33] and may have been reminded of Santa Maria del Popolo where he had also admired tombs by Andrea Bregno and his school. Perhaps too, he was acquiring a taste for the painting of Pinturicchio whose work he had also seen in the latter church. Afterwards, in the adjacent Capitoline Museum, he enjoyed seeing the originals of several figure sculptures with which he was familiar either from engravings or photographs, or from plaster casts at the Glasgow School of Art, along with some 'good ornament'.[34]

After lunch Mackintosh went to Santa Maria degli Angeli, a spacious Carthusian church adapted from the large central hall of the Baths of Diocletian by Michelangelo, and remodelled in the 18th century by Luigi Vanvitelli. He then made his way to the ancient church of San Lorenzo fuori le Mura founded by the Emperor Constantine and renewed by Pope Pelagius II in A.D. 579. He was greatly impressed by this building, particularly its chancel, where he admired the 'most beautiful Corinthian columns, and a frieze and cornice made up of various scraps from ancient temples. Very fine ornament'. He spent the whole of the following day there doing drawings.

Doorway, Santa Prassede, Rome

On Thursday Mackintosh made his only excursion outside the city, to visit the famous temples at Tivoli. To do so, he went first to the steam tramway terminus at Piazza delle Terme (now Piazza della Repubblica) and having time to spare, entered the Museo delle Terme. Set up in 1889, it contained Classical sculpture and some frescos in a few rooms adjacent to the cloister of the Carthusian convent attached to Santa Maria degli Angeli, the church he had visited two days before.[35]

The steam tramcars took two and a quarter hours to cover the 18 miles between Rome and Tivoli, passing the entrance to Hadrian's Villa en route. Mackintosh does not seem to have visited the villa as he made no mention of it in his diary. After making a steep ascent through olive groves, the tramway terminated at Porta Santa Croce from where visitors could walk to the Ancient Roman Temples of Vesta and the Sybil and take in the views of the cascades. He seems to have concentrated his attention on these features,[36] which he uninspiringly described as 'very nice' without visiting the town's other attraction, the Villa d'Este, highly recommended by the Baedeker guide with the caution that it was 'sometimes closed'.

Monday 1st May was a wasted day: there were public demonstrations and everything was closed except for St. Peter's where Mackintosh spent the late morning. Part of his afternoon was taken up with a drive on the Pincio, the most fashionable Roman *passegiata*, where one could watch the crowds in the park while listening to the band.[37] In the heat Mackintosh felt listless, 'as limp as a herring'.

On Saturday he was at last able to fulfil the promise he had made to himself and revisit the Vatican Museum, this time going early. He spent the whole morning in the Sistine Chapel revelling in the 'most marvellous' work of Michelangelo, particularly the *Last Judgement*, 'a most beautifully composed picture', but regretting its time-worn appearance. He now decided that this and Michelangelo's ceiling were 'the finest examples of pictorial art ever produced', and concluded that Raphael's frescoes in the *Stanze*, which he had previously so much admired, were 'very much inferior'.

Sunday saw Mackintosh revisiting the area around the Pantheon, taking in three churches. The first of these was Santa Maria sopra Minerva, built, as its name implies, over an ancient temple to Minerva. Mackintosh noted it was unique in Rome, as its only mediaeval Gothic church. A 13th-century Dominican foundation, owing much to the major Florentine church of Santa Maria Novella, it is the resting place of the Medici Renaissance Popes, Leo X and Clement VII. Mackintosh did not record his impressions, nor did he offer any opinion of the next church he visited, the Baroque Sant'Agnese in Agone, beyond describing it as 'small', an impression which must strike most visitors on entering after seeing the façade, with its dome and twin bell towers, which, dominating the Piazza Navona, promise a much larger interior.[38] The mainly 15th-century church of San Lorenzo in Damaso, which has no independent street presence as it shares its exterior with the Palazzo della Cancelleria, has a broad, cavernous, well-proportioned interior, of which Mackintosh approved. Finally, as it was the Sabbath, he spent the afternoon at the Presbyterian church and writing letters.

Monday was Mackintosh's last day in Rome and he used it to make one more visit to the Sistine Chapel and the Vatican Museum's picture gallery. His last Roman site was the Villa Borghese in the gardens on the Pincio near to his *pensione*. Without mentioning any specific favourites he noted that it had a fine collection, but typically, rather than picking out any of the paintings or figure sculptures for special mention, he focused on 'four most excellent little old Italian pictures, of marble', presumably in relief, which, for him, were 'quite the style'.[39] After this he headed for the railway station to board the 3 p.m. train for the Umbrian town of Orvieto.

Notes for Chapter 3

[1] Designed by Carlo Rainaldi (1611-91) and modified by Giovanni Lorenzo Bernini (1589-1680) and Carlo Fontana (1634-1714).
[2] Erected in 1814 by Giuseppe Valadier (1762-1839).
[3] The Pensione Michel charged 7 francs per day.
[4] Mackintosh, 'A Tour in Italy (1892)' in Robertson (1990), p.113
[5] Carlo Maderno (1556-1629) was commissioned to build the front in 1605; it was completed in 1612.
[6] Mackintosh, 'A Tour in Italy (1892)' in Robertson (1990), p.112.
[7] The rooms were decorated between 1508 and 1534 by Raphael and his pupils for three successive Popes, Julius II, Leo X and Clement VII.
[8] The painting was completed after Raphael's death in 1520 by his pupils.
[9] Mackintosh mistakenly identified this former custom house as a church; its columns had previously been part of the Temple of Neptune dedicated by Antoninus Pius to the Emperor Hadrian.
[10] Built between 118 and 128 under the Emperor Hadrian and consecrated as a church in 609.
[11] Mackintosh, 'A Tour in Italy (1892)' in Robertson (1990), pp.113-114.
[12] Built in 1591 by Giacomo della Porta (1539-1602) and Pier Paolo Olivieri (1515-99).
[13] Pius III died in 1503 and the monument was placed here in 1615.
[14] William James Anderson, *Italian Renaissance*, pp.83-84.
[15] By Francesco del Borgo di Santo Sepolcro (1455); Mackintosh's drawings were possibly executed on 28th April when he visited the Capitol.
[16] William James Anderson, *The Architecture of the Renaissance in Italy*, p.45; both of these examples, might be construed as a contradiction of Arts and Crafts principles which the teaching Mackintosh would have received in his design course at the Glasgow School of Art which were inimical to the technique of one craft being aped by another; it does not, however, follow that the ornamentation on both of these examples was not just as easily achievable in marble as in terracotta or in jewellers' work.
[17] Erected in AD 81 after the death of the Emperor Vespasian.
[18] Begun by the Emperor Vespasian in AD 70.
[19] *The Times* (24th April 1891), p.5.
[20] Erected in 315.
[21] Design for a Chapter House, 1892.
[22] Attributed to Giacomo della Porta (1539-1602); staircase by Giovanni Fontana (1540-1614).
[23] Dating from Sixtus IV's restoration of 1472-77 by Baccio Pontelli (1450-92) and Andrea Bregno (c.1421-1506).
[24] In the delle Rovere Chapel, the first chapel in the south aisle the tomb of Domenico (d. 1501) and Cristoforo delle Rovere (d. 1477) by Andrea Bregno with a Madonna by Mino da Fiesole (1431-85); the tomb of Bernardino Lonati in the north transept; an altar in the Costa Chapel in the south aisle (c.1505); and a baptismal font (or a repository for Holy oil) in the Capella Montemirabile, the first chapel in the north aisle.
[25] The drawing is currently untraced.
[26] Galilei (1691-1736) had been influenced by the English Palladian revival, but also by Michelangelo and Maderno.
[27] By Iacopo and Pietro Vassalletto (c.1222-32).
[28] Domenico Fontana (1543-1607) began the reconstruction of the Palace on the orders of Pope Sixtus V in 1586.
[29] John Stuart Blackie (1809-95) was Professor of Greek at Edinburgh University.
[30] San Carlo alle Quattro Fontane, interior (1638-41), façade (1664-67) by Francesco Borromini (1599-1667); Santa Maria della Vittoria, exterior (1626) by Giovanni Battista Soria (1581-1651) and an interior (1608-20) by Carlo Maderno (1556-1629); *The Ecstasy of St. Teresa* (c.1647-50) was the work of Gian Lorenzo Bernini (1598-1680).
[31] James Fergusson, *History of the Modern Styles of Architecture*, 2nd edition (London: John Murray, 1873), p.74.
[32] This watercolour is currently untraced.
[33] The church was founded before the 8th century, but most of the present building dates from c.1250, the steps from 1348; it stands on the spot where, according to legend, the Triburtine Sybil appeared to the Emperor Augustus to announce the advent of Christ, with the words "Behold the altar of God's first-born", hence the name 'Aracoeli' (Altar of Heaven).
[34] The sculptures which Mackintosh remarked on are all in the Palazzo Nuovo, one of two buildings by Michelangelo which house the Museum: the *Dying Gaul* (then generally known as 'The Dying Gladiator'), a Roman copy of a 3rd-century B.C. bronze figure from Pergamon, discovered in Rome in 1622; the *Resting Satyr*, a Roman copy of a Greek original by Praxiteles found in Hadrian's Villa at Tivoli; the *Capitoline Venus*, a Roman copy of the *Aphrodite of Cnidus* by the Greek sculptor Praxiteles, found in Rome in the 17th century; the *Pair of Centaurs* from Hadrian's Villa at Tivoli; and the *Boy with a Goose*, a Roman marble copy of a Hellenistic bronze by Boethos of Chalcedon.
[35] The contents of this museum are now in the Palazzo Massimo alle Terme in the Piazza dei Cinquecento.
[36] The Temple of the Sybil has four Ionic columns; the Temple of Vesta is a circular edifice with a colonnade of eighteen Corinthian columns – 10 of which are preserved.
[37] The Pincio was laid out by Giuseppe Valadier (1762-1839) in 1809-14 – adjacent to the Borghese Gardens and not far from Mackintosh's *pensione*.
[38] An ancient church reconstructed in 1652 by Girolamo Rainaldi (1570-1655) and his son Carlo (1611-91), then from 1653 by Francesco Borromini (1599-1667) who designed the façade, and from 1657 by Giovanni Maria Baratta (1670-1747) who completed the front and the bell towers.
[39] The Casino Borghese was begun in 1608 by Flaminio Ponzio (1560-1613); it was altered between 1775-90 by Antonio Asprucci (1723-1808) and Christopher Unterberger (1732-98) when the interiors were carried out; the major collection was begun by Cardinal Scipione Borghese (1576-1633); the 'marble pictures' are unidentified.

FOUR

The Cathedral, Florence

Orvieto, Siena and Florence

Orvieto: Monday 4th – Sunday 10th May
Mackintosh's train pulled into Orvieto Station at 5.30 p.m.. The town, in the province of Umbria, at that time had a population of around 8,000 and stands on a great 440 ft high tufa outcrop which dominates the wide Paglia valley. Leaving the station, he probably crossed the road to the funicular railway ascending through a tunnel under the 14th-century fortress to the eastern end of the town and the beginning of the main street.[1] The Corso Cavour climbs along the central spine of the rock to the Piazza del Commune (now the Piazza della Repubblica). Here Mackintosh quickly found a hotel, the Aquila Bianca, on the Via Garibaldi behind the Palazzo Communale, where he could stay for 2 francs per night.

The young architect's main focus of interest over the next five days was the town's superb cathedral. A few minutes' walk down the Corso then right along the Via del Duomo, it dominates the Piazza Santa Maria. He had nothing but praise for this masterpiece of Italian Gothic, 'especially the front.[2] Built in white marble with bands of red, purple blue black brown yellow marble, beautiful twisted columns. Bronze evangelists, and just covered with gold mosaic bands'. He filled three sheets with studies of the mosaic bands, reminiscent of the Arab work he had seen in Sicily and praised the façade for the coherence of its design, even admiring the mosaic narratives that adorned it, despite the fact that these were 'said to be modern restorations'.[3]

Although there was some rain every day, two thunderstorms and a hailstorm, Mackintosh managed to make a fine watercolour of the south façade with its semi-circular chapels and a study of the highly-ornamented jamb of its Bishop's doorway by Arnolfo di Cambio, the first architect of Florence Cathedral. On the north side he made a drawing of the eastern of two doorways. The Cathedral's

C. R. Mackintosh, Mosaic bands, west front, Orvieto Cathedral, 1891

C. R. Mackintosh, south façade, Orvieto Cathedral

interior impressed him with its fine proportions and he remarked on the beautiful painting in the chapel, presumably Lucca Signorelli's great fresco cycle of the *Last Judgement* in the Capella Nuova.[4]

Although he recorded that he found the town 'most interesting'[5] the only drawing by him which has been identified is a quick sketch of the campanile of the church of Santa Maria dei Servi[6] in the Via Belesario. Apart from this he could only comment that Orvieto was characterised by 'idleness, dirt and misery'.

Siena: Sunday 10th – Tuesday 19th May

The poor weather persisted when Mackintosh left Orvieto on the 12.45 p.m. train for Siena, a slow journey of almost six hours. The rain had cleared by the time he spotted its famous campanile[7] long before the train arrived at the station which was situated on a branch line. This required a detour around the base of the hill on which the town stands, only to reverse into a siding and then return the other way. Finally arriving at the station at 6.30 p.m., he caught a cab to the Pensione Chiusarelli, on Via San Domenico (now Viale Curtatone): at 5 francs somewhat more expensive than his previous hotel but affording a superb view of the north side of the Cathedral.

On going down to dinner, Mackintosh bumped into James Paxton[8] and Robin Dods,[9] two young Scots architects also making a study tour of Italy. He does not record whether this was planned or a completely fortuitous encounter but he knew Paxton from John Hutchison's office, where both had served their apprenticeship, and from the Glasgow School of Art where they attended some of the same classes. Dods, who had been born in New Zealand and had been trained in Edinburgh, was working with Paxton in London. The trio would travel as far as Verona together.

The city, much larger than Orvieto, had 25,000 inhabitants and was the capital of the Tuscan province of Siena. Built principally of brick on three adjoining hills, it had been an important art centre and political rival of Florence throughout the Middle Ages, only to be incorporated into the Grand Duchy of Tuscany in 1555. Mackintosh's first morning was spent in an effort to obtain permission to sketch in the Cathedral and the Palazzo Pubblico, finding it 'rather slow work as the lazy Italians didn't turn up till nearly 12'. Once permission was granted, he installed himself in the Cathedral which was much less to his taste than its sister edifice in Orvieto, despite many superficial similarities. Both churches are masterpieces of Italian Gothic with tripartite west fronts, and façades and interiors of banded stonework. Whereas Orvieto's front with its vertical and horizontal elements, the product of one architect, is a fully resolved design, Siena's was the victim of drastic changes to the articulation of its upper section in the 14th century, to accommodate its central round window, causing an uncomfortable disjunction between the two levels.[10] Mackintosh and his new companions, from the vantage point of their *pensione*, had the luxury of discussing the incongruities of the design when compared with that of a northern Gothic cathedral.

From their viewpoint it was more than obvious that the high gables of the west front did not relate to the low pitch of the nave and aisle roofs.

In his diary Mackintosh had more to say about Siena Cathedral than any other building he encountered:

> The whole church didn't strike me as very fine architecturally. On the exterior to begin with the front is a fraud as it gives no indication of the interior. Then when you examine the design you find that it is almost "not there" Then you begin to see that were it not for the fine material the whole thing would be very poor as a composition There are many nice bits of detail and there are very many bad, clumsy, & vulgar things. Which when found out detract very considerably from the effect or impression the edifice makes on you at first sight. So much for the front. Then the sides, well / they take the cake. There are no windows in the aisles so this part is plain and might look well so, but it wasn't good enough for the Sienese. No they must have windows, so they painted windows along the wall: well designed & painted in the Gothic style. Very beautiful? examples, and it is a pity that the rain is wearing some parts of them away.

He was more complimentary about the campanile,[11] admiring the plainness of its design, but could see nothing to admire either externally or internally about the dome.[12] On the lookout for further 'frauds' he also noted in the interior that the banded stonework, above a certain height, was only painted, but did find a great deal to admire. He made separate drawings of the two holy water stoups[13] at the entrance and was captivated by the floor of inlaid marble depicting biblical and mythological scenes recording that it was 'really magnificent, and makes one sorry that it is a floor'.[14] The pulpit, a masterpiece by Nicola Pisano, was 'a very good bit of work'[15] and an altar, partly adorned with figures by Michelangelo, was 'a caution in M. Angelo's usual style'.[16] Mackintosh took this to be a tomb as it was somewhat reminiscent of Julius II's which he had seen in Rome. The entrance to the library of which he also made a study was 'a very beautiful piece of Renaissance detail'.[17] Other subjects for praise were the doorway of the Baptistery, the use of marble on the high altar,[18] the font in the New Baptistery with sculptures by Donatello and Lorenzo Ghiberti[19] and the wooden stalls, with the proviso that 'like most Italian wood work' they were 'very stony'.[20]

Blind window, Siena Cathedral

Although he spent much of his time sketching at the Cathedral, Mackintosh also visited the Palazzo Pubblico, the Gothic town hall[21] where he admired the stalls in the chapel[22] and made a drawing of a pair of bronze torch bearers.[23] He also made a pencil study of one of the windows and a watercolour of the campanile. Around the streets he took an interest in the copious examples of wrought iron work and sought out the Palazzo Pollini on Via Baldassarre Peruzzi, the street named in honour of the building's Sienese architect. The three-storey edifice with its inclined base and elaborate cornice buried beneath an eave of projecting rafters had previously been studied by William James Anderson who admired it for its breadth and simplicity and the harmony of its proportions.

Florence: Tuesday 19th – Tuesday 26th May

Joining forces with his two new companions, Mackintosh's next objective was Florence where the trio arrived at Santa Maria Novella Station at 7 p.m. This great centre of the Renaissance and tourist mecca boasted 200,000 inhabitants and had been the capital of Italy briefly between 1864 and 1870. The most fashionable quarter of town for tourists was the Lungarno, along the right bank of the River Arno, but Mackintosh and his friends opted for a more modest location, a *pensione* run by a Madame Laurent fronting onto the Via del Presto, a narrow street that runs south from the Santa Trinità Bridge on the left bank.[24] Opposite was the south façade of Filippo Brunelleschi's great church of Santo Spirito, and a little way down the street the Palazzo Guadagni[25] which Mackintosh knew from his student textbooks.[26] A jotting of Santo Spirito's dome and campanile[27] alongside a sketch of a Florentine chimney appears on one sketchbook page, drawn from an upstairs window in the *pensione*, and the Palazzo Guadagni on the next, as if he could not wait to take in the delights of his new surroundings, but he seems to have developed an ambivalent attitude to the Tuscan city which he was to sum up in a letter to his friend Francis Newbery after a return visit in 1925: 'I found Florence just as artificial in a stupid way as I did 25 years ago [sic] when I went as a small lad.'[28]

As a student in 1891 he knew that he was meant to regard it as *the* art centre *par excellence* but, perhaps objecting to the uncritical attitude with which tourists were expected to marvel at its wonders and not being prepared to suspend his own artistic judgement, he reacted by describing some of the city's more revered buildings and artefacts in his diary in a very frank and perhaps overly negative way, most noticeably giving short shrift to the ground-breaking work of the architect and theorist Filippo Brunelleschi and completely failing to mention that of the other great early Renaissance architect Leon Battista Alberti (1404-72). However, conscious of his position as a young man who was only starting out on his career and needing to curry favour with an establishment which was more inclined to endorse received opinion, when he came to give a lecture on his tour in Glasgow over a year later he would feed his audience with what they would have expected from a cultured young architect, an enthusiastic description of

C. R. Mackintosh, Palazzo Pubblico, Siena, 1891

the glories of the city copying his description of Florence directly from his Baedeker guidebook: 'Like the waterlily rising on the mirror of the lake, so rests on this lovely ground the still more lovely Florence. ... Each street of Florence contains a world of art: the walls of the city are the calyx, containing the fairest flowers of the human mind: and this is but the richest gem in the diadem with which the Italian people have adorned the earth'.[29]

Wednesday, his first full day in Florence, saw Mackintosh at his most energetic, visiting the city centre and some of the most important churches. He crossed the Arno via the Santa Trinità Bridge or the Ponte Vecchio to the Piazza della Signoria. The entry in his diary is terse: 'Morning went to Piazza Signora [sic] & Pal. Vecchio, early gothic with bad tower, crib from Siena. Logia dei Lenzi [sic] very good & very large.[30] Rape of Sabins [sic] stupid thing'.

His disparagement of the tower of the Palazzo Vecchio gives no indication of his opinion of that of the Palazzo Pubblico at Siena. Whether he regarded the former simply as a poor copy of a good piece of architecture or considered that both were bad towers is unclear. In his diary he had merely mentioned the Palazzo Pubblico as 'interesting' although it had been interesting enough for him to produce a watercolour of its tower. His dismissal of Giambologna's Mannerist marble sculpture of a Roman carrying off a Sabine woman,[31] one of several pieces sited in the Loggia dei Lanzi to the right of the Palazzo Vecchio, is a possible further indication of an animosity towards the sinuosity of the Baroque style of which this was an influential precursor. From the Piazza he traced his steps to the Cathedral, again recording brief and not wholly adulatory impressions in his diary: 'Duomo very elaborate marble work liked view from [rear?] with dome and chapel best. Front modern, Giottos [sic] tower [the campanile] very good. Much dependent on effect for colour of marble. Interior a fraud. Babtistry [sic] not much. Donatella [sic] door exquisite. Interior simple & neat. Was disappointed with Florence Cathedral.'[32]

The diary does not mention any further visits, but in his 1892 Glasgow lecture he implied that he made his inspection on the Sunday. Whether this was a fictional visit, added to his narrative for effect, will never be known. His account of his impressions, however, is very different.

> On the way home I looked into the cathedral, an enormous fabric inlaid with the richest marbles and covered with panels and carving on the exterior, while the interior is plain & simple The nave is vast &

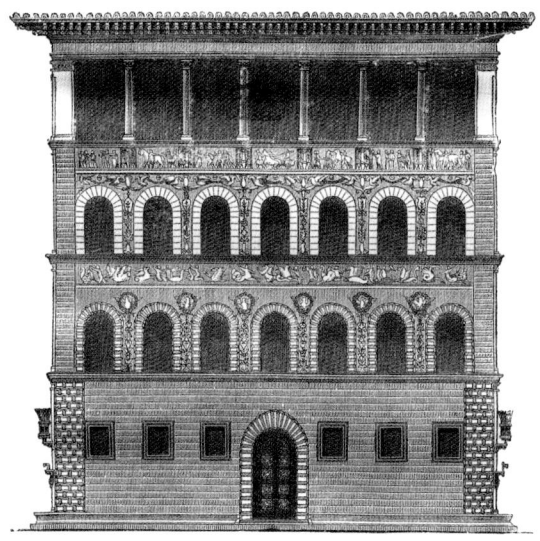

Palazzo Guadagni, Florence. Rosengarten, *A Handbook of Architectural Styles*, p.381

> solemn, the dome amazingly spacious with the high altar as a centre enclosed by a circular arcade some 200 feet in diameter There is something imposing about the decoration as it suggests the idea of sanctity into which none but the holy ought to penetrate. However profane I might feel myself I took the liberty of entering and sat down in a niche. Not a ray of light enters this sacred enclosure but through the medium of narrow windows high up in the dome and richly painted, A sort of yellow green tint predominates which gives additional solemnity to the altar and paleness to the votary before it. I was conscious of the effect and obtained at least the colour of sanctity. Having remained some time in this pious hue I left the church and went into the Battesterio [sic], a most admirable octagonal structure[33]

To return to his Wednesday itinerary, from the Duomo he walked east to Santa Croce. Although unimpressed by its bland modern west front[34] he found much to admire in the interior, in particular the 15th-century tombs, the windows in the chancel and the pulpit. Outside there was little to please him in the cloister,[35] and he only managed to note the frieze by Luca della Robbia in Brunelleschi's Pazzi Chapel which is generally regarded as an architectural masterpiece of the early Renaissance. He then made a longish walk across the city centre to Santa Maria Novella where he failed to mention the work on the upper portion of the front by Florence's other master architect, Leon Battista Alberti, reserving his encomiums for the 'exquisite glass window in the chancel'.[36] From Santa Maria Novella it was a short distance to San Lorenzo where, again making no mention of Brunelleschi,[37] he would remind himself of his admiration for Michelangelo, particularly in the Laurentian Library – 'benches & windows very good'.[38] 'Cloister' (a work attributed to Brunelleschi) 'poor'. The last church of the day was San Marco which involved a walk along the Via Cavour. Once more there was 'not much to see' in a building with an 18th-century façade and a largely 16th-century interior.[39]

If Wednesday had been used as a means of familiarising himself with the city, Mackintosh now began to tighten the focus of his studies, examining what he had already discovered in greater detail. The whole of Thursday was taken up by a return visit to Santa Croce where he made a watercolour of one of its finest tombs, that of the humanist scholar and chancellor of the Florentine Republic Carlo Marsuppini (1399-1453), an exercise in polychrome marble by Desiderio da Settignano. As an admirer of Michelangelo, he could not resist making a drawing of part of his tomb, a monument very much in the master's style designed by his biographer Giorgio Vasari and erected in 1570.

Despite finding nothing to see at the church of San Marco on the Wednesday, on Friday Mackintosh returned to inspect the adjacent Museo di San Marco, a suppressed Dominican monastery, which had been a museum since 1869. The buildings erected between 1437 and 1452 are primarily the work of the Florentine Renaissance architect Michelozzo and are adorned with frescos by his contemporary Fra. Angelico. Mackintosh could find nothing to sketch there and so decided to visit the church of San Miniato al Monte. This involved a considerable walk across the city and a trek up the hill on the other side of the Arno, but he was not disappointed. The church, built in the Tuscan Romanesque style, dates from the 11th century[40] and was regarded by Rosengarten as a notable example of an early Romanesque basilica, both for its raised choir, its painted open timber roof and its use of polychrome marbles on the exterior and interior. Mackintosh endorsed Rosengarten's judgement, making a watercolour study of its 'beautifully decorated roof' and pencil sketches of the choir screen and 'fine mosaic floor'.[41]

C. R. Mackintosh, Tomb of Carlo Marsuppini, Santo Spirito, Florence, 1891

The whole of Saturday was spent in the area close to the Piazza della Signoria, examining three sites: the Badia Fiorentina, the Bargello and the Palazzo Vecchio. The Badia, or Abbey, was a Benedictine foundation dating back to its endowment by Willa, widow of Uberto, Margrave of Tuscany, in 978. Most of the church had been drastically remodelled in the early 17th century by Matteo Segaloni and Mackintosh drew its late 15th-century doorway on the Via del Proconsolo with its enamelled terracotta lunette, which he took to be by a member of the della Robbia family.[42] He recorded no comment on the interior beyond admiring the '3 good tombs' made in the 15th century, and produced a study of an angel from that of Ugo, Margrave of Tuscany, the son of the foundress, who had died in 1001.[43]

C. R. Mackintosh, Giovanni della Robbia,
Glazed terracotta frieze, Bargello, Florence, 1891

The Bargello, which stands opposite the Badia on the Via del Proconsolo is a 13th to 14th-century fortified palazzo which from 1266 served as the residence of the Podesta, the city's chief magistrate, and was used as a prison and headquarters of the head of police from the 16th century. Between 1857 and 1865 it was restored and converted into the Museo Nazionale del Bargello to house a fine collection of Florentine sculpture and decorative art. Mackintosh noted its display of armour on the ground floor and its collection of works by Donatello, and made watercolour studies of a carpet and a piece of glazed terracotta work by Giovanni della Robbia.

The fortress–like Palazzo Vecchio is a mediaeval municipal building, mainly erected in 1291-1314 by Arnolfo di Cambio. It had served as the seat of the Signoria, the government of the Florentine Republic, until 1540 when for nine years it had been the Ducal palace. Between 1865 and 1871, when Florence was the capital of the Kingdom of Italy, it had been the National Chamber of Deputies and Foreign Ministry. Mackintosh commented on the 'beautiful quadrangle', designed by Michelozzo in 1453 and its vaults and columns ornamented by Giorgio Vasari in 1565.

Sunday was given over to a visit to Florence's major galleries, the Uffizi and Palazzo Pitti, both of which, 'especially' the Palazzo degli Uffizi were 'crammed full of good pictures & statuary'. Sunday was a free day when the entrance fee of 1 franc was waived. The Uffizi was erected in 1560-74 by Giorgio Vasari on behalf of Grand Duke Cosimo I de' Medici to house the offices of the municipal government. The Loggia on the third floor was developed as a gallery containing the Medici sculpture and painting collections by Cosimo's son Francesco I in 1574. It consists of two long corridors connected by a third shorter one which overlooks the Arno, with the two long east and west corridors giving access to a series of galleries. Entering the east corridor Mackintosh was not only struck by the sculptures arrayed along its length, several of which he already knew from plaster casts in Glasgow School of Art, but was impressed by the 13th and 14th-century paintings by Giotto and the Sienese school which then adorned the walls. He also enjoyed the collection of paintings by Michelangelo, Raphael and Titian in the galleries adjacent to the west corridor, singling out Titian's works as most to his liking, in particular his half-length depiction of a goddess known as 'Flora' which he described as 'exquisite'. He did not record his opinion of the Palazzo Pitti, probably sated with impressions from the Uffizi by the time he arrived at its sister gallery.

Monday, the last full day, was again filled with activity. He began it with a watercolour sketch of the Ponte Vecchio,[44] probably his daily view from the Santa Trinità Bridge. Then he set out to make a series of jottings in various parts of the town. Several of the surviving drawings of Florentine palaces may have been made on this day. Of these buildings he judged the Palazzo Strozzi, and the Palazzo Medici-Riccardi[45] to be the best, admiring their 'large masses of plain masonry small windows, surmounted by tremendous cornices' which gave them 'a simple but dignified grandeur'.[46] He also revisited the Bargello and in the afternoon bought photographs to supplement his sketches.

Notes for Chapter 4

[1] The Fortezza was constructed in 1364 by Cardinal Albornoz; by 1890 it had been converted into a garden with an amphitheatre for public performances.
[2] The façade is attributed to the Sienese architect and sculptor Lorenzo Maitani (1270/75-1330).
[3] The mosaics as they exist, almost all of which depict the life of the Virgin Mary, were produced by different artists from the 14th to the 19th centuries; some are restorations .
[4] The decoration of the chapel was commenced by Fra. Angelico (c.1400-55) and Benozzo Gozzoli (1420-97) in 1447; Signorelli (c.1441-1523) was responsible for most of the scheme which he produced between 1499 and 1504.
[5] Mackintosh, 'A Tour in Italy (1892)' in Robertson (1990), p.114.
[6] The church dates from 1265 but was completely reconstructed in a Neo-Classical style by the architect Virginio Vespignani in 1857.
[7] The Torre del Mangia, the campanile of the Palazzo Pubblico was constructed between 1325 and 1345 by Lippo Memmi (fl. 1317-47) and Agostino di Giovanni (1285-c.1347).
[8] James Paxton (c.1864-?).
[9] Robin (Robert) Smith Dods (1868-1920).
[10] The portals, designed between 1284 and 1296, are believed to be the work of Giovanni Pisano; the work on the façade was only recommenced in 1376 under Giovanni di Cecco.
[11] Completed 1264.
[12] The dome was completed in 1264; its lantern was added in 1664.
[13] Executed by Antonio Federighi (1420/5-83) in the last quarter of the 15th century.
[14] 1370s to mid-16th century.
[15] The pulpit (1265-68) by Nicola Pisano (c.1200- after 1278) has a Renaissance staircase constructed in 1543 by Bartolomeo Neroni (c.1505-71).
[16] The altar was commissioned by Cardinal Francesco Piccolomini and executed in 1481 by Andrea Bregno; Michelangelo carved four of the figures: Saints. Paul, Peter, Pius and Gregory between 1501 and 1504.
[17] Executed in 1497 by Lorenzo di Mariano (1476-1534).
[18] Designed in 1506 by Baldassarre Peruzzi (1481-1537).
[19] Executed between 1427 and 1429 with a marble shrine by Jacopo della Quercia (1371/4-1438).
[20] These were the work of several artists between 1363 and 1397.
[21] Built 1297-1310.
[22] Carved by Domenico di Niccolo dei Cori (c.1362-before 1453) in 1429.
[23] Both 1509-12 by Giacomo Cozzarelli (1453-1515) from Palazzo del Magnifico, Piazza San Giovanni.
[24] The address was Via del Presto 11 with another entrance at Via Maggio 28; Mackintosh noted the price as 4.50 to 5 francs.
[25] By Cronaca (Simone del Pollaiolo; 1454-1508) c.1505.
[26] Albert Rosengarten, *A Handbook of Architectural Styles*, p.381, illus.; James Fergusson, *History of the Modern Styles of Architecture*, p.99, illus.
[27] The Dome was designed by Filippo Brunelleschi (1337-1446) but completed after his death in 1484; the campanile (1503) was the work of Baccio d'Agnolo (1462-1543).
[28] Mackintosh, Letter to Francis Newbery, 27th December 1925, in Neat and McDermott, *Closing the Circle: Thomas Howarth, Mackintosh and the Modern Movement: a Biography*, p.129.
[29] Karl Baedeker, *Northern Italy* (1899), p.416 and Mackintosh, 'A Tour in Italy (1892)' Robertson (1990), p.115.
[30] The Loggia dei Lanzi was built 1376-82 by Benci di Cione (d. 1388) and Simone Talenti (14th century).
[31] *Rape of the Sabine Women*, 1581-83, by Giambologna (1529-1608).
[32] Begun in the 13th century, its architects included Arnolfo di Cambio,

Giotto, Francesco Talenti, Orcagna and Brunelleschi; the west front was built 1876-87 to the design of Emilio de Fabris (1808-83); the campanile was begun by Giotto in 1334, continued by Andrea Pisano in 1343 and completed by Francesco Talenti, 1348-59; the Baptistery (11th to 13th century) has bronze doors by Andrea Pisano and Lorenzo Ghiberti; the east door (1425-52) by Ghiberti is the best known and is probably that admired by Mackintosh as the work of Donatello.

[33] Mackintosh, 'A Tour in Italy (1892)' in Robertson (1990), p.116.
[34] 1857-63 by Niccolo Matas (1798-c.1872).
[35] Presumably the 14th-century first cloister attributed to Arnolfo di Cambio (c.1245-1302); the second cloister, completed in 1453, is the work of Brunelleschi.
[36] By the workshop of Domenico Ghirlandaio (1449-1494) in the Tornabuoni Chapel (1486-90).
[37] Rebuilt (1425-46) by Brunelleschi for the Medici family.
[38] Constructed (1559-71) by Giorgio Vasari (1511/12-74) and Bartolomeo Ammannati (1511-92) to Michelangelo's design.
[39] Front designed by Agostino Nobili in 1778, interior (1588) by Giambologna (1529-1608).
[40] Façade c.1090; interior (1018-63); floor (1207).
[41] Albert Rosengarten, op.cit. pp.166-167 and pp.253-254.
[42] Door by Benedetto da Rovezzano (1495) with lunette relief by Benedetto Buglioni (1461-1521).
[43] Mino da Fiesole produced the other two tombs, one in the left transept dating from 1481, the other dedicated to Bernardo Giugni (1466) in the right transept.
[44] The bridge was constructed in 1345, replacing an earlier structure.
[45] Palazzo Strozzi, begun in 1489 by Filippo Strozzi; Palazzo Medici-Riccardi designed by Michelozzo (1396-1472) after 1444 for Cosimo il Vecchio de' Medici.
[46] Mackintosh, 'A Tour in Italy (1892)' in Robertson (1990), p.117.

Florence

FIVE

Campo dei Marcoli, Pisa

Pisa to Ferrara

Pisa: Tuesday 26th May
Mackintosh was up at 4.30 a.m. to finish his watercolour of the Ponte Vecchio, before returning to the *pensione* for breakfast in time to catch the 9.30 a.m. train for Pisa. A halt en route at Empoli, the junction for trains to Siena and the south, allowed him enough time to make a quick sketch of part of the late-mediaeval Torre Sant'Agostino of the church of San Stefano degli Agostiniani, a notable landmark in the town which would be destroyed in 1944.[1]

In the 12th century, Pisa had been one of the great maritime powers of the Mediterranean, dominating the Italian coast from La Spezia to Civita Vecchia, with an empire that included Sardinia, Corsica and the Balearic Islands. Its most notable buildings, the Cathedral, the apogee of the Pisan Romanesque style with its rich employment of polychrome marble and multiple arcading, together with its baptistery, campanile – the famous leaning tower – and the Campo Santo – its cloistered cemetery – all date from this period. They are grouped together in a large space, the Campo dei Miracoli (Field of Miracles) which consciously echoed the Temple Mount in Jerusalem. Although in the 1890s Pisa was still the capital of a province, the see of an archbishop and the seat of a university, the Baedeker Guide described it as 'a quiet town with 30,000 inhabitants'. The Baedeker recommended a stay of at least one night, but on arrival at 11 a.m., the three young architects determined on seeing the town in a few hours, left their luggage at the station and headed through the arcaded streets to the Campo dei Miracoli.

Crossing the River Arno by the Ponte di Mezzo on the way, they had a good view of the Palazzo Agostini on the opposite bank. This Gothic building was the subject of a watercolour by Ruskin, painted in 1845, and housed the Caffè del'Ussero, the meeting place of Italian patriot writers of the *Risorgimento*, the movement which had led to the unification of the country. Impressed by its brick and terracotta façade, Mackintosh made a quick sketch of one of its bays together with a detailed study of a first-floor window. Arriving at the Campo dei Miracoli he found the sacred buildings 'a very interesting group' but was 'very much disgusted with [the] exterior of the Cathedral'[2] which was 'all arcade and no design': there was 'no place to rest the eye'. Entrance to the building was opposite the leaning tower through the Porta di San Ranieri, where he stopped to sketch before finding the interior 'indifferently good', although there was 'some nice glass' and the wooden stalls in the choir[3] were 'very good indeed'. The circular baptistery[4] to the west of the Cathedral, however, he voted 'better' than its neighbour. He made most use of his sketchbook in the adjacent Campo Santo,[5] built in the form of a cloister, decorated with mediaeval frescoes and lined with Roman sculptures and sarcophagi. At the western end he made a jotting of the early 15th-century tomb of Archbishop Pietro Ricci,[6] and on another page he sketched a 12th-century mosaic fragment from the workshop of Rainaldo, the second architect of the Cathedral. This fragment had been previously copied by Mackintosh, before his visit to Italy, from the measured study in Anderson's book, but was now re-examined with added colour notes.[7] At the bottom of the page, he drew a study of one of the capitals on the eastern arcade of the cloister.

Leaving Pisa at 8.20 p.m. and travelling via Lucca,[8] the three students arrived at the small Tuscan town of Pistoia at 11.30 p.m.

Pistoia: Wednesday 27th May
Mackintosh does not record where they stayed in Pistoia, but most of the hotels were situated in the area around Piazza Cino (now Piazza Gavinana) and Via Cavour, close to the major buildings, mostly examples of the Pisan Romanesque which were explored next morning and early afternoon. In the Piazza del Duomo, the Cathedral and octagonal Baptistery earned the accolade of 'fairly good'

Upper: Palazzo Agostini, Pisa
Lower: Detail of entrance bay, San Giovanni Fuorcivitas, Pistoia

and the campanile merited a careful drawing. Although 'nothing else' was 'up to much', the 14th-century Gothic Palazzo del Comune in the same square was the subject of a more rapid jotting. The Pisan Romanesque was acknowledged by a sketch of a bay of the heavily arcaded 12th-century church of San Giovanni Fuorcivitas; and the 14th-century campanile of San Paolo was recorded by another sketch. For Mackintosh, one exception to the general mediocrity, was the glazed terracotta frieze (1514-27) on the exterior of the Ospedale del Ceppo by Giovanni della Robbia, whose work he had previously admired in Florence.

Keeping up their punishing schedule, Mackintosh and his companions left the town at 3.30 p.m. for Bologna, the populous capital of the Emilia, where they arrived at 5.15 p.m. for a visit of two and a quarter hours.

Bologna: Wednesday 27th May
The short stay took them from the station down the Via dell' Indipendenza to the Piazza del Nettuno and the adjacent Piazza Vittorio Emanuele (now Piazza Maggiore) at the centre of town. There Mackintosh commented on San Petronio, the vast church in the Tuscan-Gothic style that the Bolognese began in 1390 in emulation of the Cathedral of Florence and left with only its nave completed in 1659. He favourably noted one of the marble screens which enclose several of the side chapels, the unfinished early Renaissance front and the mediaeval brick sides. He drew the Romanesque campanile of the Baroque Cathedral of San Pietro, sketched two of the numerous capitals, which ornament the loggias that shade the streets, and one of the two leaning towers which are a feature of the town. In their vicinity he was charmed by the 'very nice little brick ch[urch]', probably Santi Vitale e Agricola, one of a complex of three ancient churches dedicated to St. Stephen the Martyr, dating from 887. Having seen little else that was 'calculated to keep' them 'any longer' there was time for dinner before catching the 7.30 p.m. train for Ravenna.

Ravenna: Wednesday 27th May – Monday 1st June
Ravenna was more to Mackintosh's taste, a 'very delightful place' which came upon the travellers 'like an oasis in a desert'. In 1891 it was only a small town with a mere 12,000 inhabitants, but between the 5th and 8th centuries, due to its impregnable position protected by marshes and its proximity to the major naval port of Classis on the Adriatic, it had been successively the capital of the Western Roman Empire, of Odoacer the Hurian,

King of Italy, of Theodoric the Ostrogoth, and from 539 till 752 the seat of the Exarch of the Eastern Roman Empire. The silting up of its port had resulted in its decline but also guaranteed the survival of a group of remarkable churches and a large number of their outstanding mosaics.

Mackintosh did not record where he stayed but it might have been in the centre of town, either at the Byron, on Piazza Byron (now Piazza Caduti), or the Spada d'Oro e San Marco on Via Farini (now Via Diaz), which was slightly nearer to the railway station. Following the same plan as in Florence, he spent the Thursday, his first full day, familiarising himself with the town. His diary indicates that he reconnoitred at least five churches: Sant'Apollinare Nuovo, San Vitale, San Giovanni Evangelista, the Cathedral and south of the town, Sant'Apollinare in Classe. As with Monreale Cathedral, Mackintosh noted that both churches dedicated to Sant'Apollinare had uninteresting exteriors, but was impressed by the 'ripping mosaic work in both'.

From this point onwards Mackintosh's diary entries become quite terse and he no longer bothers to record what he has done each day, but does inform us that the remainder of his stay in Ravenna was spent making drawings of the buildings he had previously identified.

C. R. Mackintosh, Mosaic frieze, Sant'Apollinare Nuovo, Ravenna, 1891

The 'ripping' mid-6th century mosaic work in Sant'Apollinare Nuovo and Sant'Apollinare in Classe both merited watercolour studies. These schemes date from the period soon after the reconquest of most of Italy under the Byzantine Emperor Justinian I and are in the hieratic style of the period. The mosaics in the Baptistery, however, in the more naturalistic style of the mid-5th century when they were commissioned by Bishop Neon, also gained the same attention. San Vitale, the octagonal court church of the Byzantine Exarchate attracted a more summary treatment. Mackintosh remarked on its 'quite distinctive form' but merely noted its important mosaics in the choir as 'some mosaic in side chapel'. Its eastern façade, though, was recorded in a sketch which includes a depiction of a group of local women and children finished with a watercolour wash. There were also drawings of the 10th-century campanile of San Giovanni Evangelista, the exteriors of Sant'Apollinare in Classe and the Neonian Baptistery. While describing the Baptistery as 'very fine' Mackintosh dismissed the adjacent Cathedral, largely rebuilt in the 18th century, as 'very poor'. His sharp eye focused on the details of a 12th-century lattice screen displayed in the Archbishop's

Palace, rescued from the original Cathedral which had been destroyed in an earthquake. The sketchbook also contains summary drawings of two doorways, jotted down at the early 16th-century secularised monastery of Classe, which had been converted into the municipal museum.

Ferrara: Monday 1st June
Leaving Ravenna at 9.30 a.m. the three companions headed for Venice, stopping at Ferrara on the way, where they arrived at 10.50. Ferrara, from the 13th to the 16th century had been the seat of the Este family, great patrons of the arts. In its heyday it had a population of 100,000, but in 1598 it had lost its importance and became an appendage of the Papal States. When Charles Dickens visited in the 1840s he saw it as 'a desert of a place' with the grass growing in its silent streets.[9] In 1859 it was annexed by the Kingdom of Italy and by 1891 had recovered to the extent that the town had a population of 29,000.

The route to the town centre along the Viale Cavour took Mackintosh direct to the great brick Castello, a 14th-century edifice achieving its final form in the 16th century. Once the stronghold of the Este family this was now occupied by the local authority and also served as the telegraph office. After crossing the drawbridge over the moat to the south-west gate and paying the entrance fee, the custodian showed him the dungeons and took him to the first floor. Here he saw the Hall of Games and admired its frescos (at that time attributed to Dosso Dossi). He also viewed a small passageway which featured the Cabinet of the Bacchanalia, with its fresco which he heard was painted by Titian.[10]

After drawing the Castello, Mackintosh examined the Cathedral with his usual mixed reactions. The 13th-century Gothic west front received the accolade of 'very good', whilst the south elevation was 'very poor', the 18th-century interior[11] was passed over as 'modern', and the campanile, an unfinished edifice attributed to the major Renaissance architect and theorist Leon Battista Alberti, was 'about as ugly as they make em'.

Mackintosh also visited the Palazzo Schifanoia in the south-western area of the town, built by the Este between 1391 and 1469 as a summer residence. A group of drawings and details of the elaborate marble doorway commissioned by Borso d'Este from Francesco del Cossa and erected around 1470 – the only ornamental element in an austere brick façade – along with a study of a window in its garden front, found their way into the sketchbook. Inside the building the frescoes of the months by Francesco del

Above: Castello Estense, Ferrara
Opposite: Baptistery, Pistoia

Cossa and others merited the remark 'worth seeing'. Mackintosh's summing up of the town was that it contained 'some nice bits' but that they were 'few and far between'. The nice bits, apart from the major buildings that caught his attention, were two doorways, one opposite the Castello, the other en route to the Palazzo Schifanoia, a marble well head and the 1621 campanile of San Benedetto close to the railway station. All of these stood out as ornamental elements against the town's plain brick façades. Returning to the station for 5.30 p.m. the three men left for Venice.

Notes for Chapter 5

[1] Elaine Grogan, *Beginnings: Charles Rennie Mackintosh's Early Sketches* (Oxford: Architectural Press in Association with National Library of Ireland, 2002), pl. 30.
[2] Begun in 1063 by Buscheto (fl. 11th century) and continued by Rainaldo (fl. 12th century).
[3] Attributed to Giuliano da Maiano (1432-90).
[4] Begun 1152, designed by Diotisalvi (fl. 12th century), with Gothic features added by Nicola and Giovanni Pisano in the 13th century; the dome was added in the 14th century.
[5] Designed by Giovanni di Simone (fl. 13th century) and built between 1278 and the 15th century.
[6] The monument is now in the Museo dell'Opera del Duomo
[7] William James Anderson, *Architectural Studies of Italy*, pl. IV; Mackintosh, Sketchbook, National Library of Ireland, 2011 TX, p.1 and Mackintosh, Sketchbook, National Library of Ireland, 2009 TX, p.72.
[8] Mackintosh, 'Memoir on the Italian Tour' in Robertson (1990), p.235; the Memoir contains the only mention of Lucca which was on Mackintosh's train route between Pisa and Pistoia; there are no extant sketches and it is unlikely that Mackintosh stopped there.
[9] Charles Dickens, *Pictures from Italy*, 1846.
[10] Dosso Dossi (1480-1542) was court painter to the Este from 1514; the frescos, including that once attributed to Titian, are now thought to be the work of Camillo Filippi (1500-74) and his sons Cesare (1536-1604) and Sebastiano (Bastianino) (c.1532-1602).
[11] Remodelled 1712-18.

SIX

The Doge's Palace from the Lagoon, Venice

Venice to Como

'I like this odd town of Venice, and find, every day, some new church or palace of interest & beauty'[1]

Well head, Campo SS. Giovanni e Paolo, Venice

Venice: Monday 1st June – Wednesday 10th June
There are several discrepancies between the brief, presumably accurate, account of Mackintosh's visit to Venice in his diary and the lengthy more imaginative description of his impressions given in his lecture over a year later. What follows is an attempt to reconstruct the visit from both sources relying, where possible, on the chronology supplied by the diary.

Venice is situated on a close-knit archipelago of 117 islands in a shallow lagoon some 3 km from the mainland. In the lecture, Mackintosh recorded his approach to the city via Fusina on the shore of the Lagoon. This required the companions to leave their train at Padua where they would board a steam carriage to convey them along the bank of the Brenta Canal. At Fusina, according to the lecture, they stepped on board a gondola which followed a clockwise course around the city and passed the islands of San Giorgio in Alga, Murano and the cemetery of San Michele before finally entering the Grand Canal, which divides the city, opening up a vista of churches and palaces 'suffused with the rays of the setting sun and reflected with all their glory of colour'. Then, as night fell, they were treated to a lamp-lit procession of singing gondoliers moving down the Grand Canal from the Rialto before they finally entered their lodgings in the Hôtel Milan et Pensione Anglaise at midnight:

> Innumerable lights began to appear on the canal, every boat had its lantern, and the gondolas moving rapidly along, were followed by tracks of light which played and danced upon the waters.

I was gazing in rapturous delight at those dancing fires, when the sounds of music were wafted along the canal towards us, as they grew louder and louder a barge, illuminated with numerous lights of various hues, filled with musicians issued from the Rialto, and stopping under one of the palaces, began serenading which stilled every clamour & suspended all conversation in the galleries and porticos: till, rowing slowly away it was heard no more. The gondoliers catching the air, imitated its cadences, and were answered by others at a distance, whose voices, echoed on the palaces on either side acquired a plaintive and interesting tone. I retired to rest full of sound and long after I was asleep the melody seemed to vibrate in my ear. And thus ended my first experiences of Venice.[2]

Throughout most of its history Venice was a great maritime republic run by its chief citizens with a doge, or duke, at its head. Its trading empire stretched as far as the Aegean, the Black Sea and Cyprus in the Eastern Mediterranean with a land empire in northern Italy. Along with Venetia, its Italian possessions, it was conquered by Napoleon in 1797 and after being annexed to Austria in 1814 was incorporated into the Kingdom of Italy in 1866. The city had a population of 200,000 at its apogee in the 15th century but by 1890 this had fallen to 158,000. Then as now, it was an important tourist centre with an art and architectural heritage rivalling Florence and Rome.

On his first morning in the city, Mackintosh followed his usual plan of familiarising himself with its major buildings before embarking on a programme of sketching. The first part of the project would take four days, followed by four more making drawings. The hotel, whose entrance was on the narrow Calle Traghetto, faced onto the Grand Canal directly opposite the prominent church of Santa Maria della Salute, but leaving this landmark for another day Mackintosh took an excursion up the canal to view the façades of its palaces which 'quite charmed' him with their 'delightful colouring and grouping'. He would have been familiar with Ruskin's monumental three-volume *Stones of Venice* which analysed their architecture through three phases, the Byzantine, the Gothic and the Renaissance. Agreeing with Ruskin, he saw the Gothic buildings as derived from the Doge's Palace,[3] picking out the Ca'd'Oro as the 'best', and singling out the Palazzi Contarini, Foscari, Pisani and Spinelli as particularly 'interesting'. Of the Renaissance palaces he only noted the universally admired Palazzo Grimani, a building that even Ruskin, despite his hatred of Renaissance Classical architecture, had praised.[4]

The afternoon was spent in the Piazza and Basilica of St. Mark. In his diary Mackintosh had nothing to say about the Piazza and its buildings but in the lecture he praised the Classical design of the Procuratie Nuove by the Florentine architect and sculptor Jacopo Sansovino,[5] 'an uninterrupted series of arches & marble columns exquisitely wrought', which occupies the south side of the square. With his focus on Sansovino, he mistakenly attributed the bronze pedestals of the three flagstaffs which stand before the front of the Basilica of St. Mark to this master, admiring their 'bold and elegant' relievos 'in the true spirit of the antique'.[6] He also picked out the architect's elegant marble Logetta whose arcaded façade, adorned with bronze sculptures of Peace, Apollo, Mercury and Pallas, acts as an entrance to St. Mark's campanile. Like many tourists before and after him Mackintosh ascended the 322 ft high tower, climbing its winding inclined plane of 38 bends to make 'a leisurely survey of Venice beneath, with its azure blue sea, its great stretch of flat red tiled roofs, broken and diversified by innumerable towers, domes & cupolas...'.[7]

St. Mark's Basilica itself was an overwhelming experience even exciting praise in Mackintosh's diary: 'The exterior – well its S Marco. The interior is a caution it's simply superb as a piece of mosaic architecture. The gold ground has a magnificent effect.'

He had far more to say in the lecture where he recalled the experience of entering 'the most gorgeous but about the darkest church in Europe [which] is glorified by the sun. The contrast is the more striking, as the rest of the church is so dark and like a gloomy wilderness, through which you might wander long enough before you discovered that all around you were columns of porphyry of malachite and verde antique, panels glowing with gold and gems & pavements dazzling in mosaics.'[8] Despite his rapturous admiration he still found time to record that the 'modern work' (presumably the 17th and 18th-century mosaics on the façade and in some sections of the interior) was 'abominable'.

On the Wednesday morning, Mackintosh was on the steps of Santa Maria della Salute waiting for its doors to open. With its white dome sitting on an unusual voluted drum, this Baroque church[9] is one of the glories of the Venetian cityscape, presiding over the south bank of the Grand Canal just before it emerges into the Basin of Saint Mark. As Mackintosh noted, it had been 'erected by the Senate in performance of a vow to the Holy Virgin who begged off a terrible pestilence in 1630',[10] hence its dedication. He had little else to say only commenting that it made a 'good effect outside' and that there was a 'fine Titian' in the interior.[11]

He then took a gondola to the Island and Church of San Giorgio Maggiore. Here, after walking through the church designed by Andrea Palladio in 1566, and passing through the cloister of the suppressed monastery, he entered the refectory[12] where, in his lecture, he stated that Paolo Veronese's *chef d'oevre*, *The Wedding Feast at Cana*, could be seen. This, however, had been looted by Napoleon in 1797 and perhaps Mackintosh had mistaken Tintoretto's *Marriage of the Virgin* which still adorned its walls for this canvas.[13] Once more stepping into a gondola, Mackintosh moved on to another of Palladio's churches, Il Redentore, 'a simple and elegant structure' on the adjacent Giudecca, before embarking for the journey across to St. Mark's

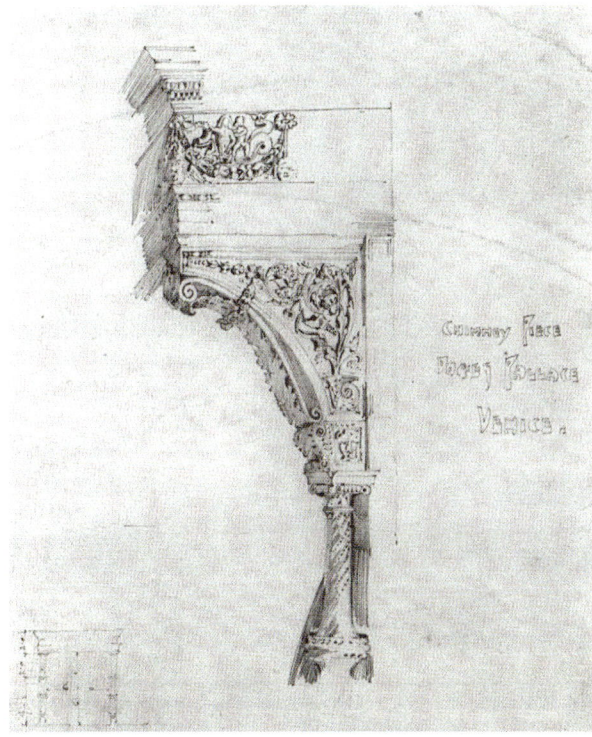

William James Anderson, Chimney piece, Sala Grimani, Doge's Palace, Venice; Anderson, *Architectural Studies in Italy*, pl. 35

C. R. Mackintosh, Chimney piece, Sala Grimani, Doge's Palace, Venice, 1891

Square where he had an argument with the gondolier over his fare.

From there his schedule took him to the Scuola di San Rocco, famous for its display of vast canvases by Tintoretto. Mackintosh duly admired these, also picking out Titian's *Annunciation* (1525) as 'very fine'. His last visit of the morning was to the Accademia di Belle Arte, the city's art gallery and the world's greatest repository of Venetian art, much of it placed there after Napoleon's suppression of many of the city's monasteries and churches in 1797. He merely described it as 'worth seeing'.

After such a busy morning in 'the excessive heat of Venice' the three companions were ready to relax, so they took a boat to the Lido, where they bathed in the Adriatic, and Mackintosh painted a small watercolour of the distant city from across the Lagoon.

On the Thursday Mackintosh visited three buildings, the churches of Santa Maria dei Miracoli, Santi Giovanni e Paolo and the Doges' Palace. Santa Maria dei Miracoli, with its marble-clad exterior reflected in the waters of a canal was much to Mackintosh's taste, as he noted in his diary: 'most exquisite Renaissance church. Most beautiful carving, most complete little ch[urch] in Venice or anywhere else'. Built by Pietro Lombardo between 1481 and 1489, it was designed like a reliquary to enshrine a miraculous image of the Virgin. Not far away is the vast but plain Gothic church of Santi Giovanni e Paolo, built for the Dominicans between 1333 and 1390; the burial place of doges whose Gothic and Renaissance tombs had been the subject of a long discussion by Ruskin on the decline of Venetian art.[14] Mackintosh merely noted that some of the tombs 'both gothic and Renaissance' were 'very fine' but seems not to have drawn them. Perhaps his need to record the appearance of sepulchral monuments had been sated in Rome and Florence. Instead, at some point in his stay he would paint the church's south transept window[15] and ignoring Verrocchio's great equestrian statue of Bartolomeo Colleoni[16] in the square outside, turn his attention to a handsome Renaissance well head as a subject for his sketchbook.

In his lecture, he indicated that he visited the Ducal Palace late in the day, allowing him time to see some of the interior where he noted its 15th-century chimney pieces: intriguingly he picked out the same example that William James Anderson had drawn two years earlier. He also admired the bronze well heads in the courtyard and the Giant Stair, which then gave visitors access to the main apartments, before he was ejected by a custodian.[17]

Eager to complete his inspection of the Ducal Palace he returned next morning. Entering from the Piazzetta via the Porta della Carta, he ascended the Giant Stair with its statues of Mars and Neptune by Sansovino to take a more leisurely tour of the apartments with their huge canvases by Tintoretto, Veronese and others depicting the triumphs of the Venetian Republic, then crossed the Bridge of Sighs to explore the prisons and torture chamber.

Afterwards he took the steamer to Murano, the seat of the Venetian glass industry where he would have examined the Cathedral of San Donato completed in 970. This was discussed by Ruskin in his *Stones of Venice*, with its great apsidal mosaic of the Virgin. From there he visited the more remote, sparsely inhabited island of Torcello. Here he explored its ancient Cathedral (639-1008) with its fine Byzantine mosaics: a great *Last Judgement* on the west wall, a *Virgin and Child and Apostles* in the apse and a *Christ in Majesty* in a side chapel; and the adjacent 11th-century church of Santa Fosca. He arrived back in Venice on the Fondamenti Nuovi 'about sunset,… a vast quay or terrace of white marble, which commands the whole series of islands from S. Michele to Torcello, That rise and glitter o'er the ambient tide…'[18]

Saturday 6th June was Mackintosh's 23 birthday, but his diary just records that he spent the day sketching. In his lecture, he listed several additional churches as amongst the most interesting in Venice. One of these was San Zaccaria.[19] Here he entered the Capella di San Tarasio to the right of the high altar to make a study of one of three gilded Gothic altars (1443). Others were the great Franciscan church of Santa Maria dei Frari, close to the Scuola di San Rocco and noted for its paintings, particularly an *Assumption of the Virgin* (1516-18) by Titian; Santa Maria del Carmine; and the Greek Orthodox church of San Giorgio dei Greci. There are no known sketches that relate to these.[20] He did, though, draw the interior of the Renaissance church of San Giovanni Crisostomo[21] close to the Rialto, and sketched the Dogana di Mare and the apse of the Monastery of San Gregorio across from his hotel.[22]

More ambitious were two watercolours of palaces, one of which was the Ca'd'Oro.[23] On the Monday and Tuesday he concentrated on Santa Maria dei Miracoli, filling four sheets with drawings of decorative details in the interior.

Padua: Wednesday 10th June

Having completed their nine days in Venice, the three companions set out for a busy day exploring Padua and Vicenza. The old university town of Padua with a population of over 47,000 was twice the size of Vicenza. No drawings appear to have resulted from Padua and once again, Mackintosh had little to say in his diary beyond noting that there was little of interest except for San Lorenzo and Sant'Antonio. There is no important church dedicated to San Lorenzo in Padua so it is difficult to decide which church he was thinking of. The Scrovegni Chapel and the Eremitani, the two most significant ecclesiastical buildings closest to the railway station, the former housing the greatest expression of Giotto's genius, the latter containing an important cycle of frescoes by Mantegna, both well-known by the 1890s, might have been mentioned by Mackintosh had he visited them. The most probable candidate, therefore, is Santa Giustina which he would indicate in his lecture as being 'the only other edifice [apart from Sant'Antonio] that calls for mention in Padua'.

Sant'Antonio, the shrine of St. Anthony of Padua, is one of the most important pilgrimage sites in Italy and in the lecture Mackintosh, after giving a brief description of the exterior of the church, suggested a possible reason for having produced no drawings there:

> The first object which arouses interest is a confused pile of turrets and domes which are dedicated to the blessed St. Anthony. On entering the nave is full of women & children kneeling by baskets of vegetables and other provisions which by good St Anthony's interposition they hope to sell advantageously during the day. Beyond these nearer the choir and in a gloomier part of the edifice, knelt a row of rueful penitents, smiting their breasts and lifting their eyes to heaven. Further on in front of the dark recess in which the sacred relics are deposited, a few desperately melancholy sinners lay prostrate. A lofty altar decked with the most lavish magnificence supports the shrine. Those who are profoundly touched with its sanctity may approach and walking round may look into the various corners and crevices.

C. R. Mackintosh, Ca' d'Oro, Venice, 1891

But supposing a traveller ever so heretical I would advise him by no means to neglect this pilgrimage, since every part of the recess he visits is decorated with exquisite sculptures. Sansovino and other renowned artists have vied with each other in carving the alto relievos of the arcade, which for design and execution cannot be surpassed.

The above record will give you some idea of the circumstances under which ecclesiastical architecture is studied in Italy. This is no exceptional case, but may be taken as true generally.[24]

Despite his seeming lack of interest in the diary, Mackintosh does appear to have been impressed by one other edifice in the town, the Palazzo della Ragione that, a year later, he mistakenly remembered as the work of Palladio, the architect of the exterior of 'the Basilica', or Palazzo della Ragione, a similar edifice in Vicenza, which he would examine later in the day and mention briefly in his diary as 'very good'. Both buildings have enormous wooden 'ship's-keel' roofs, the one in Padua by Fra. Giovanni degli Eremitani dating from 1306-08 and the other in Vicenza by Domenico da Venezia which was constructed in the latter half of the 15th century.

Mackintosh's description of the interior of the hall in Padua in his lecture indicates how his memory had confused the two:

> The next interesting structure is the great hall of the town a most spacious place designed by the great Palladio. Timber casts a solemn gloom, which is not diminished by the wan light admitted through windows of pale blue glass. The size & shape of this colossal chamber, the arching of the roof, the enormous rafters stretching across it, and above all the watery gleams that glanced through the casement, possessed my fancy with ideas of Noah's Ark, and almost persuaded me, I beheld that extraordinary vessel.[25]

Vicenza: Wednesday 10th June
The small compact town of Vicenza was 'better than Padua', being a 'good place to study Palladio's work' despite 'all the churches' being 'very poor'. Andrea Palladio, the last great architect of the Renaissance, was born in the town where he is well-represented by his domestic and civic architecture. In his lecture, Mackintosh's memory seems to have played tricks with him as he recalled being there on a wet morning. This seems hardly possible if he had already spent time 'wandering all over' Padua. He indicated that in Vicenza he had taken shelter in Palladio's Teatro Olimpico in the north-eastern corner of the town, designed by the architect on the model of an Ancient Roman theatre and completed after his death in 1584. Its interior received rare praise from Mackintosh, given that it relied so heavily on long-dead historical precedents and precepts: 'It is impossible to see this building without feelings of sincere admiration or conceive a structure more truly classical, or to point out a single ornament which has not the best antique authority. I am not in the least surprised that the citizens of Vicenza enthusiastically gave into this architect's plan & sacrificed large sums to erect so beautiful a model.'[26]

There are only two positively identifiable sheets of drawings from Vicenza.[27] One contains studies of details of buildings but the other, appropriately, is a sketch of a house, then known as the 'Casa di Palladio' at the eastern end of the Corso Principe Umberto (now the Corso Andrea Palladio), not far from the Teatro Olimpico.[28] A third, however, a rough sketch resembles the Palazzo Thiene which has been attributed to Palladio.[29] Late in the day, the three left for Verona.

Verona: Thursday 11th – Sunday 14th June
Early next morning, the young architects were 'on the tramp again' around Verona's churches and palaces. This beautiful town of some 60,800 inhabitants, almost encircled by the River Adige, had been the stronghold of the powerful Scaligeri family in the 13th and 14th centuries and is noted for their Gothic tombs. It possesses a group of fine Lombard Romanesque and Gothic churches and was rated by the Gothic Revival architect George Edmund Street, who had visited in the 1850s, as equal to Venice and Florence in interest.[30] Ruskin had gone even further, declaring it to be his 'dearest place in Italy'.[31] The companions' tramp took in Sant'Anastasia, the Cathedral, Santa Maria in Organo and San Zeno Maggiore, all to Mackintosh's taste. He began a new sketchbook, filling the first page with drawings made at the Castelvecchio, halfway along the route from Sant'Anastasia to San Zeno. Standing on the north bank of the Adige he sketched a domestic chimney, part of the great fortified mediaeval bridge and a tower of the 14th-century castle.[32] On six of the seven following pages he concentrated on San Zeno itself, a church of which George Edmund Street wrote 'I think it may certainly be regarded as on the whole the noblest example of its class; indeed, except the best Gothic work of the best period, I doubt whether any work of the Middle Ages so much commands respect and admiration as this Lombard work'. From the number of sketches he drew and from his few adulatory remarks, it is clear that Mackintosh agreed with him. He produced separate drawings of the west front and campanile, a 'very beautiful example of Italian gothic brick and stone work', an elevation of a bay of the nave and a cross-section of the 'ship's-keel' roof in the 'very simple & nice interior', and two studies of the 'exquisite wooden stalls in the choir'. The next two pages of the sketchbook feature drawings made in the town's civic centre at the Piazza dei Signori where he sketched three heraldic bas-reliefs on the buildings and studies of early-Renaissance details from the Palazzo della Ragione. Several pages further on is a drawing of a major feature of the Palazzo, the Torre dei Lamberti, its square 84-metre campanile, built in 1172 with a mid-15th century octagonal upper stage.

On Friday 12th June, Paxton and Dods left for Munich but Mackintosh continued his sketching with a visit to Santa Maria in Organo on the left bank of the river, drawing its campanile and elaborately inlaid wooden stalls.[33] On the Friday or Saturday, he also probably revisited the large Dominican Gothic church of Sant'Anastasia to draw its marble western doorway and a bay of its brick and stone nave.[34] On his last day, he was up at 5 in the morning to sketch the door of the Cathedral[35] before leaving the province of Venetia and taking the 10 a.m. train for Mantua in Lombardy.

Mantua: Sunday 14th June
The train took Mackintosh across Mantua's Ponte dei Molini that divides two of the three lakes which, together with the marshes to the south of the town, made it a strongly fortified place. Before the formation of the Kingdom of Italy, Mantua, along with Verona, had been one of the fortified towns of the Quadrilateral which had safeguarded the Austrian possessions in the north of the peninsula. In the Renaissance period, the Gonzaga Marquises and Dukes of Mantua had made it an

important artistic centre through their patronage of Mantegna, Lorenzo Costa, Titian, Giulio Romano and Primaticcio. Architecturally, apart from the fine brick Gothic palace of the Gonzaga, the town is the location of Giulio Romano's Palazzo del Tè and two churches by Leon Battista Alberti, San Sebastiano and Sant'Andrea. None of this appears to have moved Mackintosh. His diary entry is to say the least, unenthusiastic: 'Went all over the town and then all the churches but found nothing of interest'. In his lecture he only managed to mention that he had been there and his sketchbook contains one page of meagre ornamental details. Mackintosh's failure to respond to Alberti's Sant'Andrea, one of the most notable early exercises in Renaissance Classicism, is hard to understand considering that he was prepared to pay homage to Palladio. By the late afternoon he had had enough of Mantua and took the train to Cremona where at 6 p.m. he paid 2 francs to book into the Albergo Italia e Capello on the Corso Campi. His train journey had refreshed him sufficiently for him to take a quick look around before dinner, enough to find the Cathedral 'disappointing'.

A further possible reason for his lack of interest may have been that thoughts of securing the funding for his planned nine months' stay on the Continent, which would include a visit to the South of France, were now beginning to occupy him. It was possibly after his meal that he sat down to write an important letter to John Shields,[36] the Secretary to the Thomson Trustees in Glasgow who had agreed to award the remaining £30 of the prize money, once they had approved of the drawings to be sent from Italy at the end of his tour. Mackintosh was concerned over the reliability of the postal service and asked Shields if the money could be sent without his forwarding any sketches. In his letter he stressed his conscientiousness, listed all of the towns that he had visited, and hoped that this would be enough to warrant the Trustees sending the money.[37] He indicated that he would be in Milan in around 10 days' time and gave the address of his hotel there.

Cremona: Sunday 14th – Monday 15th June

Early next morning he was ready to go on the tramp again and despite 'ransacking the whole town' found nothing worth seeing except for the Cathedral, even if that had initially been a disappointment! He made a rapid sketch of its marble west front with its two conical brick turrets and captioned it 'a caution'. In late 19th-century parlance the word 'caution' was quite commonly used to denote something humorous, surprising, or exceptional. Mackintosh had used it when giving high praise to the

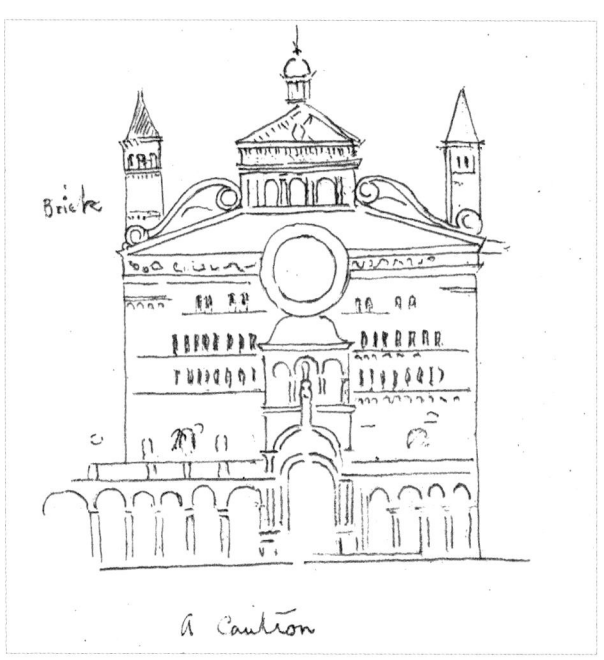

C. R. Mackintosh, West Front, Cremona Cathedral, 1891

interior of St. Mark's. Was he coming round to an appreciation of this building? It displays a mixture of styles from Lombard Romanesque through Gothic to Renaissance. He stayed long enough to make another more considered drawing of the tabernacle over the main doorway with its Madonna and Child and two saints which is more reminiscent of French than Italian Gothic.[38] Inside he made studies of details from one of the Basilica's two pulpits and from a 17th-century monument in the north transept. One of the only objects in his perambulation of the town he deemed worthy of his attention was a brick Renaissance palazzo which merited a drawing of its façade with ornamental terracotta details from its door and frieze.[39] He also found his way to San Michele, the oldest church in the town, where he drew its 12th-century apse, but he was still not really in the mood and had to force himself to sketch. By 3 p.m. he had nothing to do and was utterly tired out. One building that did exceed his expectations and earned the accolade of two drawings was the Cathedral Baptistery which he mentioned in his diary almost as an afterthought as being 'very good'. This plain octagonal brick structure, partly faced in marble and dating from 1167, stands at the south-west corner of the Cathedral.

George Edmund Street, Broletto, Brescia; Street, *Notes of a Tour in Northern Italy*, p.75.

Mackintosh's train for his next destination, Brescia, left at 6.20 p.m. and arrived at 8.35 p.m. Here he paid another 2 francs to book into the town's Albergo Capello near the Piazza del Duomo.

Brescia: Monday 15th – Tuesday 16th June
Mackintosh spent all the next day in Brescia, not leaving until 5.50 p.m. From the evidence of his sketchbook, most of his time was concentrated on the central area around the Piazza del Duomo (now Piazza Paolo VI) with its two cathedrals and Broletto, the centre of municipal government in the mediaeval period. Of the two cathedrals, the Duomo Nuovo, a mainly 17th-century structure with a cupola dating from 1825, did not appeal as he described it as 'poor'. Its neighbour, the Romanesque Duomo Vecchio, an 11th-century circular building constructed above a 6th-century basilica, was 'not so bad' but unfortunately, was being 'frightfully restored'. Only one feature of the two churches was worthy of being recorded in the sketchbook: the early 16th-century tomb of the bishop St. Apollonius which had been transferred to the new Cathedral in 1674 from the crypt of the Duomo Vecchio.[40]

The 12th-century brick and stone Broletto was occupied by law courts and a prison at the time of Mackintosh's visit. He made a rapid sketch of its crenellated stone bell tower, the Torre del Popolo, but far more of his time was taken up by a two-page study of the small redundant brick church of Sant'Agostino in the narrow street to the north of the piazza. Mackintosh was probably familiar with details from its west façade from illustrations in Fergusson's *History*[41] and a perspective drawing of the church and Broletto, captioned 'Broletto, Brescia' was illustrated in George Edmund Street's book on Northern Italy.[42] Mackintosh's inscription 'A brick house, Brescia' on his study of its 15th-century street frontage, may indicate its use as a domestic building in 1891, although it is more probable that it was part of the Broletto at this time.

From the Broletto, it was a short walk for Mackintosh to view the picturesque castle of the Visconti Dukes of Milan on its hill at the north-east corner of the town, to make his only other drawing. He did not comment on the Municipio or Loggia (1492-1508) close to the Piazza del Duomo, a building attributed to Palladio, but on his way to the station along the Corso Vittorio Emanuele (now Corso Martiri della Liberta) he noticed the elaborately-carved Renaissance façade of Santa Maria dei Miracoli (1488-1560), its ornamentation reminiscent of that in the interior of its namesake in Venice that he had so much admired.[43]

Bergamo: Wednesday 17th June
Arriving at Bergamo at 7.35 p.m. he made his way along the Viale della Stazione (now Viale Giovanni XXIII) to the Hotel Capella d'Oro in the Citta Bassa, the lower part of the town, close to the Piazza with its two Doric temples erected in 1837. From there he had a view of the upper town, the Citta Alta, where most of the significant buildings are located. He saved his exploration of the town for the next day. Then as now, the Citta Alta is approached via a funicular railway which was only completed in 1887 and takes the visitor up a steep incline through the city walls to the Piazza Mercato delle Scarpe, a short distance from the Piazza Vecchia, a sloping rectangular space, with the 12th-century Torre Civica on the right and the Gothic Broletto at the top. Like George Edmund Street before him, Mackintosh admired the Broletto, then occupied by a library, praising it as 'good gothic' and recording its façade

and details of its balcony, window sill, and cornice in his sketchbook. Street had commended the Broletto for the simplicity of its design and admired the way in which the vaulted arcade on which it stands not only terminated the piazza, but cast an air of mystery and suggestion over the architectural treasures that lay beyond it.[44] Mackintosh walked the few steps through its open loggia and came face-to-face with the entrance of the Romanesque Santa Maria Maggiore and the elaborate Renaissance façade of the Capella Colleoni. Street had regarded this as too bizarre to be good, seeing its design as lacking any true style and Ruskin saw it as 'encrusted to the point that it was impossible to think of it without exhaustion.'[45]

Mackintosh was more terse in his dismissal, merely remarking that it was 'poor Renaissance, overloaded'. He was no more polite about the exterior of Santa Maria Maggiore, regarding it as 'early and crude', but he liked its massing enough to make a charming drawing of it from a vantage point along the Via Donizetti. Continuing down this street he found more to interest him in the elegant marble frontage of the Casa dell'Arciprete, declaring it 'good Renaissance' and filling one page of his sketchbook with a careful drawing of its street façade and the opposite page with details and notes of the different coloured marbles employed.

His diary does not mention his impressions of the only other building he drew in the town, the Gothic entrance front of the suppressed monastery of Sant'Agostino, which then served as a barracks. Mackintosh recorded its function by including a comical figure of a sentry at one of its gateways.

Lake Como: Thursday 18th - Friday 26th June
After a further night at Bergamo, Mackintosh took the short journey to Lecco at the bottom of the eastern arm of Lake Como. Still on the lookout for architectural subjects he found nothing there, but managed a drawing of boats in the harbour before going up the lake to Colico. En route he made sketches of the sailing boats and mountainous landscape, the campanile of Santa Maria del Tiglio at Gravedona on the western shore, and the outline of a church at Bellano on the eastern side. Disembarking at Cadenabbia, a 'very nice place', he checked into the palatial Hotel Belle Ile on the waterfront at a cost of 7 francs per night. This was to be his home for the next week. The diary gives no information on his activities. All that survives are three pages of sketches, one of boats with outlines of landscape, another taken from the shore near

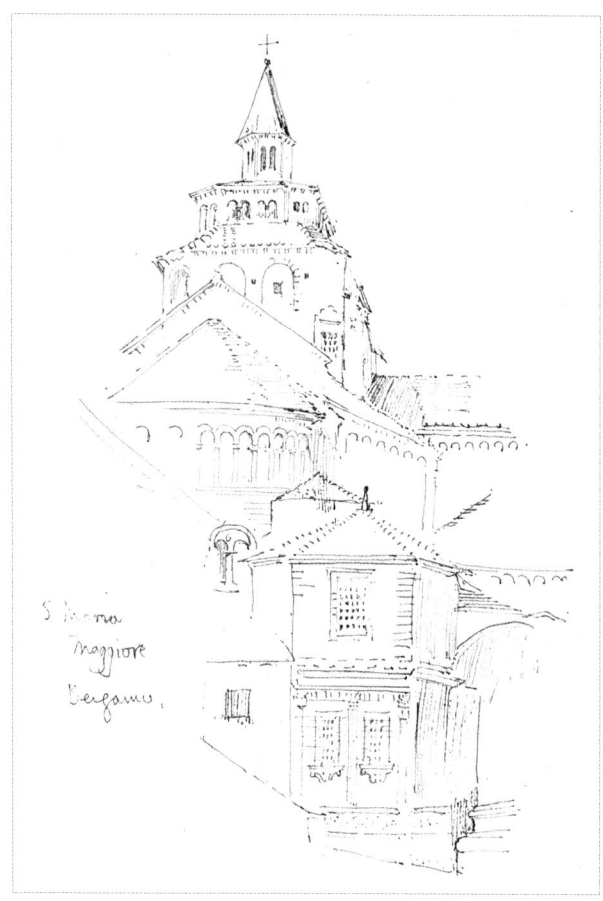

C. R. Mackintosh, Santa Maria Maggiore, Bergamo, 1891

Cadenabbia looking across to Bellagio and Varenna and a third of wrought iron gates at the Villa del Balbiano at Campo which was just south of Cadenabbia and easily accessible by boat.

Como: Friday 26th - Saturday 27th June
Mackintosh left Cadenabbia at 2.15 p.m. for Como which lies on the southern shore of the western arm of the Lake. The small fortified city has several fine architectural monuments, and suitably refreshed from his vacation, Mackintosh was ready to appreciate them. The white marble Cathedral, an amalgam of Gothic, early and late Renaissance, with an 18th-century cupola, was deemed 'very good'. The building was a particular favourite of William James Anderson who would use his own drawing of it as the frontispiece of his book on Italian Renaissance architecture. Anderson remarked on how the 'massive solidity and simplicity of the lower part of the building'

Apse San Fedele, Como

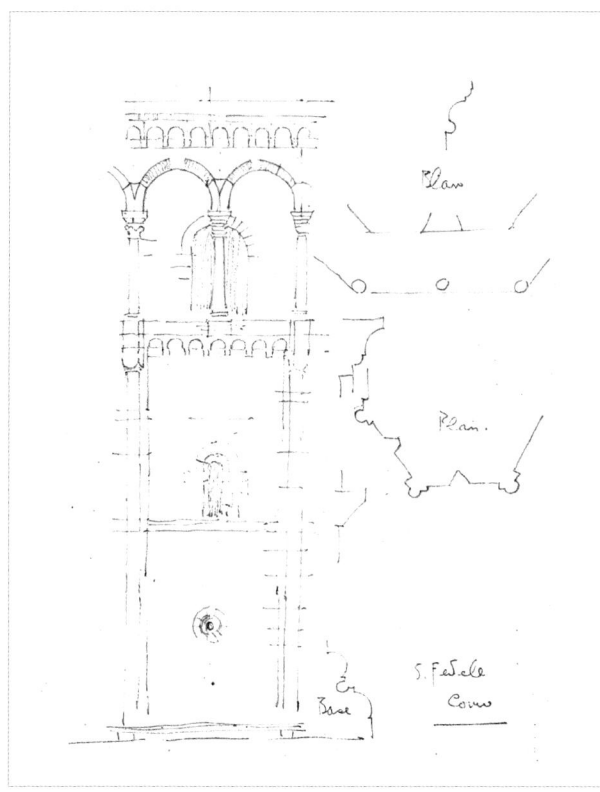

C. R. Mackintosh, Apse, San Fedele, Como, 1891

was opposed to 'the delicate richness of the sky-line' and felt that it demonstrated the 'restraint of the true architect' in the control of the elements of the design in its use of 'deep buttresses...corbelled-out figures, fanciful pinnacles'.[46] Mackintosh found its two exquisitely ornamented side doors with their paired concentric arches on pilasters set in a square reveal 'very suggestive'. He would, however, find the massing of the tri-apsidal east end even more suggestive, making two drawings, one of the interior, the other of the exterior elevation, using the exterior as the basis for a later competition design.[47]

Adjoining the Cathedral was another subject for the sketchbook, the Gothic Broletto, its façade composed of courses of red, white and dark grey marbles. Similar to that in Bergamo, its ground floor is an open arcade with a second stage containing three windows, its central opening giving onto a balcony.

The two other buildings worthy of attention were the Romanesque churches of Sant'Abbondio and San Fedele.

The 11th-century Sant'Abbondio, above the town on the slope of a hill with its five-aisled plan and twin campaniles, was a 'very charming old church' and merited two sheets of drawings. In the interior of the apsidal presbytery is a series of 14th-century frescoes depicting the life of Christ which were perhaps too early and too provincial for Mackintosh's taste: he found them 'not up to much'. San Fedele also received a mixed reception. It was 'very good, what's left of it'. Its front, facing onto the Piazza del Mercato and its apsidal east end on the Via Vittorio Emanuaele II were mediaeval, but the restored interior with its 17th-century vault was 'very bad classic'. The five-sided apse was generally admired, receiving praise in the Baedeker, and meriting an illustration with the erroneous caption 'Santa Maria' in Street's book.[48] Mackintosh's study of it would be another source for a future design.[49]

Following an afternoon, a stay of one night and a further morning of exploration in Como, Mackintosh left at noon for Milan where he had booked into the Hotel Biscione e Bellevue.

Notes for Chapter 6

[1] Mackintosh, 'A Tour in Italy (1892)' in Robertson (1990), p.121.
[2] Ibid., p.118.
[3] John Ruskin, *The Stones of Venice*, Vol. 2: *The Sea Stories* (The Works of John Ruskin, Vol. 10), edited by E. T. Cook and Alexander Wedderburn (London: George Allen, 1904), p.272.
[4] John Ruskin, *The Stones of Venice*, Vol. 3: *The Fall* (The Works of John Ruskin, Vol. 11), edited by E. T. Cook and Alexander Wedderburn (London: George Allen, 1904), pp.43-44.
[5] Mackintosh, 'A Tour in Italy (1892)' in Robertson (1990), p.119; the building was commenced in 1582 by Vincenzo Scamozzi (1552-1616) following a plan by Jacopo Sansovino (1486-1570) and completed in 1640 by Baldassare Longhena (1604-82).
[6] Ibid., p.119; the relievos were executed by Alessandro Leopardi (14??-1521) in 1504.
[7] Ibid., p.121.
[8] Ibid., pp.121-2.
[9] Erected 1601-82 by Baldassare Longhena (1604-82).
[10] Mackintosh, 'A Tour in Italy (1892)' in Robertson, op.cit., p.118.
[11] *Descent of the Holy Spirit* (c.1550).
[12] Andrea Palladio, 1560-62.
[13] Veronese (1528-88); *The Wedding Feast at Cana* (1562-63) is now in the Louvre in Paris.
[14] John Ruskin, 'Roman Renaissance', *The Stones of Venice*, Vol 3; *The Fall* (The Works of John Ruskin, Vol. 11), edited by E. T. Cook and Alexander Wedderburn (London: George Allen, 1904), p.69 et seq.
[15] Depicting warrior saints it was made at Murano in 1515 to designs by Bartolomeo Vivarini (fl. 1450-99) and Gerolamo Mocetto (c.1470-after 1531).
[16] Andrea del Verrocchio (c.1435-88); sculpture c.1479-88.
[17] The Doge's Palace closed at 3 p.m.; Mackintosh, however, suggests in his lecture that he was ejected at dusk, Mackintosh, 'A Tour in Italy (1892)' in Robertson, (1990), p.120.
[18] Ibid., p.121.
[19] Completed 1480-1515 by Mauro Codussi (c.1440-1504) in the transition style between Gothic and Renaissance.
[20] Mackintosh showed an illustration of San Giorgio dei Greci at his lecture; this could have been a photograph; his diary note that he purchased photographs in Florence might suggest that he habitually did so to supplement his sketches.
[21] Commenced by Mauro Codussi (1440-1504) in 1497 and completed by his son Domenico in 1525.
[22] Dogana da Mar (1677-78) by Giuseppe Benone (1618-84); San Gregorio (9th century, rebuilt in 15th century).
[23] Both were exhibited at the Royal Glasgow Institute of Fine Arts in 1892.
[24] Mackintosh, 'A Tour in Italy (1892)' in Robertson (1990), p.123.
[25] Ibid.
[26] Ibid., pp.123-4.
[27] There is also an uncaptioned drawing of a Renaissance palace which resembles Palazzo Thiene which was commissioned from Giulio Romano (1499-1546) in 1542; it is conjectured that the upper storeys were designed by Palladio after 1546; Mackintosh, *North Italian Sketchbook*, p.4 (Glasgow School of Art Archives and Collections, MC:G57).
[28] The Casa Palladio is now known as Casa Cogollo (1559-62), 165-7, Corso Andrea Palladio, and is generally regarded as the work of Giovanni Antonio Fasolo (1530-72); in the 19th century it was attributed to Palladio.
[29] Appendix 1, 150.
[30] George Edmund Street, *Notes of a Tour in Northern Italy (Artists Abroad)* (London: Waterstone, 1986), p.138.
[31] John Ruskin, Letter to Charles Eliot Norton, 1857.
[32] Built by Cangrande II Della Scala as his home in 1354-57; in 1891 the castle was a barracks.
[33] Santa Maria in Organo, dating from the 7th century, was rebuilt by the Olivetan order after an earthquake in 1117, with a white marble façade designed by Michele Sanmicheli in 1481; the campanile, completed in 1533, is believed to be the work of Fra. Giovanni da Verona (c.1457-1525) who was responsible for the church's interior woodwork.
[34] The church was erected between 1290 and 1323 to the designs of Fra. Benvenuto da Imola and Fra. Nicolo da Imola; Mackintosh was familiar with Sant'Anastasia from James Fergusson's *A History of Architecture in all Countries*, vol. 2, p.326, where it is described as 'one of the purest and most perfect types of an Italian Gothic church' and where a similar drawing of a bay appears; he has, however, noted the bands of painted ornamentation against a plain white ground, not featured in Fergusson's illustration, but mentioned in Street's *Notes of a Tour in Northern Italy*, p.97, as a major feature of the interior.
[35] This drawing is untraced.
[36] John Shields (1821-1912) was a retired quantity surveyor.
[37] Mackintosh, Letter to Shields, dated Cremona 14th June 1891 in Robertson (1990), p.229; in his list of towns he missed out Florence and unaccountably included Paestum and Amalfi, which are not mentioned in the diary and which could not have been reached from Naples in the time allowed to him.
[38] The west front (1274-1606) with a rose window (1274); the tabernacle (c.1310) is considered to be by Marco Romano (fl. 14th century).
[39] There are several similar palazzi in Cremona, but Mackintosh's source is unidentified.
[40] Dated to 1504 and attributed to Maffeo Olivieri (1484-1543/4).
[41] James Fergusson, *A History of Architecture in all Countries*, vol. 2, p.360.
[42] Street, op.cit., pp.75-78.
[43] Giovanni Antonio Amadeo (1447-1522); Mackintosh mistakenly referred to this as Santa Maria del Carmine; there is a Renaissance church of that name in a different part of the town with a far more restrained façade.
[44] Street, op.cit., pp.66-67.
[45] John Ruskin, *The Seven Lamps of Architecture* (The Works of John Ruskin, Vol. 8), edited by E. T. Cook and Alexander Wedderburn (London: George Allen, 1903), pp.50-51.
[46] William James Anderson, *The Architecture of the Renaissance in Italy*, pp.53-4.
[47] Design for a Chapter House, Royal Institute of British Architects Soane Medallion Competition entry, 1892.
[48] Street, op.cit., p.400.
[49] Glasgow Art Galleries, Competition entry, 1892.

SEVEN

The Cathedral, Milan

Milan and Pavia

'In Milan there is a lot that is worth seeing and a great lot that isn't... the Cathedral... has many good points'[1]

Milan: Saturday 27th June – Tuesday 7th July
Milan was Italy's third largest city and its financial centre. It had been the capital of the Western Roman Empire in the 4th century. Later, from 1277 to 1535, it was the seat of the Visconti and Sforza Dukes of Milan and after being ruled by the Spanish and then the Austrians with an interlude as a Napoleonic capital at the turn of the 18th century, it had reverted to Austrian rule which had only ended with the establishment of the Kingdom of Italy in 1859. Mackintosh would have arrived at the Stazione Ferrovio Nord from where trams were available to the Piazza del Duomo, close to his hotel.[2]

After checking in at 6 p.m. he found the expected letter from John Shields awaiting him. Shields had been staying in Callander, north of Glasgow, and as he had been unable to consult with the Trustees was prevented from giving Mackintosh a definite answer on whether they would release the remainder of the prize money without seeing his drawings. He explained, however, that this was doubtful as they were bound by the regulations of the Trust and that the best course for Mackintosh would be to send the drawings on at once, taking precautions for their safety. As Shields had offered to put Mackintosh's case to the Trustees when he returned from Callander, Mackintosh wrote that he would await their decision before sending on his work, pointing out that he would be in Milan 'for some days' before going on to Pavia and Genoa. Shields' reply that came a fortnight later would alter his plans.

In the meantime, Mackintosh pursued his busy schedule. His hotel was in the Piazza Fontana, centrally placed behind the Cathedral and its exploration was his first objective next morning. He 'was surprised at the splendour of' this huge building, after Seville the largest Gothic cathedral in Europe, only surpassed in size as an ecclesiastical building in Italy by St. Peter's. Commissioned by the powerful Duke of Milan, Gian Galeazzo Visconti in 1386, it was designed by a committee of Italian, German and French master masons and mathematicians. It had been built over several centuries and entirely faced with white marble, its exterior, mainly completed in the 19th century, ornamented with a filigree of panelling, surmounted by a forest of 98 pinnacles and spires and adorned with over 2,000 figure sculptures. It was bound to impress, even if Mackintosh found it 'overdone'. Nevertheless he pronounced 'the old bits' to be 'really rather good' and singled out the side aisle windows for special praise. On the other hand, the parapet tower he dismissed as 'all restoration' and 'very much inferior', but made no comments on the Classically-influenced west front, planned in the 17th century and only completed to a modified Gothic design on the command of Napoleon in 1805. The interior was 'disappointing' and lacked 'the grand solemnity associated with large gothic cathedrals': although the chancel, 'with light behind' had 'a good effect' the work was inferior, and the windows were filled with 'very poor painted glass'.[3] Equally to be deplored, because it was dishonest, was the painted tracery in the vaulting of the side aisles which detracted 'very considerably from the internal effect'.[4] Yet Mackintosh did like the originality of the 52 huge piers which each have niches above their capitals containing figure sculpture, and made a rapid sketch of one. He also made a more considered study of one of the 'old bits', a 14th-century Gothic wall tomb in the south aisle,[5] and in the north transept, the Trivulzio Candelabrum, a huge seven-branched bronze candlestick with a 12th-century base.[6] Leaving the Cathedral, he passed through the Piazza del Duomo into the grand shopping arcade, the Galleria Vittorio Emanuele II.[7] One might have

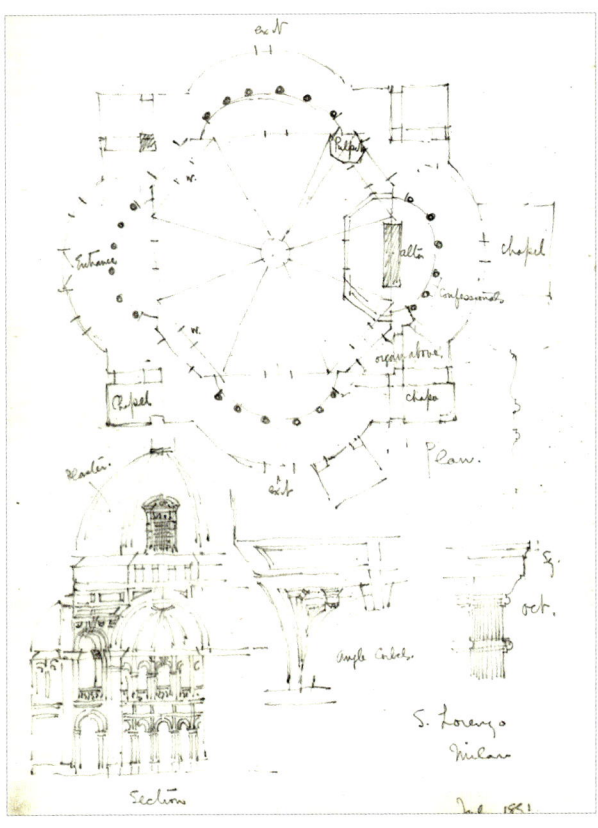

C. R. Mackintosh, San Lorenzo Maggiore, Milan, 1891

expected that he would have praised this, the first such structure to be erected in Italy and a forerunner of the one he had admired in Naples, but compared with the latter he found it 'much inferior'. His destination, the Brera, the city's art museum, fared slightly better. Mackintosh made a long list of the painters in the permanent collection whose work caught his eye[8], but he found a temporary exhibition of modern Italian art to be of distinctly uneven quality, the painting being 'mostly very weak' – although the Venetian work was better than the rest, with the sculpture 'much better than the paintings'.

During the 10 days he spent in Milan he visited several other churches and art galleries. Of the churches there was the Lombard Romanesque Sant'Ambrogio, 'a quaint old thing in stone brick and plaster'. Founded by the powerful bishop St. Ambrose in the 4th century, it had been substantially rebuilt between the 8th and 12th centuries. Approached through an open atrium which seals it off from the outside world and a five-bay narthex (porch) under a wide gable flanked by two campaniles, the church has a rib-vaulted nave, a triple apse and side aisles, these last surmounted on both sides by a women's gallery, or matroneum, an unusual feature which Mackintosh would encounter again in Pavia. He made a cursory sketch of the front from the west side of the atrium with subsidiary jottings of one of the capitals in the atrium, two in the nave and studies of two of the three doorways in the narthex. He also made a more considered drawing of an interior bay at the dome noting the decorative combination of brick and plaster.

Then there was Sant'Eustorgio to the south-west of the city centre: 'also very nice'. Like Sant'Ambrogio it had a long history. Having been consecrated in the 6th century much of it was in the Gothic style of the 12th to 13th centuries with 15th and 16th-century additions. Mackintosh filled a whole page of his sketchbook with a detailed analysis of a bay of the nave with notes on its ornamentation. He also made drawings of two tombs, one of a Renaissance example in the nave and another of the most important monument in the church, the elaborate 14th-century Gothic shrine of St. Peter Martyr.[9] Mackintosh's rapid sketch, merely suggesting the main forms is, unusually for him, a perspective study.

San Lorenzo Maggiore, close to Sant'Eustorgio along the Corso di Porta Ticinese, had an 'interesting plan'. Ignoring the fine Roman colonnade which stands in the small piazza before the entrance, Mackintosh concentrated on the interior. The octagonal plan incorporating an ambulatory and four semicircular apses, dates from the 4th century, but the muscular grey stone interior elevation, a Mannerist Classical edifice by Martino Bassi dates from the late 16th century. Mackintosh not only made a drawing of the plan, but despite its late date felt it worthwhile to make a careful study of Bassi's elevation with details of an arch and cornice.

Santa Maria delle Grazie, further on Corso Magenta, was 'worth seeing'. This brick Gothic church received a Renaissance dome and crossing, and a fine marble porch in 1472, all of these attributed to Bramante. They drew a mixed reception from Mackintosh who made a detailed analytical drawing of the 'good Renaissance porch', but dismissed 'the Renaissance work on the exterior of the dome & transepts' as 'mildly comical'. He was aware of Leonardo's famous fresco of *The Last Supper* in the adjacent refectory but if he saw it he left no comment on what was then a shadow of what the painter had intended.

Luigi Scrosati, Ornamentation, Studiolo Dantesco, Museo Poldi Pezzoli, Milan; destroyed by allied bombing in 1944, restored 2002

C. R. Mackintosh, Ornamentation, Studiolo Dantesco, Museo Poldi Pezzoli, Milan, 1891

Mackintosh regretted that the other churches were 'mostly late of a very inferior quality', but despite this found two 17th-century examples of particular interest. One was the small church of Santa Maria alla Porta,[10] not far south of the Castello Sforzesco, the great ducal castle which dominates the city. Without going into any details he remarked that it had 'some rather inspiring decoration'.[11] The other was Sant'Alessandro, Milan's major Baroque church.[12] He made no mention of it in his diary or the subsequent lecture, but his sketchbook contains two almost identical plans of its interior.

For the civic and domestic buildings, Mackintosh reverted to his interest in earlier architecture. Immediately to the west of the Piazza del Duomo is the Piazza de' Mercanti, the centre of the mediaeval city. It contains the Lombard Romanesque Palazzo della Ragione, constructed in brick and similar to the Broletto in Como and its counterpart in Bergamo. His drawing of its northern façade typically took in the two 13th-century storeys but omitted the 18th-century upper floor. He was equally selective in picking out features of the Ospedale Maggiore. Known locally as 'Ca'Granda' (the big house), it was commissioned by the Duke Francesco Sforza in 1456 and designed in the Renaissance style by the Florentine architect Antonio Filarete with two matching wings, one for women the other for men, each containing four courts, with a central court and chapel. Filarete only had time to build the south wing which was also worked on by the Milanese architect Guiniforte Solari, who had been partly responsible for the Gothic work in Santa Maria delle Grazie. The remainder was built in the 17th century, with a Neo-Classical façade completed between 1797 and 1804. Mackintosh's study of the building contains a miniature sketch of the whole façade but focuses on the decorative treatment of the 15th-century wing with its terracotta ornamentation and heavy cornice. The other building that caught his eye also dated from the 15th century, the Palazzo Fontana-Silvestri along the Corso Venezia, north-east of the Cathedral. With its plaster rendered brick façade, terracotta ornamentation

C. R. Mackintosh, blind window, west front, Certosa di Pavia, 1891

on its window jambs, and a stone portico surmounted by an iron balcony, it was attributed to Bramante.

For his work in the museums, Mackintosh returned to the Brera whose ground floor was devoted to the Museo Archeologico which contained a collection of architectural fragments from demolished Milanese buildings, both domestic and ecclesiastical.[13] Here he found porticoes of palazzi, chimney pieces, sarcophagi and examples of carved ornament, all from the Renaissance period of the late 15th to early 16th century, and recorded several in his sketchbook. Another discovery was the Museo Poldi Pezzoli on the Via Manzoni. This had been the private residence of the art collector Gian Giacomo Poldi Pezzoli who had bequeathed it and its contents to the city on his death in 1879. Mackintosh revelled in the rich collection of textiles, armour, ceramics, jewellery and bronzes, describing it as 'for its size the finest collection of art treasures [he had] seen anywhere'. It was, however, the design and treatment of one of Poldi Pezzoli's private apartments that particularly took his eye. This was the Studiolo Dantesco, designed by the Milanese artist-craftsmen Giuseppe Bertini and Luigi Scrosati. Poldi Pezzoli had it constructed in the style of the 14th century between 1854 and 1856 to display some of his mediaeval artefacts and to celebrate Italy's great poet and patriot Dante Alighieri. Despite its mid-century date the treatment of the walls, particularly the plant-based ornamentation in gilded and painted gesso and ceramic by Scrosati, looks forward to Art Nouveau and it was probably Mackintosh's interest in the conventionalisation of plant form, its use of different materials and its display of craftsmanship which drew him to make two studies of this interior.

Having spent over a week in Milan, Mackintosh made his last entry in his diary: 'Tuesday 7th July left for Pavia'. It is highly likely, however, that by 'Pavia' he meant the Certosa di Pavia, a group of monastic buildings 8 km north of the city, as his only dated drawing from Pavia bears the inscription '21st July' and he was staying at the Certosa by the 12th.[14] The monastery is also nearer to Milan and direct tram and train services from there rendered it easily accessible. From the large number of drawings Mackintosh produced at the Certosa a longish stay seems likely and although it lies in the countryside the Hotel–Ristorante Milano, which Mackintosh was to make his new address, was conveniently situated just outside its walls.

Certosa di Pavia: Tuesday 7th? – Tuesday 21st July?
No reply had come from Mackintosh's last letter to Shields while he was staying in Milan, but one was forwarded to him at the Certosa. This unequivocally stated that the drawings must be examined and approved by the Committee before the prize money could be dispatched. Shields offered sympathetic advice on finding the best means of sending the work to Glasgow and assured Mackintosh that the Trustees would cover the cost. If Mackintosh had been intending to use the hoped-for addition to his finances to enable him to continue touring the Continent, which would probably have begun with a trip to Genoa[15] and a sea voyage to a southern French port, he now decided to abandon his plans and wait for the balance of his prize after an early return home.[16]

Whatever his feelings, he was still determined to make the best use of the time left to him in Italy. In fact, the Certosa would be the subject of more drawings than any other building he had visited on the whole tour: 28 sketches, many of them finished in watercolour, all except one, a drawing of the interior of the dome in its church, being studies of decorative details.

The monastery had been commenced under the patronage of Gian Galeazzo Visconti in 1396, the same Duke of Milan who had endowed its Cathedral. Situated in the ducal hunting grounds adjacent to Pavia, the Certosa was intended as a grandiose mausoleum church for his dynasty. The building of the complex was continued by Ludovico, the last of Milan's Sforza dukes who, from 1492 to 1497, employed a multitude of artists and craftsmen who were largely responsible for the sumptuous ornamentation to be found throughout the huge complex. Subsequently the Carthusian community, which occupied the monastery up until its expulsion in 1782, had been required to use part of the revenue of its lands for the embellishment of the buildings, with the result that the site contained a huge collection of artworks dating from the 14th to the 18th centuries.

The buildings are approached via an entrance vestibule embellished with frescos by Bernardino Luini, a Milanese follower of Leonardo da Vinci. This opens onto a large garden court, at the far end of which rises the west front of the church built in the antique Classical style. Faced entirely with coloured marbles and adorned with sculpture, it had been described as 'perhaps the most masterly work of its kind of the fifteenth century'.[17] Its interior is a vaulted Gothic structure on a Latin cross plan with a dome over the crossing. The adjacent conventual buildings include a lavishly ornamented lavabo, sacristy and refectory, an impressive small cloister and an immense great cloister around which were built the separate houses of the Carthusian monks.

The Certosa had been greatly admired throughout the 19th century and was a frequent source of sketches by architectural students. The boundless admiration of Mackintosh's friend, George McKenzie, on his own tour of Italy a few months earlier had caused him to write: 'The façade as a whole and its parts in detail, are so beautiful in design and execution that this building might be called 'The Poem'…the effect of light and shade in the loggia [of the small cloister?] was finer than anything I have yet seen'.[18] The convinced Gothicist Ruskin, on the other hand, after a visit in 1845, had been far less impressed: 'The Certosa… is, in elaborateness and quantity of labour, far more marvelous than my recollection of it. In *quality* of art, far inferior. … It is an attempt by people without mind or feeling to imitate what is good. But it is all done to be *fine*, nothing for a simple or great purpose'.[19]

From the number of sketches Mackintosh produced, and if his lecture, which related to the features he had chosen to draw, was a true reflection of his own feelings, it would seem that his sentiments were closer to McKenzie's:

The façade of this edifice, by Ambrogio Bergognone,[20] an example of the richest Renaissance style, is entirely covered with marble of different colours, and most tastefully decorated. At the base are medallions of Roman emperors, and above them scenes from sacred history, beyond them are the magnificent windows, which for beauty & delicacy of workmanship cannot be equalled anywhere.

The interior, which has a very gorgeous effect, was also decorated by Bergognone. Every chapel contains valuable pictures & other objects of interest and are separated from the nave, as is the transepts & choir, by beautiful iron & brass screens. The choir stalls are covered with intarsia which is perhaps the best in Italy. A beautiful door to the right of the choir leads to the lavatorio where there is an exquisite marble fountain, which perpetuates the memory of the architect of this noble pile. The cloisters which are got at through another beautiful door, are surrounded by marble columns and charming decorations, in terracotta.[21]

Certosa di Pavia, entrance front

Pavia: Tuesday 21st July

After his stay at the Certosa, Mackintosh made the short journey to Pavia where his main objective was the 12th-century Lombard Romanesque church of San Michele. Just off the Corso Garibaldi, one of the town's main east-west arteries, it lies hidden in its own small piazza. James Fergusson had described the church as 'one of the most interesting of its age' presenting 'in itself all the characteristics of a perfect round-arched Gothic church', adding 'indeed there is hardly a feature worth mentioning which was invented after this date except the pointed arch – a very doubtful improvement …'.[22] Mackintosh agreed, remarking in his lecture that it was a 'beautiful old church, certainly the best of its kind in Italy'. His three drawings of the building include one of the west front, with its three elaborately ornamented doors; another of the plan which indicates its early adoption of groin vaulting, its wide nave and transepts; and details of the ornament on the south door, the '*Porta Speciosa*' and some of the capitals.

San Michele is adorned by a quantity of anthropomorphic and zoomorphic ornament, but Mackintosh typically ignored this to concentrate on the botanically-derived carvings in the sandstone of which the basilica is constructed.

From Pavia he returned to Milan where he took the train to Paris, then via Brussels to Antwerp where he stayed for a few days. The images in the sketchbook are an indication of what he might have chosen to study had the remainder of the prize money been available to him. While in Paris he took a detour to visit the French Renaissance Chateau d'Écouen where he drew a chimney piece, and in Antwerp he sketched the Flemish Renaissance buildings on its main square and museum objects from the same period.[23] His colleagues John Keppie and George McKenzie had recently visited the Renaissance Chateau de Blois on the River Loire and had probably inspired Mackintosh, who was interested in Scottish Baronial and Elizabethan buildings, to extend his knowledge of northern Renaissance architecture. As this was not to be, after a few days in Antwerp, he boarded the ferry to London from where he took the train back to Glasgow.[24]

Notes for Chapter 7

[1] Mackintosh, 'A Tour in Italy (1892)' in Robertson (1990), p.124.
[2] Hotel Biscione e Bellevue, Piazza Fontana.
[3] Much of the Cathedral's 15th- and 16th-century glass had been restored by Giovanni Battista Bertini and his sons who had worked for 70 years from the 1830s extensively applying enamels, a system which reduced the translucency of the glass.
[4] Mackintosh would have been familiar with Ruskin's castigation of this feature: 'the roof of Milan Cathedral is seemingly covered with elaborate fan tracery, forcibly enough painted to enable it, in its dark and removed position, to deceive a careless observer. This is, of course, gross degradation; it destroys much of the dignity even of the rest of the building, and is in the strongest terms to be reprehended', John Ruskin, *The Seven Lamps of Architecture*, (The Works of John Ruskin, Vol. 8), edited by E. T. Cook and Alexander Wedderburn (London: George Allen, 1903), p. 72.
[5] Tomb (1406) of Marco Carelli (d. 1394) attributed to Filippino degli Organi (fl. 1400-50) and Jacopino da Tradate (fl. 1401-40).
[6] Mackintosh, 'A Tour in Italy (1892)' in Robertson (1990), p.124.
[7] Built 1865-77 by Giuseppe Mengoni (1829-77).
[8] Mackintosh's list comprised Giovanni Bellini (c.1435-1516), Francesco Francia (c.1450-1517), Benedetto da Maiano (1442-97), Dosso Dossi (1480-1542), Paolo Veronese (1528-88) 'not very strong', Perugino (1446-1523), Giotto (1266/7-1337), Tintoretto (1519-94) 'very fine', Gentile Bellini (c.1429-1507), Titian (1480/5-1576) 'not very good', Ambrogio Bergognone (1455?-1524?), Vincenzo Foppa (fl. 1427-1515), Salvatore Rosa (1615-73) 'very like Titian' and Giulio Campi (c.1502-72).
[9] Tomb (1339) by Giovanni di Balduccio (c.1290-after 1339).
[10] Built 1652 by Francesco Maria Richini (1583-1658).
[11] Mackintosh, *North Italian Sketchbook*, p.63b note (Glasgow School of Art Archives and Collections, MC:G57).
[12] Begun 1601, designed by Lorenzo Binago (1554-1629) and Francesco Maria Richini (1583-1658).
[13] Most of the exhibits are now in the Museo d'Arte Antica in the Castello Sforzesco.
[14] Mackintosh, Letter to Shields, dated Certosa di Pavia, 12th July 1891 in Robertson (1990), p.231.
[15] Mackintosh, Letter to Shields, dated Milan, 27th June 1891; Mackintosh stated that he would go next to Pavia and Genoa, ibid., p.230; and Letter from Shields to Mackintosh, 30th June 1891, ibid., p.230.
[16] Mackintosh, Letter to Shields dated Milan, 12th July 1891, ibid., p.231.
[17] Karl Baedeker, *Italy: Handbook for Travellers: first part: Northern Italy*, 11th remodelled edition (Leipsic: Karl Baedeker, 1899), p. 135.
[18] Clark, *The McKenzie Sisters* (Duns: Black Ace Books, 1996), p. 27.
[19] John Ruskin, Letter to John James Ruskin dated Milan, 16th July 1845, in Shapiro, Harold I., editor, *Ruskin in Italy: Letters to his Parents 1845* (Oxford: Clarendon Press, 1972), p.148.
[20] The façade is largely the work of Giovanni Antonio Amadeo (1447-1522) and Cristoforo Lombardo (fl. 16th century; Ambrogio Bergognone (fl. 1480-1522) was responsible for much of the decoration of the interior.
[21] Mackintosh, 'A Tour in Italy (1892)' in Robertson (1990), p.125.
[22] James Fergusson, *A History of Architecture in all Countries*, vol. 2, pp.303-4.
[23] Elaine Grogan, 'Charles Rennie Mackintosh's Antwerp Sketches', *Charles Rennie Mackintosh Society Journal* 85, Winter 2003, pp.12-16.
[24] Mackintosh, 'A Tour in Italy (1892)' in Robertson (1990), p.125; there were sailings to London two or three times per week by the General Steam Navigation Company: Karl Baedeker, *Belgium and Holland*, (Leipsic: Karl Baedeker, 1891), p.137.

Lavatorio, Certosa di Pavia

EIGHT

The Rose Boudoir, Turin, 1902

Influence of the Tour

By 12th August Mackintosh was home at 2 Firpark Terrace, Glasgow writing to Shields to ask when the Committee could examine his sketches. Shields quickly arranged for him to hang them in the Religious Institution Rooms at 200 Buchanan Street on the 20th. Room 10, 'up two floors', had been hired from 1 till 4 p.m. and Mackintosh was asked to attach his drawings to the walls with small drawing pins prior to the meeting at 3 p.m. He was also required to supply the Committee with a memoir of his tour to be read at the event.[1] Although he was not allowed to be present during the examination, Shields advised him that he could visit the rooms at 3.15 to await the Committee's decision.[2] This came quickly. After the members had approved the drawings and the memoir, the balance of the prize money was duly awarded. If the Trustees had been happy to award the prize, they had, however, one concern: they minuted that the second clause of the Trust should be strictly adhered to in future, namely: 'That the Studentship or prizes shall be awarded for the furtherance of the study of Ancient Classic architecture as practised prior to the third century of the Christian era and with special reference to the principles illustrated in the works of the late Alexander Thomson'.[3] Mackintosh had obviously flouted this rule, but perhaps some guilt attached itself to the Trustees themselves who had previously given permission to the first prize-winner, William James Anderson, to concentrate on 16th-century Renaissance architecture.

This was not the end of the hoped-for benefits of the Italian tour: Mackintosh was eager to capitalise on his experiences. In its 7th August issue, the *British Architect* advertised his forthcoming lecture to the Glasgow Architectural Association, entitled 'A Tour in Italy' scheduled for 2nd January 1892.[4] In the event the talk was postponed until 6th September but received a good review in the same journal for its 'racy' criticism of individual buildings and the 'admirable pencil and water-colour sketches and some good photographs' which the lecturer used as illustrations.[5]

Mackintosh had further uses for his drawings. The first of these was to enter them for the Royal Institute of British Architects' 1891 Pugin Travelling Scholarship whose winner not only received a silver medal but also a £60 prize which would have enabled him to continue his studies of Continental architecture, but despite the panel's judgement that 'the pencil work of Mr Charles R. McIntosh [was] broad and dignified in manner' and that his 'selection of subjects and method of execution' were 'good... The colour examples [being] daintily done', he was unsuccessful.[6]

The other major use for the drawings was as sources for his own architectural designs, particularly in the two years immediately following the tour. Mackintosh was a student at the Glasgow School of Art until summer 1894 and entered three more student competitions. The first of these was for the 1892 Royal Institute of British Architects' Soane Medallion. The project was to design a chapter house. Mackintosh's scheme, a domed octagonal building, was in the Renaissance style, all of its elements, from its base to the lantern on its cupola, except for a row of Flemish dormers which adorned its parapet, sourced from Italy: a bricolage of spolia, almost as if Mackintosh, like an 18th-century grand tourist was displaying his culture via the souvenirs he had amassed on his travels. The most common Italian ecclesiastical polygonal building was the baptistery and Mackintosh had examined several, most notably at San Giovanni in Laterano in Rome, at Ravenna, Florence, Pisa, Pistoia and Cremona, and would have been familiar with that at Bergamo. However, the main influence on his design was none of these: it was an apse from Como Cathedral. Using his sketch as the source, he changed the relative proportions of the wall's horizontal elements and added more ornament whilst retaining the sculptured figures from the entablature, one of which he had noted in his sketchbook. Amongst the ornament he added was a choir of angels similar to those in a photograph

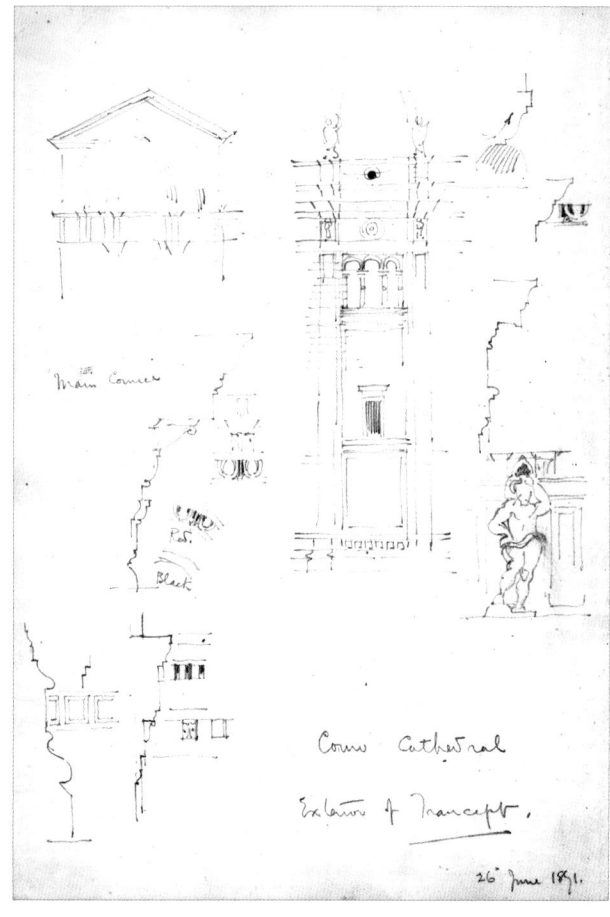

of the influential Italianate Pre-Raphaelite painter Burne-Jones' *Days of Creation*.[7] The interior had a Cosmatesque pavement, such as he had seen in Santa Maria Maggiore at Rome; stalls taken from his drawings of those at San Zeno in Verona; candelabra sourced from the Trivulzio Candelabrum in Milan Cathedral; and two figure sculptures, one of Moses the other of St. Jerome, sketched from the south transept of the same building, which adorned the arcade of its gallery. There was also a design for a doorway to a cloister copied directly from his careful study of the door to the small cloister in the Certosa di Pavia. The arcade of the cloister itself was also reproduced with little modification from that in the Certosa's small cloister. The scheme, reviewed as 'skillful' and 'clever' in the *British Architect*[8] was unsuccessful in the competition but won the only gold medal awarded for an architectural design in the 1892 National Competition run by the Department of Science and Art for work produced in schools of art. The examiners remarked that the design showed 'considerable artistic power', but regretted that Mackintosh had copied his candelabra directly from an ancient example; a comment that was not lost on him when he noted in his lecture that the beautiful bronze candelabrum in the transept of Milan Cathedral was 'evidently very well known'.[9]

In the same year Mackintosh was working on Honeyman and Keppie's unsuccessful competition entry for the new Glasgow Art Galleries. While deriving a great deal from Aston Webb's 1891 winning design for the South Kensington (now the Victoria and Albert) Museum,[10] Mackintosh's scheme was peppered with Italian details.

Above left: Tomaso Rodari, Eastern Apse, Como Cathedral
Above right: C. R. Mackintosh, Eastern Apse, Como Cathedral, 1891
Opposite above: C. R. Mackintosh, Design for a Chapter House, *British Architect*, vol. 37, 4th March, 1892
Opposite below left: C. R. Mackintosh, Detail, Design for a Chapter House, *British Architect*, vol. 37, 4th March, 1892
Opposite below right: Moses, Milan Cathedral

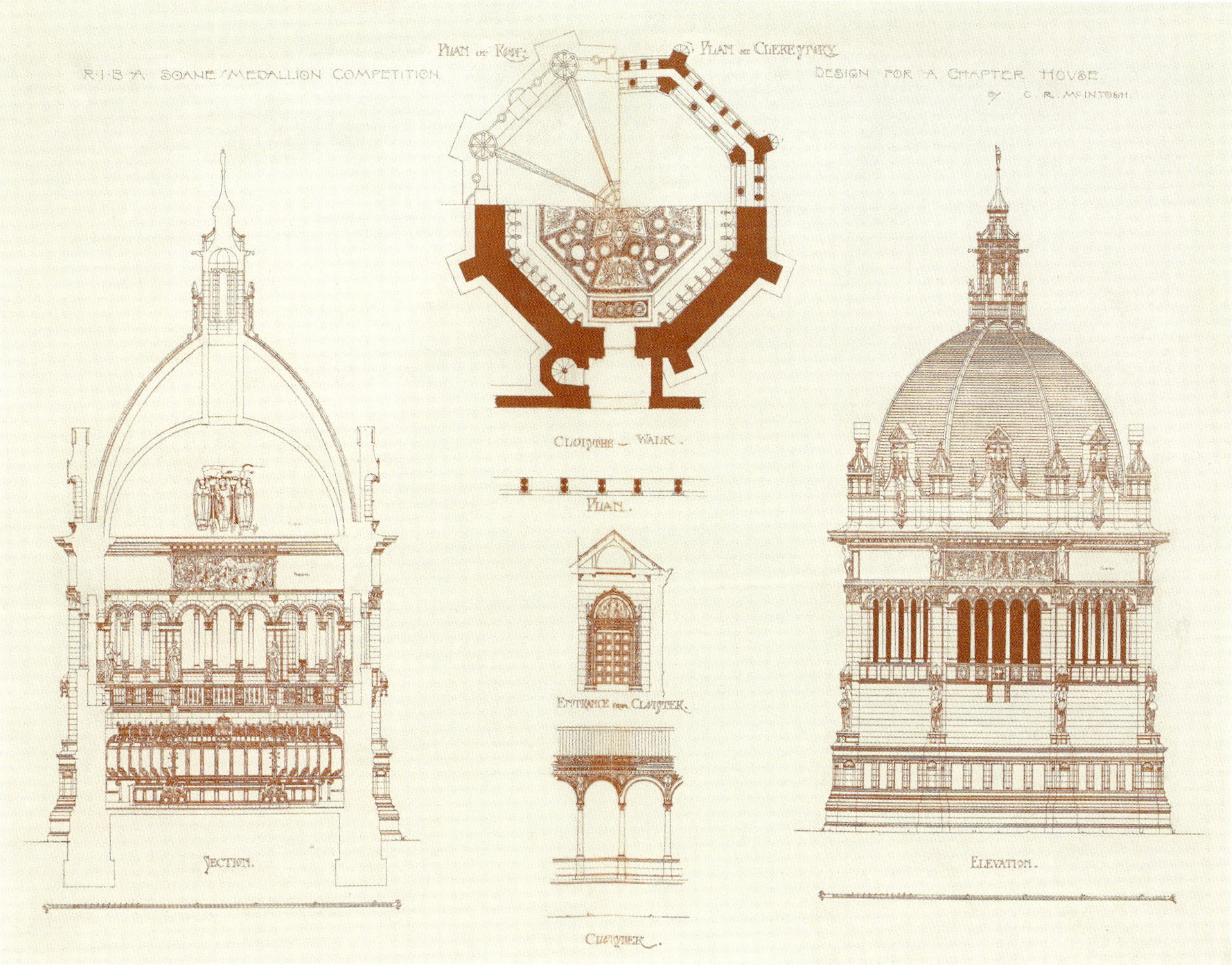
PLAN OF ROOF
PLAN AT CLERESTORY
R·I·B·A· SOANE MEDALLION COMPETITION
DESIGN FOR A CHAPTER HOUSE
BY C. R. McINTOSH
CLOISTER WALK
PLAN
ENTRANCE FROM CLOISTER
SECTION
ELEVATION
CLOISTER

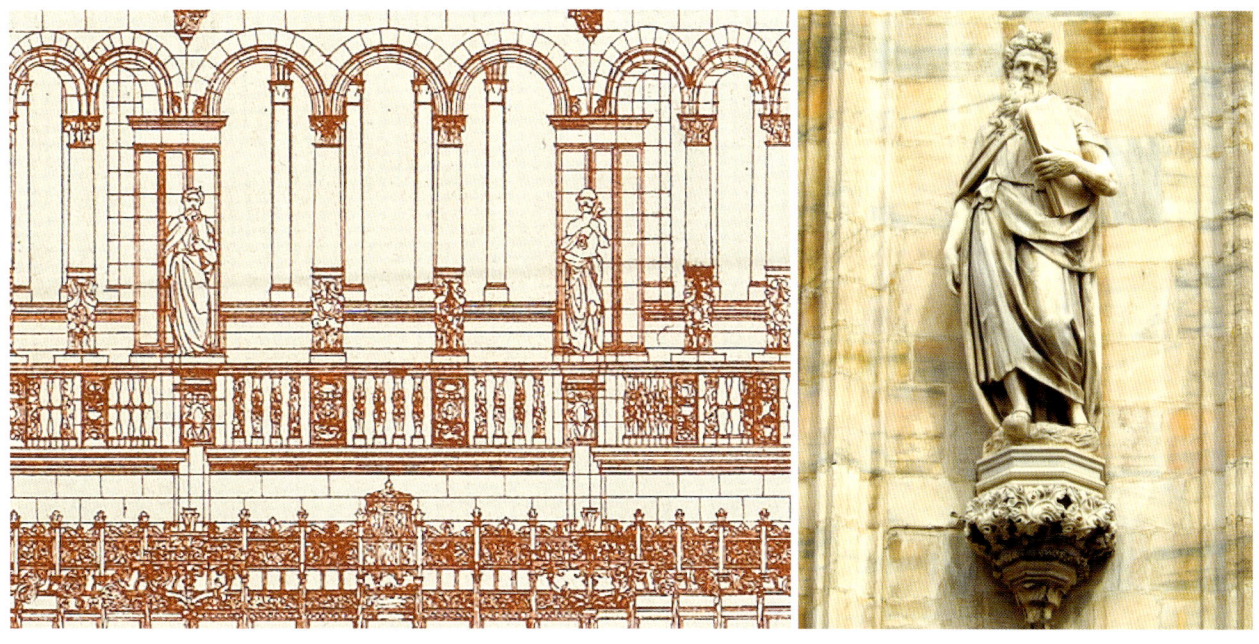

The Central Hall bears a strong resemblance to the naves of Sant'Ambrogio in Milan and San Michele in Pavia and a staircase turret on the eastern façade is an only slightly amended copy from Mackintosh's drawing of the Romanesque apse of San Fedele in Como. The towers either side of the entrance contain elements from the campaniles of San Zeno in Verona and San Marco in Venice. The balcony on the entrance front is an elaborated version of the balcony on the Broletto in Bergamo and the sculptural decoration of the building's exterior is a palimpsest of spolia from the tour. There are nudes from Michelangelo's Sistine chapel ceiling, a seated figure inspired by the same master's sculpture of Moses but with a different head, reclining female nudes which bear a strong resemblance to Michelangelo's figures from the Medici tombs in Florence's San Lorenzo and ubiquitous Italian cartouches. Mackintosh's only surviving graphic design from 1892 featuring Sybils, male nudes and balusters from the Sistine Chapel ceiling further demonstrates his admiration for Michelangelo.

Honeyman and Keppie's scheme for the Manchester Municipal Technical Schools' competition of the same year, in which Mackintosh also had a hand, has more Italianate features. Its main inspiration was the recently completed Glasgow Central Station Hotel by the Scottish architect Robert Rowand Anderson who had incorporated twinned Italianate wndows on the first floor which are reminiscent of those on the Palazzo Medici Riccardi in Florence. These and much else were carried over to Honeyman and Keppie's scheme, but the tower which was to have graced a corner of the proposed technical school owed nothing to Anderson's hotel and was a modified version of the towers of the Castello Estense in Ferrara. By 1893 Mackintosh was beginning to shake himself free from the overt influence of Italy. His work on the decorative details of the interior of the Glasgow Art Club that year is in the Free Renaissance style but without any obvious direct references. The stencilled frieze in the hall, based on thistle motifs, seems to be a new departure even if it contains forms which might be based on Italian cartouches. The finger plates on the doors displaying elongated female figures are even more innovative and are amongst the first examples of the Glasgow Style that Mackintosh and his friends pioneered that year. Perhaps the only direct reference to drawings made on the tour are the astragals, also on the doors, which are taken from balusters on a Flemish Renaissance bed that Mackintosh sketched in a museum in Antwerp.[11] Another move away from overt Italian sources was his unsuccessful entry for the Soane Medallion in the same year, a design for a railway station which he made in the Modern Gothic style, an adaptation from English Mediaeval Perpendicular Gothic favoured by contemporary British architects. Even here, however, he included an aesthetic echo from Italy in his employment of matching towers either side of the train shed, a memory of the placing of the twin campaniles of Sant'Abbondio in Como.

A built scheme commenced in 1893, his first major building, was the extension to the premises of the *Glasgow Herald*, a six-storey warehouse block dominated at one end by an octagonal water tower. Mackintosh had drawn many campaniles on his tour but his water tower bears little resemblance to any of them. The preliminary sketches, however, indicate how he was experimenting with ideas from Italy. In his earliest surviving drawing, he has a doorpiece at the corner derived from the one he had admired at Santa Maria delle Grazie in Milan. He abandoned this feature in a later finished perspective drawing but in line with his comments on the campanile of the cathedral of Siena, which he praised for its simplicity and the gradual increase in the number of window openings as it rose, he arranged his vertical sequence of openings in the tower increasing their width at each stage, placing a triple Romanesque window at the top; although this was not incorporated into the finished building. The two uppermost floors of the warehouse have been seen as experiments in a free interpretation of the Scottish Baroque, but in the same early sketch there is a suggestion that Mackintosh was considering something different, a colonnaded loggia reminiscent of those on the upper storeys of Florentine palazzi, such as on the Palazzo Guadagni. If all of these ideas were abandoned, Mackintosh was still interested in employing Italiante cartouches as decorative features, but by now he was experimenting with their forms, elongating those on the eighth stage of the tower until they came close to resembling elephants' ears and trunks, perhaps a humorous comment on the tower's function.

Mackintosh, as a practising architect was constantly aware of the latest developments in design ideology. In 1891, he lectured on Scottish Baronial architecture, arguing that it had been the last indigenous national style and that its forms were adaptable to the needs of modern requirements: in another lecture he had similarly commended Elizabethan architecture as a genuine national style and praised it for

INFLUENCE OF THE TOUR

Left: C. R. Mackintosh, Detail of principal entrance elevation, Competition design for Glasgow Art Gallery, *British Architect*, vol. 38, 8th July, 1892
Right: C. R. Mackintosh, Great Hall, Competition design for Glasgow Art Gallery, *Building News*, 10th June, 1892
Bottom: C. R. Mackintosh, Invitation card to Glasgow School of Art Club meeting, 1892

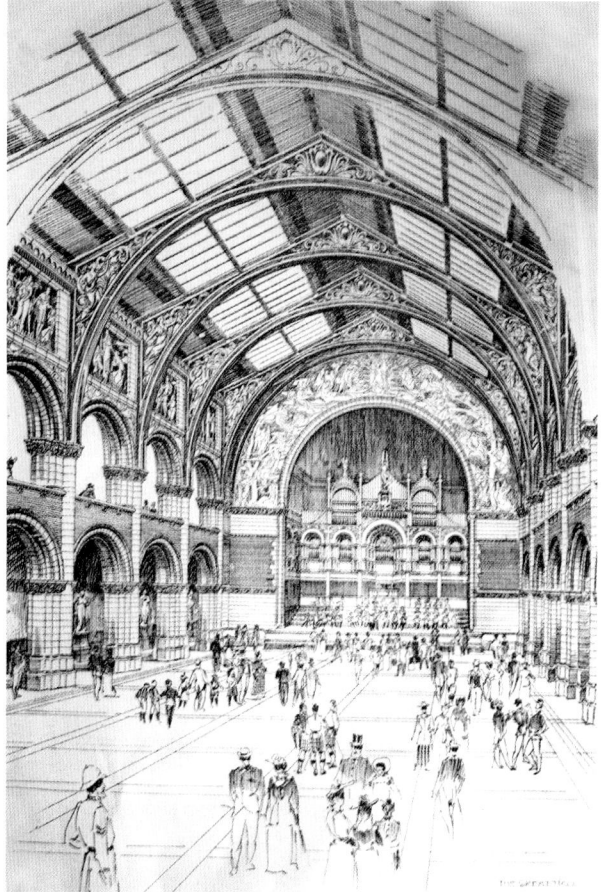

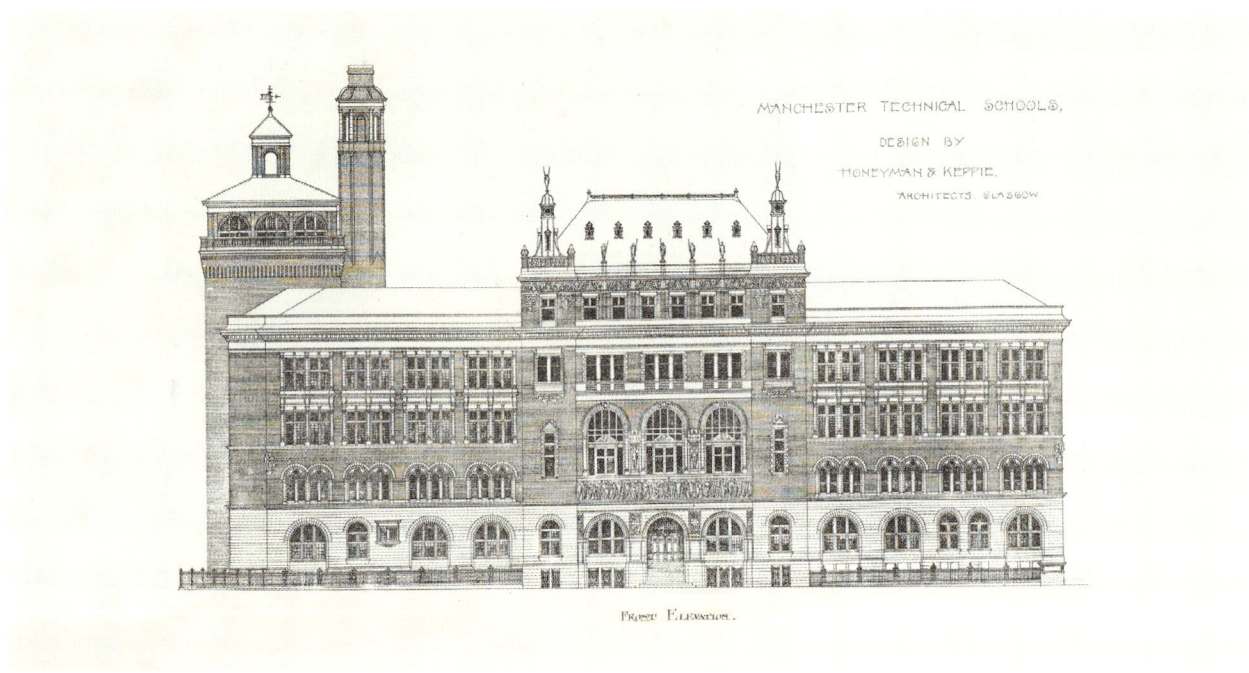

Above: C. R. Mackintosh, Competition design for Glasgow Art Gallery, *British Architect*, vol. 37, 10th June 1892, showing towers and central staircase turret
Below: C. R. Mackintosh, Competition design for Manchester Municipal Technical Schools, 1892, *British Architect*, 4th November, 1892

Opposite top left: C. R. Mackintosh, Sant'Abbondio, Como, 1891
Opposite top right: C. R. Mackintosh, Design for a Railway Terminus, *British Architect*, vol. 39, 17th February, 1893
Opposite bottom left: C. R. Mackintosh, Preliminary design for *Glasgow Herald* building, c.1893
Opposite bottom right: Doorway, Santa Maria delle Grazie, Milan

INFLUENCE OF THE TOUR

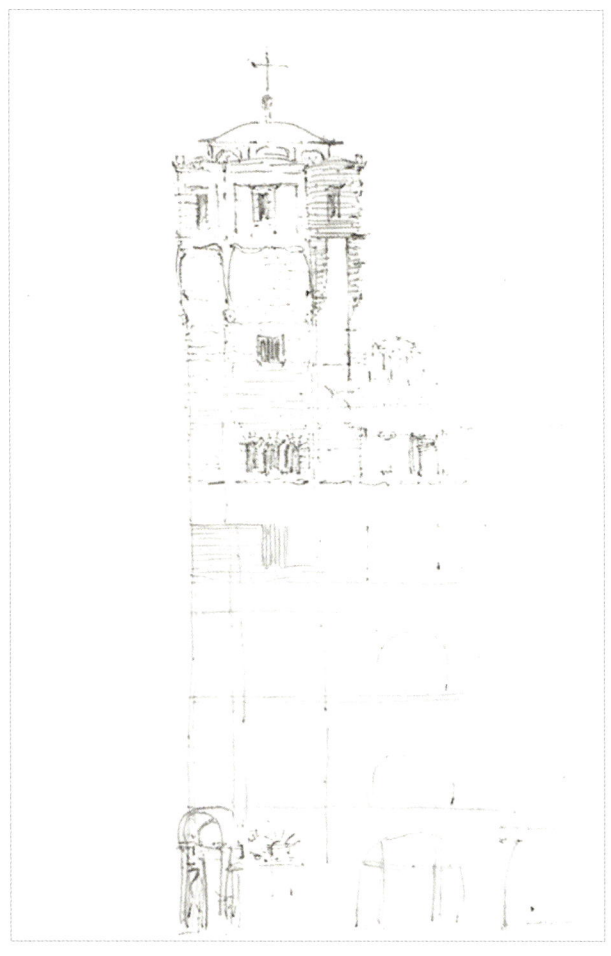

83

its aura of domesticity.[12] In two lectures on the subject of architecture also delivered soon after the Italian tour, he argued strongly for an architecture which reflected the needs and belief systems of his own times, respecting local building traditions and materials, just as he believed architecture up until the end of the 15th century had done. Participating in the vernacular revival espoused by many Arts and Crafts architects, he toured the Northern Cotswolds in 1894, followed in 1895 by a tour of Dorset, examining English domestic buildings of the 16th to 18th centuries. When, in 1896, he came to design his most important work, the new Glasgow School of Art, while following and improving on government guidelines for schools of art and keeping to the locally imposed competition requirements for a simple building, he incorporated, in modified form, much of what he had studied and held dear. There were Scottish Baronial references on the southern and eastern façades, a quotation from Dorset vernacular in the oriel window at the northern entrance, a reminiscence of the Elizabethan Montacute House, which he had visited the previous year, in the northern elevation with its great studio windows, and the inclusion of long oriels on the east and west façades. Yet this was not an exercise in historicism: it was an attempt to produce a well-designed school of art closely adapted to the needs of its users. The references to historical styles were subordinate to this and subtle, a means of symbolically placing the building in its national context. If there is a debt to Italy on the exterior, it must be the projecting cornices over the studio windows, seen in no other British art school. He had encountered this feature in Siena on Peruzzi's Palazzo Pollini, but they were also a common element in Florentine architecture, where they serve to shade the streets, hardly a requirement in Glasgow. Was this, in part, a suggestion that the new building with its profile so similar to that of a Renaissance palace built during Florence's golden age would foster equally great art?

Mackintosh's use of space in his interiors might also owe something to his months spent tramping the streets of Italian towns looking for their architectural treasures. These towns tend to hide their secrets: a narrow thoroughfare will suddenly emerge into a piazza dominated by a magnificent church whose looming presence was not apparent a minute before. Mackintosh was playing the same games when he made a staircase climb from the sombre entrance hall in the School of Art into the much larger daylit space of the Museum, or where he inserted an unnecessary and unexpected delicate wrought iron balcony

Upper: C. R. Mackintosh, Glasgow School of Art, first stage, 1899
Lower: Giuliano da Maiano and Baccio di Agnolo, Palazzo Antinori, Florence

C. R. Mackintosh, Design for wall stencil, Buchanan Street Tearooms, 1896

part way down the western staircase in the same building to reveal a surprise view along a corridor, or where he only suggested the existence of the corridor which is part of, but distinct from, the drill hall in his board school on Scotland Street in Glasgow.

By the late 1890s, the influence of Italy had been internalised, its forms had undergone a metamorphosis in Mackintosh's creative imagination and any attempt to relate his work back to Italian sources becomes increasingly open to conjecture. His 1896 stencilled frieze of Japanese figures for the Buchanan Street Tea Rooms is a possible reference, however distant, to the great procession of saints in Ravenna's Sant'Apollinare Nuovo that he had studied in a watercolour. Even later, in 1902, his design for Liverpool Cathedral, based largely on those of Glasgow and Durham featured buttresses containing massed figures of saints, suggestive of the unusual treatment of sculptured figures high up on the nave piers of Milan Cathedral that Mackintosh had also sketched.

The Buchanan Street frieze, however, marks the first of two further associations with Italy now no longer as inspiration, but in a geographical sense. 1895 saw the inauguration of the Venetian biennales, which in 1897 featured a consignment of paintings from the Glasgow School of Painters. Francis Newbery, headmaster of the Glasgow School of Art, also showed work and seems to have used the occasion to persuade the organisers to feature decorative art from Scotland in their 1899 biennale. Mackintosh showed three works: a poster design for a music journal and two mural designs, one of which was of Japanese inspiration for a restaurant, almost certainly the above-mentioned 1896 work produced for Miss Cranston's Buchanan Street Tea Rooms.[13]

Mackintosh's next, more high profile association with Italy occurred in 1902 when he was appointed by Newbery as the designer of the Scottish section of the International Exhibition of Modern Decorative Art which was held in Turin. By this time Mackintosh, working alongside Margaret Macdonald, whom he had married in 1900, had brought the Glasgow Style interior to its apogee. He divided the Scottish space into three separate rooms, the first two of which were bisected by a corridor punctuated by banners featuring stencilled female figures. Each of the three spaces had its own colour treatment. The largest, at the end, in purple and white, housed the bulk of the exhibits from Glasgow and further afield. The central space, in grey, gold and white contained a room setting, a 'Lady's writing room' by Herbert and Frances Macnair on one side, and a selection of embroideries on the other. However, the first space that the visitor would have

Above: C. R. Mackintosh and Margaret Macdonald, Rose Boudoir, Scottish Section, International Exhibition of Modern Decorative Art, Turin, 1902
Opposite: C. R. Mackintosh, Corridor detail, Scottish Section, International Exhibition of Modern Decorative Art, Turin, 1902

encountered in white, silver, rose pink and green, displayed the work of the Mackintoshes, with, on the right, a room setting entitled 'the Rose Boudoir'. This sparsely furnished space contained a selection of chairs, a table, electric light fittings, vases, a writing cabinet and gesso panels all on the theme of the rose. It met with a mixed reception. One Italian commentator Alfredo Melani, regarded it as 'the most charming thing at the International Exposition,'[14] whilst another critic Ugo Ojetti, reacting to the innovative nature of Mackintosh and Margaret Macdonald's work remarked, 'All this is not new art: in fact it is not art'.[15] Turin demonstrated that Mackintosh had come of age as a mature confident artist. Like so many truly creative individuals, he had been able to absorb and move beyond his student experience to a point where his work could not be ignored by critics and practitioners but where it would not always be understood.

Mackintosh's 1891 tour of Italy had helped him to complete his education as an architect and designer. By examining the masterpieces that had informed the work of his fellow professionals over the previous four centuries, Mackintosh had absorbed what was useful to him and begun to gain the courage to discard that which was not in the development of a personal language. As he himself was to put it in 1902:

> The artist may gather from a close study of old work a great deal that will refine his tastes, that will help him to a more adequate appreciation and therefore a fuller enjoyment of art and nature and life.

But there was a caveat:

> Let us look upon the result of the world's artistic achievements as the beginning the morning of our lives – not the grave of our aspirations the death knell of our ambitions.[16]

Notes for Chapter 8

[1] Mackintosh, 'Memoir on the Italian Tour' in Robertson (1990), pp.235-236: in the Memoir Mackintosh claimed to have visited Paestum, which his diary rules out; he also included Lucca which he would have at least passed through on the train between Pisa and Pistoia, but does not mention in his diary, and forgot to include Cremona.

[2] The committee on this occasion was William Leiper, President of the Glasgow Institute of Architects in the chair, John Keppie, Alexander Petrie, James Chalmers, Henry Edward Clifford, Malcolm Stark and John Shields; Keppie, seconded by Chalmers, moved that the seond half of the prize be awarded.

[3] Robertson (1990), pp.232 and 234 f.n. and Alexander Thomson Memorial Minute Book, 1, p.128.

[4] *British Architect*, vol. 36, 7th August 1891, p.100.

[5] *British Architect*, vol. 38, 9th September 1892, p.198; the lecture was repeated at the Architectural Section of the Philosphical Society of Glasgow on 28th November; see Appendix 2 for a list of illustrations used in the lecture.

[6] Ibid., vol. 37, 22nd January 1892, p.59; the prize was awarded to Detmar Blow (1867-1939).

[7] Mackintosh's interest in Burne-Jones' painting is clear; in 1896 he displayed a photograph of the work above his mantelpiece; Roger Billcliffe, *Charles Rennie Mackintosh: the Complete Furniture, Furniture Drawings & Interior Designs* (London: Lutterworth Press, 1979) p.35.

[8] *British Architect*, vol. 37, 4th March 1892, p.173, and vol 38, 1892, p.59.

[9] Glasgow School of Art, *Annual Report*, 1893, p.13 quoting National Competition Examiners' report (G. Aitchison, T. G. Jackson, J. J. Stevenson) (Glasgow School of Art Archives and Collections, GSAA//GOV/1/2); and Mackintosh, 'A Tour in Italy', Robertson, p.124.

[10] David Walker, 'The Glasgow Years', in Wendy Kaplan, editor, *Charles Rennie Mackintosh* (New York: Abbeville Press, 1996) pp.125-7.

[11] Elaine Grogan, 'Charles Rennie Mackintosh's Antwerp Sketches'; *Charles Rennie Mackintosh Society Journal*, 85, Winter 2003, pp.14-15.

[12] Mackintosh, 'Scotch Baronial Architecture' in Robertson (1990), pp.49-63 and Mackintosh, 'Elizabethan Architecture', ibid., pp.141-151.

[13] Jude Burkhauser, 'Sala M'Arte Decorativa Scozzese: Charles Rennie Mackintosh and the Glasgow Group at the Venice Biennale Exhibition of 1899', *Charles Rennie Society Newsletter*, 58, Spring, 1992, pp.9-13; the poster design was probably that for the Scottish Musical Review illustrated by Burkhauser.

[14] Alfredo Melani, 'L'art nouveau at Turin', *Architectural Record*, 1902, pp.739-40.

[15] Ugo Ojetti, 'L'Arte Nuova a Torino', *Corriere della Sera* (Milan), 1st June 1902.

[16] Mackintosh, 'unuterred utterances' appended to his lecture 'Seemliness (1902)' in Robertson (1990), p.225.

Forum, Pompeii

Appendices

APPENDIX 1
CATALOGUE OF DRAWINGS
Over 200 sheets of drawings in pencil, or in pencil and watercolour, survive from the tour and can be divided into two groups: sketches and more finished drawings, among which are the majority of the watercolours.

Most of the former are contained in two sketchbooks. The first of these, covering the earlier part of the tour from Naples to Venice, came into the possession of the Glasgow glass painter, Oscar Paterson who gave it to Dr. Henry George Farmer in 1916. Farmer in turn bequeathed it to the National Library of Ireland in Dublin in 1963 (PD 2009 TX). The sketchbook was already in use before Mackintosh went to Italy and the Italian drawings appear on 45 of its 93 pages, beginning at page 42.

The Italian sketches for the second part of the trip, from Vicenza to Pavia, including drawings made in Paris and Antwerp, are on 75 pages of a 97-page sketchbook in the Glasgow School of Art Archives and Collections (MC: G 57). The book was purchased in 1930 by Professor William James Smith from the architectural firm of Keppie Henderson & Partners, previously Honeyman, Keppie and Mackintosh. Smith, who was Professor of Architecture at the Glasgow School of Architecture, gave it to the Glasgow School of Art in 1959.

Other sketches and more finished drawings and watercolours now exist as independent works in public and private collections. The bulk of these were presented to Dr. Thomas Howarth, Mackintosh's first biographer, by an unnamed donor in 1943.[1] Howarth sold the larger part of his Italian drawings at public auction in 1994. Other Italian drawings remained part of the Mackintosh estate or were purchased from the architect during his lifetime or from his Memorial Exhibition in 1933. Intriguingly, in 1977, Howarth noted that Glasgow's Royal Technical College (now the University of Strathclyde) possessed a folio of the Italian drawings which had been found in a skip and which he believed was lodged in its library but, if it had ever existed, there is now no trace of this collection.[2] The catalogue, therefore, contains references to all known drawings but it is hoped that others will come to light in the future.

Mackintosh would often draw from different subjects or motifs on the same page, thus, occasionally, buildings or details from different locations appear together and these are not always captioned and are sometimes captioned incorrectly. Moreover, the two existing sketchbooks do not follow a strict chronological sequence, so the catalogue is arranged chronologically by city and building rather than by sketchbook page, correcting Mackintosh's attributions where necessary. This means that several sketchbook pages and sheets of drawings are cited more than once.

Images of the drawings held by the National Library of Ireland can be found on their website. The Glasgow School of Art's sketchbook can also be found on their website.

Notes
[1] Thomas Howarth, *Charles Rennie Mackintosh and the Modern Movement*, 2nd edition (London: Routledge & Kegan Paul, 1977) p.10, footnote: 'Many years later a fine collection of sketches was presented to the author in 1943 and these, with the Royal Technical College portfolio constitute the major part of the work executed by Mackintosh in Italy.'

[2] Ibid.: '...a portfolio containing many of these sketches found its way into a Glasgow office, and in due course was thrown out with the rubbish. By a stroke of good fortune it was noticed lying on the top of a well-filled dustbin in one of the city's alleyways and was promptly salvaged. It is now safely housed in the library of the Royal Technical College, Glasgow'.

POMPEII

1. Studies from Pompeii Museum, inscribed top left 'POMPEII MUSEO', signed with monogram and dated lower right 'APRIL 7th/ 1890 [sic]', pencil
272 x 185 mm
Provenance: Dr. Thomas Howarth by 1943; his sale Christie's London, Thursday 17th February 1994 (2), illus., p.15
Exhibited: Art Gallery of Ontario, Toronto, 1978. (3), illus.
Collection: Unknown
The studies include two friezes, a water spout, an oil lamp and five wine jars.

2. Studies from Pompeii, inscribed top left 'SKETCHES FROM POMPEI [sic]', signed with monogram and dated lower right 'APRIL 7th/1891', pencil
271 x 188 mm
Provenance: Dr. Thomas Howarth by 1943; his sale Christie's London, Thursday 17th February 1994 (1), illus., p.13
Exhibited: Art Gallery of Ontario, Toronto, 1978 (2)
Collection: Unknown
The studies include a pedestal, a candelabrum, a trough, a Corinthian capital and a statue of Hercules.

3. Study from Temple of Vespasian
Collection: Unknown
Mackintosh recorded that he made a drawing in this temple on 7th April.

4. Studies from Pompeii, inscribed top left 'SKETCHES FROM POMPEI [sic]', signed with monogram and dated lower right '9 APRIL 1891', pencil
257 x 340 mm
Provenance: Dr. Thomas Howarth by 1943; his sale Christie's London, Thursday 17th February 1994 (3), illus., p.15
Exhibited: Art Gallery of Ontario, Toronto, 1978. (6)
Collection: Unknown
The sheet includes studies of a table leg from the House of Cornelius Rufus, a frieze from the Street of Tombs and a street sign.

5. Tomb of Naevolaeia Tyche, inscribed top [?] 'SKETCHES FROM POMPEI [sic]', and lower centre 'MONUMENT', signed with monogram and dated lower right '9 APRIL 1891', pencil
273 x 186 mm
Provenance: Dr. Thomas Howarth by 1943
Exhibited: Art Gallery of Ontario, Toronto, 1978 (4 or 5)
Literature: Finucci, 1981, vol.1, illus., p.9
Collection: Unknown

6. Monument, Pompeii, inscribed 'SKETCHES FROM POMPEI [sic]', 'MONUMENT', signed with monogram and dated lower right '9 APRIL 1891', pencil
273 x 213 mm
Provenance: Dr. Thomas Howarth by 1943
Exhibited: Art Gallery of Ontario, Toronto 1978 (4 or 5)
Collection: Unknown
This untraced drawing could possibly be a study from the Street of Tombs.

NAPLES

7. Candelabrum, Museo Archeologico Nazionale, inscribed centre right 'NAPLES MUSEUM', signed with monogram and dated lower right '10th APRIL 1891', pencil
335 x 255 mm
Provenance: Dr. Thomas Howarth by 1943; his sale Christie's London, Thursday 17th February 1994 (6), illus. p.17
Exhibited: Art Gallery of Ontario, Toronto, 1978 (7)
Literature: Robertson, 1990, illus., pl. 24
Collection: Unknown

8. Studies of pottery, Museo Archeologico Nazionale, inscribed lower left 'EGYPTIAN [sic] POTTERY NAPLES MUSEUM', signed with monogram and dated lower right 'APRIL 1891', pencil
272 x 185 mm
Provenance: Dr. Thomas Howarth by 1943; his sale Christie's London, Thursday 17th February 1994 (7), illus., p.18; Christie's London, Thursday, 3rd May 2012 (24)
Exhibited: Art Gallery of Ontario, Toronto, 1978 (9)
Collection: Unknown
The drawing could have been produced on any of Mackintosh's visits to the Museum on 6th, 10th or 11th April. Unaccountably Mackintosh captioned these studies of mostly Greek pottery as 'Egyptian'.

9. Bronze tabernacle, Museo Archeologico Nazionale, Naples, inscribed upper left 'BRONZE TABERNACLE/NAPLES MUSEUM', signed and dated lower right 'CRM/1891', pencil
342 x 255 mm
Provenance: Dr. Thomas Howarth by 1943; his sale Christie's London, Thursday 17th February 1994 (9). illus., p.18
Collection: Unknown
The drawing could have been produced on any of Mackintosh's visits to the Museum on 6th, 10th or 11th April.

10. Central doorway, Santa Trinità Maggiore (Gesù Nuovo), inscribed lower centre 'TRINITA MAGGIORE NAPLES / ENTRANCE DOOR', signed with monogram and dated lower right '9th APRIL 1891', pencil and watercolour
240 x 190 mm
Provenance: Dr. Thomas Howarth by 1943; his sale Christie's London, Thursday 17th February 1994 (4), illus., p.16
Exhibited: University of Toronto School of Architecture, Toronto, 1967 (114); Art Gallery of Ontario, Toronto, 1978, (11)
Literature: Billcliffe, 1978 (14)
Collection: Unknown
In his diary Mackintosh recorded making this drawing on 8th April.

11. Porta Capuana, inscribed top 'PORTA CAPUANA/NAPLES 1535', signed with monogram and dated lower right '8th APRIL 1891', pencil
305 x 209 mm
Provenance: William B. O'Neal, Charlottesville, Virginia from 1980s by whom bequeathed to Virginia Museum of Fine Arts, Richmond, 16th September 1987
Literature: Rubis, 2005, illus., p.19
Collection: Virginia Museum of Fine Arts, Richmond (87.210)
Although dated '8th April', in his diary Mackintosh recorded making his drawing on 9th April.

12. Campanile, Santa Maria del Carmine, inscribed and dated centre left 'MARINA [sic] DEL CARMINE/NAPLES/APRIL 1890 [sic]', pencil
126 x 175 mm
Provenance: Oscar Paterson by 1916, by whom presented to Dr. Henry George Farmer, who bequeathed the sketchbook containing the drawing to the National Library of Ireland, Dublin, 1963
Literature: Grogan, 2002, p.174 (50), illus., pl. 25; Macaulay, 2010, illus., pl. 77
Collection: National Library of Ireland, Dublin (PD 2009 TX 50)
Mackintosh visited the church, and probably made the drawing on 8th April. His viewpoint is from the Strada Nuova.

13. Campanile, Santa Maria del Carmine, inscribed left 'MARIA DEL CARMINE / NAPLES', signed with monogram and dated lower centre '9 APRIL 1891', pencil
341 x 260 mm
Provenance: Dr. Thomas Howarth by 1943; his sale Christie's London, Thursday 17th February 1994 (5), illus., p.17
Exhibited: Art Gallery of Ontario, Toronto, 1978 (10)
Collection: Unknown
Mackintosh recorded visiting the church on 8th April. The date suggests

that the drawing, a more considered work than no. 12, was made on a return visit on the following day. His viewpoint is from the corner of the Piazza del Carmine.

14. Well in Great Cloister, Certosa di San Martino, inscribed top 'CERTOSA DI SAN MARTINO. NAPOLI/WELL IN COURTYARD', signed and dated bottom right 'CRM/11th APRIL 1891', pencil
272 x 189 mm
Provenance: Dr Thomas Howarth by 1943; his sale Christie's London, Thursday 17th February 1994 (8), illus., p.18
Exhibited: Art Gallery of Ontario, Toronto, 1978 (8), illus., p.17
Collection: Unknown

PALERMO
15. Entrance Porch, Palermo Cathedral, inscribed upper left 'PALERMO CATHEDRAL/ENTRANCE PORCH', signed and dated lower right '15 APRIL 1891/CRM.', pencil and grey wash
252 x 337 mm
Provenance: Dr. Thomas Howarth by 1943; his sale Christie's London, Thursday 17th February 1994 (12), illus., p.20
Exhibited: Art Gallery of Ontario, Toronto, 1978 (15)
Collection: Unknown
Mackintosh recorded finishing this drawing on 15th April. He had begun it on 13th April.

16. Eastern turrets, Palermo Cathedral, inscribed top left 'PALERMO CATHEDRAL./EASTERN TURRETS.', signed and dated lower right 'CRM./APRIL 1891', pencil
267 x 317 mm
Provenance: Dr. Thomas Howarth by 1943
Exhibited: Art Gallery of Ontario, Toronto, 1978 (13)
Collection: Private collection
Mackintosh recorded finishing sketches of the Cathedral on 17th April.

17. Campanile, La Martorana (**Santa Maria dell'Ammiraglio**), inscribed and signed with monogram and dated lower right 'CAMPANILE/ MARTORANA./ CRM. PALERMO 1891', pencil and watercolour
340 x 210 mm
Provenance: Dr. Thomas Howarth by 1943; his sale Christie's London, Thursday 17th February 1994 (13), illus., p.21
Exhibited: University of Toronto, School of Architecture, Toronto, 1967 (16); Art Gallery of Ontario, Toronto, 1978 (16), illus., p.15
Literature: Billcliffe, 1978 (16), illus., p.52
Collection: Unknown
Drawn on 15th April.

18. Bay, Monreale Cathedral [?], inscribed lower left 'MONREALA' [sic], signed and dated lower right 'CRM./APRIL 1891.', pencil
174 x 265 mm
Provenance: Dr. Thomas Howarth by 1943
Collection: Private collection
The drawing would have been made on one of Mackintosh's two visits to Monreale, either on 14th or 16th April. The source of the sketch is unidentified and conjectural.

19. Capital in the nave, Monreale Cathedral, inscribed centre left 'MONREALE', pencil
126 x 175 mm
Provenance: As for no. 12
Literature: Grogan, 2002, p.174 (51), illus., pl. 26
Collection: National Library of Ireland, Dublin (PD 2009 TX 51)
The drawing would have been made on one of Mackintosh's two visits to Monreale, either on 14th or 16th April.

20. Cloisters, Monreale Cathedral, pencil and watercolour
368 x 165 mm
Provenance: Acquired by William Meldrum after Memorial Exhibition 1933; by family descent

Doorway, Gesù Nuovo, Naples

Exhibited: Hunterian Art Gallery, Glasgow, 1990 (54)
Literature: Robertson, 1990, illus., pl. 28; Billcliffe, 1978 (15), illus., p.55
Collection: Unknown
The drawing would have been made on one of Mackintosh's two visits to Monreale, either on 14th or 16th April.

21. Fountain in the Cloisters, Monreale Cathedral, inscribed centre right 'FOUNTAIN IN CLOISTER/MONREALA [sic]', signed and dated lower right 'CRM./APRIL 1891', pencil
257 x 359 mm
Provenance: Dr. Thomas Howarth by 1943; his sale Christie's London, Thursday 17th February 1994 (14), illus., p.21
Exhibited: Art Gallery of Ontario, Toronto, 1978 (17)
Collection: Unknown
The drawing would have been made on one of Mackintosh's two visits to Monreale, either on 14th or 16th April.

22. Doorway and window of Archiepiscopal Palace and Porta Nuova, inscribed left 'SKETCHES FROM PALERMO', signed and dated lower right 'CRM/APRIL 1891', pencil
270 x 184 mm
Provenance: Dr. Thomas Howarth by 1943; his sale Christie's London, Thursday 17th February 1994 (10), illus., p.19
Exhibited: Art Gallery of Ontario, Toronto, 1978 (10)
Collection: Unknown

The drawings, which include at bottom right a sketch of a detail of the adjacent Cathedral tower, could have been made on 17th April when Mackintosh was making sketches of the Cathedral. A thumbnail sketch of the 17th-century Porta Nuova is at top right. All of the motifs on this page were visible from the door of Mackintosh's hotel.

23. Study of two doors and a window, Santa Maria della Catena, inscribed lower left 'S. ANTONIO. [sic] PALERMO', signed with monogram lower right, pencil
271 x 188 mm
Provenance: Dr. Thomas Howarth by 1943; his sale Christie's London, Thursday 17th February 1994 (11), illus., p.19
Exhibited: Art Gallery of Ontario, Toronto, 1978 (14)
Collection: Unknown

ROME

24. Studies of architectural ornament, possibly sketched at the Vatican Museum, inscribed centre right 'VATICAN.', pencil
126 x 175 mm
Provenance: As for no. 12
Literature: Grogan, 2002, p.174 (56)
Collection: National Library of Ireland, Dublin (PD 2009 TX 56)
The drawing was probably made on Mackintosh's first visit to the Vatican Museums on 21st April. He made further visits on 2nd and 4th May.

25. Studies from Galleria dei Candelabri, Vatican Museum, inscribed lower left 'VATICAN. MUSEO/ROME.', pencil
126 x 175 mm
Provenance: As for no. 12
Literature: Grogan, 2002, p.174 (57)
Collection: National Library of Ireland, Dublin (PD 2009 TX 57)
The drawing was probably made on Mackintosh's first visit to the Vatican Museums on 21st April. He made further visits on 2nd and 4th May. The studies are from an urn stand (top right), the base of a triangular candelabrum (top left) and another urn stand (bottom).

26. Window, Palazzo Ruspoli, Via del Corso, inscribed centre right 'PAL./ RUSPOLI' at top right of a sheet of studies of façades and architectural details, inscribed lower right 'NOTES FROM/ ROME.', signed and dated upper right 'CRM/APRIL 1891', pencil
269 x 183 mm
Provenance: Dr. Thomas Howarth by 1943; his sale Christie's London, Thursday 17th February 1994 (19), illus., p.24; Christie's London, Thursday 3rd May 2012 (19)
Exhibited: Art Gallery of Ontario, Toronto, 1978 (24)
Collection: Unknown.

27. Column and entablature from the Pantheon, inscribed lower right 'SKETCH/FROM THE/PANTHEON ROME.', signed and dated bottom right 'CRM./APRIL 1891.', pencil
27 x 18.4 cm
Provenance: Dr. Thomas Howarth by 1943; donated by him to Professor James Grady, Atlanta, Georgia, 7th December 1951
Collection: Unknown

28. Tomb of Pius III, Sant'Andrea della Valle, Corso Vittorio Emanuele II, inscribed centre left 'MONUMENT ST ANDREWS CH ROME' at top left of a sheet of studies of two monuments and a church façade, inscribed lower right 'NOTES FROM/ ROME.', signed with initials and dated 'APRIL 1891', pencil
270 x 184 mm
Provenance: Dr. Thomas Howarth by 1943; his sale Christie's London, Thursday 17th February 1994 (16), illus., p.22
Exhibited: Art Gallery of Ontario, Toronto, 1978 (23)
Collection: Unknown
Mackintosh visited Sant'Andrea on 22nd April.

29. Window, Palazzo della Cancelleria, inscribed top left 'PALAZZO CANCELLERIA/ROME', signed and dated bottom right 'CRM/APRIL 1891.', pencil
27 x 18.4 cm
Provenance: Dr. Thomas Howarth by 1943; donated by him to Professor James Grady, Atlanta, Georgia, 7th December 1951
Collection: Unknown
Mackintosh recorded making this sketch from a shop doorway on 22nd April.

30. Arch of Titus, signed and dated lower left 'CRM. 1891', pencil and watercolour
241 x 318mm
Provenance: Dr. Thomas Howarth by 1943; his sale Christie's London, Thursday 17th February 1994 (17), illus., p.23
Exhibited: University of Toronto School of Architecture, Toronto 1967 (119); Art Gallery of Ontario, Toronto, 1978 (25)
Literature: Billcliffe, 1978 (17)
Collection: Unknown
Drawn on 22nd April.

31. The Colosseum, inscribed top left 'THE COLOSSEUM/ROME.', signed and dated lower right 'CRM./APRIL 1891.', pencil
173 x 260 mm
Provenance: Dr. Thomas Howarth by 1943
Collection: Private collection
Mackintosh recorded a visit to the Colosseum on 22nd April.

32. Arch of Constantine, waterclour
Collection: Unknown
Mackintosh recorded beginning this drawing on 23rd and completing it on 27th April.

33. Tomb of Cardinal Philippe de Levis de Quelus and his brother Archbishop Eustache (1489), Santa Maria Maggiore, inscribed top right 'S. MARIA MAGGIORE' at top right of a sheet of studies of two monuments and a church façade, inscribed lower right 'NOTES FROM/ ROME.', signed and dated 'CRM./APRIL 1891.', pencil
270 x 184 mm
Provenance: Dr. Thomas Howarth by 1943; his sale Christie's London, Thursday 17th February 1994 (16), illus., p.22
Exhibited: Art Gallery of Ontario, Toronto, 1978 (23)
Collection: Unknown
Mackintosh visited Santa Maria Maggiore on 24th April. The drawing of the tomb is at top right.

34. Campanile, Santa Maria Maggiore, from Piazza di Santa Maria Maggiore, inscribed 'CAMPANILE/S. MARIA MAGGIORE/ROME.', signed and dated lower right 'CRM/APRIL 1891.', pencil
272 x 189 mm
Provenance: Dr. Thomas Howarth by 1943; his sale Christie's London, Thursday 17th February 1994 (18), illus., p.24
Exhibited: Art Gallery of Ontario, Toronto, 1978 (22)
Collection: Unknown
Drawn on 24th April.

35. Doorway, Santa Prassede, inscribed 'DOORWAY/S. PRASSEDE ROME.', signed and dated lower right 'CRM/APRIL 1891.', pencil
Provenance: Dr. Thomas Howarth by 1943
Literature: Finucci, 1981, vol. 1, illus., p.15
Collection: Unknown
Mackintosh visited Santa Prassede on 24th, 25th and 27th April.

36. Monument, Santa Prassede
Collection: Unknown
Mackintosh visited Santa Prassede on 24th, 25th and 27th April and recorded finishing this sketch on his third visit.

37. Façade, Trinità dei Monti, inscribed centre left 'TRINITA/DI [sic] MONTI' at bottom of a sheet of studies of two monuments and a church façade, inscribed lower right 'NOTES FROM/ ROME.', signed and dated 'CRM.APRIL 1891.', pencil
270 x 184 mm

The Vestibule of St. Peter's, Rome

Provenance: Dr. Thomas Howarth by 1943; his sale Christie's London, Thursday 17th February 1994 (16), illus., p.22
Exhibited: Art Gallery of Ontario, Toronto, 1978 (23)
Collection: Unknown
The drawing could have been made at any time during Mackintosh's stay in Rome as the church was very close to his pensione. He recorded visiting the church on 24th April.

38. Porta del Popolo, from Piazzale Flaminio, inscribed centre 'PORTA DEL POPOLO. ROME.' at top of a page containing three architectural studies from Rome and Florence, pencil
126 x 175 mm
Provenance: As for no. 12
Literature: Grogan, 2002, p.174 (54), illus., pl. 28
Collection: National Library of Ireland, Dublin (PD 2009 TX 54)
Mackintosh mentions visiting the Porta del Popolo on 24th April.

39. Façade, Santa Maria del Popolo, Piazza del Popolo, inscribed lower left 'S. M. DEL POPOLO', at lower left of a sheet of studies of façades and architectural details, inscribed lower right 'NOTES FROM/ ROME.', signed and dated upper right 'CRM/APRIL1891', pencil
269 x 183 mm
Provenance: Dr. Thomas Howarth by 1943; his sale Christie's London, Thursday 17th February 1994 (19), illus., p.24; Christie's London, Thursday 3rd May 2012 (24)
Exhibited: Art Gallery of Ontario, Toronto, 1978 (24)
Collection: Unknown
Mackintosh recorded visiting the church on 24th April.

40. An altarpiece two monuments and a baptismal font in Santa Maria del Popolo, Piazza del Popolo, inscribed lower right 'MOMUMENTS [sic]/S. MARIA DEL POPOLO/ROME.' and signed and dated lower 'CRM/1891.', pencil
268 x 185 mm
Provenance: Dr. Thomas Howarth by 1943; his sale Christie's London, Thursday 17th February 1994 (20), illus., p.25
Exhibited: Art Gallery of Ontario, Toronto, 1978 (21)
Collection: Unknown
Mackintosh recorded visiting the church on 24th April. The altarpiece (c.1505), dedicated to Saints Vincent, Catherine of Alexandria and Anthony of Padua, is by Giovanni Cristoforo Romano and is in the Costa Chapel. One monument, by Andrea Bregno, is in the delle Rovere Chapel and is dedicated to Cardinal Domenico delle Rovere (d.1501) and Cristoforo delle Rovere (d.1477). The other monument in the north transept is dedicated to Bernardino Lonati.
The baptismal font is in the Capella Montemirabile.

41. Façade and a doorway of Lateran Palace on Piazza San Giovanni in Laterano, inscribed centre left 'THE LATERN [sic]/ROME.', signed and dated lower right 'CRM/1891.', pencil
269 x 182 mm
Provenance: Dr. Thomas Howarth by 1943; his sale Christie's London, Thursday 17th February 1994 (21), illus., p.25
Exhibited: Art Gallery of Ontario, Toronto, 1978 (19)
Collection: Private collection
Mackintosh visited the Lateran Palace on 25th April.

42. Doorway, Palazzo di Venezia, inscribed lower right 'DOORWAY/PALAZZO DI VENEZIA/ROME', signed and dated 'CRM/APRIL 1891', pencil
269 x184 mm
Provenance: Dr. Thomas Howarth by 1943; his sale Christie's London, Thursday 17th February 1994 (15), illus., p.22
Exhibited: Art Gallery of Ontario Toronto 1978 (20)
Collection: Unknown
Mackintosh probably made this drawing on 28th April when he visited buildings in the area of the Capitol.

C. R. Mackintosh, Doorway, Palazzo di Venezia, Rome, 1891

43. Doorway and jamb, Palazzo di Venezia, inscribed 'PAL. VENEZIA. ROME' at top of a page of studies of doorways from Rome and Florence, pencil
126 x 175 mm
Provenance: As for no. 12
Literature: Grogan, 2002, p.174 (55), illus., pl. 29
Collection: National Library of Ireland, Dublin (PD 2009 TX 55)
Mackintosh probably made this drawing on 28th April when he visited buildings in the area of the Capitol.

44. Chancel frieze and capital, San Lorenzo fuori le Mura, inscribed lower left 'S. LORENZO/ ROME.', signed and dated lower right 'CRM/APRIL 1891', pencil
235 x 355 mm
Provenance: Dr. Thomas Howarth by 1943 who presented it to the University of Stirling, 1981
Collection: University of Stirling Art Collection (1981.2)
Mackintosh visited San Lorenzo on the afternoon of 28th April and spent all day there sketching on 29th April.

45. Chancel frieze, San Lorenzo fuori le Mura, inscribed at top 'S. LORENZO ROME.', pencil
126 x175 mm
Provenance: As for no. 12
Literature: Grogan, 2002, p.174 (59)
Collection: National Library of Ireland, Dublin (PD 2009 TX 59)
Mackintosh visited San Lorenzo on the afternoon of 28th April and spent all day there sketching on 29th April.

46. Campanile, San Francesco Romana, inscribed lower left 'ROME' at lower left of a page of studies from Rome and Florence, pencil
126 x175 mm
Provenance: As for no. 12
Literature: Grogan, 2002, p.174 (54), illus., pl. 28
Collection: National Library of Ireland, Dublin (PD 2009 TX 54)

47. Bay of an unidentified palazzo and a doorway, at top of a sheet of studies of façades and architectural details, inscribed lower right 'NOTES FROM/ ROME.', signed and dated upper right 'CRM/APRIL 1891', pencil
269 x 183 mm

Provenance: Dr. Thomas Howarth by 1943; his sale Christie's London, Thursday 17th February 1994 (19); Christie's London, Thursday 3rd May 2012 (19), illus., p.24
Exhibited: Art Gallery of Ontario, Toronto, 1978 (24)
Collection: Unknown

ORVIETO

48. Part of South façade, Orvieto Cathedral, signed and dated lower right 'CRM/ 1891', inscribed lower left 'ORVIETO', pencil and watercolour
318 x 241 mm
Provenance: Mackintosh Estate
Exhibited: Edinburgh Festival Society, Edinburgh, 1968 (13); Hunterian Art Gallery, Glasgow, 1990 (53); National Galleries of Scotland (Dean Gallery), Edinburgh, 2005 (8)
Literature: Billcliffe, 1978 (18), illus., p.54; Robertson, 1990, illus., pl. 27; Macaulay, 2010, illus., pl. 78
Collection: Hunterian Art Gallery, University of Glasgow (GLAHA 41430)

49. Studies of mosaic bands on west front, Orvieto Cathedral, extensively inscribed with colour and size indications, pencil
335 x 248 mm
Provenance: Dr. Thomas Howarth by 1943; his sale Christie's London, Thursday 17th February 1994 (23), illus., p.26
Collection: Unknown

50. Studies of mosaic bands on spiral column on south side of south-west doorway, Orvieto Cathedral, inscribed at top 'ORVIETO CATHEDRAL/MOSAIC BANDS IN SPIRAL COLUMN/ FRONT DOOR.', pencil and watercolour
245 x 334 mm
Provenance: Dr. Thomas Howarth by 1943; his sale Christie's London, Thursday 17th February 1994 (24), illus., p.27
Exhibited: Art Gallery of Ontario, Toronto, 1978 (33)
Literature: Billcliffe, 1978 (18a)
Collection: Unknown

51. Studies of mosaic bands, Orvieto Cathedral, inscribed at top 'MOSAIC BANDS' and at bottom 'ORVIETO CATHEDRAL. INTERIOR.', pencil and watercolour
334 x 248 mm
Provenance: Dr. Thomas Howarth by 1943; his sale Christie's London, Thursday 17th February 1994 (25), illus., p.27
Exhibited: Art Gallery of Ontario, Toronto, 1978 (34)
Literature: Billcliffe, 1978 (18b)
Collection: Unknown
The source of these studies, although similar to nos. 49 and 50, has not been identified.

52. North-east doorway, Orvieto Cathedral, inscribed top left 'ORVIETO CATHEDRAL./DOORWAY.', signed and dated bottom right 'CRM/MAY 1891', pencil
275 x 170 mm
Provenance: Dr. Thomas Howarth by 1943; his sale Christie's London, Thursday 17th February 1994 (22), illus., p.26
Exhibited: Art Gallery of Ontario, Toronto, 1978 (32)
Collection: Unknown
The doorway is also known as 'the Doorway of the Corporal'.

53. Jamb of south doorway, Orvieto Cathedral, signed and dated bottom right, 'CRM/MAY 1891', inscribed 'ORVIETO CATHEDRAL/DOOR JAMB', pencil
153 x 228 mm (approx.)
Provenance: Dr. Thomas Howarth by 1943
Exhibited: Art Gallery of Ontario, Toronto, 1978 (33)
Literature: Finucci, 1981, vol. 1, illus., p.23
Collection: Unknown

This doorway, also known as 'the Door of the Bishop's House', was made by Arnolfo di Cambio.

54. Holy water stoup, Orvieto Cathedral, inscribed upper right 'FOUNTAIN/ORVIETO CATHEDRAL.', signed and dated bottom right 'CRM/MAY 1891', pencil
320 x 250 mm
Provenance: Dr. Thomas Howarth by 1943 who presented it to the University of Stirling, 1981
Collection: University of Stirling Art Collection (1981.3)
The holy water stoup (1485) is situated at the western end of the nave and is the work of Antonio Federighi (c.1420-90).

55. Campanile, Santa Maria dei Servi, at bottom left of a page of architectural studies, inscribed lower right 'ORVIETO', pencil
175 x 126 mm
Provenance: As for no. 12
Literature: Grogan, 2002, p.174 (58), illus., p.52, fig. 7
Collection: National Library of Ireland, Dublin (PD 2009 TX 58)
Only the drawing of Santa Maria dei Servi on this sheet has been positively identified as Orvieto.

SIENA

56. Southern buttress, west front, Siena Cathedral, inscribed lower right, 'Siena', pencil and watercolour
305 x 115 mm (approx.)
Provenance: Dr. Thomas Howarth by 1943
Exhibited: University of Toronto School of Architecture, Toronto, 1967 (113); Art Gallery of Ontario, Toronto, 1978 (30)
Literature: Billcliffe, 1978 (20)
Collection: Unknown

57. Campanile, Siena Cathedral, inscribed upper left 'SIENA CATHEDRAL/CAMPANILE', signed and dated lower right 'C.R.M./MAY 1891', pencil
257 x 169 mm
Provenance: Dr. Thomas Howarth by 1943; his sale Christie's London, Thursday 17th February 1994 (27), illus., p.28
Exhibited: Art Gallery of Ontario, Toronto, 1978 (29)
Collection: Unknown

58. Southern holy water stoup, nave, Siena Cathedral, inscribed at top 'FONT/SIENA CATHEDRAL', signed and dated lower right 'CRM/MAY 1891.', pencil
215 x 303 mm
Provenance: Dr. Thomas Howarth by 1943
Literature: *Glasgow Architectural Association Sketchbook*, vol. 4, 1894, illus., pl. 21
Collection: Private collection

59. Northern holy water stoup, nave, Siena Cathedral, inscribed at top 'SIENA CATHEDRAL. FONT'
Literature: *Glasgow Architectural Association Sketchbook*, vol. 4, 1894, illus., pl. 21
Collection: Unknown

60. Pedestal at right hand of doorway of Chapel of San Giovanni, Siena Cathedral, inscribed at bottom 'SKETCH OF PEDESTAL/ SIENA CATHEDRAL', pencil
339 x 258 mm
Provenance: Dr. Thomas Howarth by 1943; his sale Christie's London, Thursday 17th February 1994 (26), illus., p.28
Exhibited: Art Gallery of Ontario, Toronto, 1978 (27)
Collection: Unknown

61. Capital on pulpit and panels from stalls, Siena Cathedral, inscribed upper right 'CAP.PULPIT/SIENA CATHEDRAL' and lower centre 'PANELS FROM STALLS/SIENA.', signed and dated lower right 'C.R.M./MAY 1891', pencil
355 x 254 mm

Provenance: Dr. Thomas Howarth by 1943
Literature: Finucci, 1981, vol. 1, illus., p.32
Collection: Unknown
The capital is from the north side of the pulpit.

62. Entrance to Piccolomini Library, Siena Cathedral, inscribed lower centre 'ENTRANCE TO LIBRARY. SIENA CATHEDRAL', signed and dated lower right 'CRM MAY 1891', pencil and watercolour
384 x 272 mm
Provenance: Professor Randolph Schwabe by 1933; by family descent
Purchased by British Museum from Sir Harry and Lady Barnes, 1981
Exhibited: MacLellan Galleries, Glasgow, 1933 (77)
Literature: Billcliffe, 1978 (21)
Collection: British Museum (1981, 1212.21)

63. Baptistery, Siena Cathedral, signed lower left 'C. R. McINTOSH', pencil and watercolour
391 x 279 mm
Provenance: acquired by William Meldrum after Memorial Exhibition, 1933; by family descent
Exhibited: Hunterian Art Gallery, Glasgow, 1990. (57)
Literature: Billcliffe, 1978 (19), illus., p.51; Robertson, 1990, illus., pl. 21.
Collection: Unknown

64. Palazzo Pubblico, watercolour
folded to 369 x 165 mm
Provenance: Miss Nancy Mackintosh, 1933; by family descent
Exhibited: MacLellan Galleries, Glasgow, 1933 (127); Edinburgh Festival Society, Edinburgh 1968 (12)
Literature: Edinburgh, 1968, illus., pl. 3; Billcliffe, 1978 (22), illus., p.52
Collection: Private collection
The viewpoint is from the bottom of Chiasso del Bargello in the Piazza del Campo.

65. Studies of a window and a corbel, Palazzo Pubblico, at bottom of a sheet of studies from Siena inscribed lower left 'WINDOW PAL. PUBLICO [sic] SIENA', signed and dated lower right 'CR.M/MAY 1891', pencil
330 x 248 mm
Provenance: Dr. Thomas Howarth by 1943; his sale Christie's London, Thursday 17th February 1994 (28), illus., p.29
Exhibited: Art Gallery of Ontario, Toronto, 1978 (28)
Collection: Unknown

66. Palazzo Pollini, at top of a sheet of studies from Siena inscribed upper right 'PALAZZO POLLINI/SIENA.', signed and dated lower right 'CR.M/MAY 1891', pencil
330 x 248 mm
Provenance: Dr. Thomas Howarth by 1943; his sale Christie's London, Thursday 17th February 1994 (28), illus., p.29
Exhibited: Art Gallery of Ontario, Toronto, 1978 (28)
Collection: Unknown

67. Studies of two bronze torch bearers and ironwork, inscribed lower left 'SOME SIENA/IRON WORK', signed and dated lower left 'CRM. MAY 1891', pencil on buff paper
354 x 269 mm
Provenance: Dr. Thomas Howarth by 1943; his sale Christie's London, Thursday 17th February 1994 (29), illus., p.29
Exhibited: Art Gallery of Ontario, Toronto, 1978 (31), illus., p.18
Collection: Unknown
The bronze torch bearers were in the Palazzo Pubblico which Mackintosh visited on 11th May. Most of the ironwork is from the Piazza and Palazzo Tolomei.

C. R. Mackintosh, Holy Water stoup, Siena Cathedral
Glasgow Architectural Association Sketchbook, vol. 4, pl. 21

FLORENCE

68. Dome and Campanile, Santo Spirito, with study of a chimney, at centre and bottom of a page of studies from Florence and Empoli inscribed top right 'FLORENCE', lower left, 'FLORENTINE CHIMNEY' and lower right 'DOME FLORENCE', pencil
126 x 175 mm
Provenance: As for no. 12
Literature: Grogan, 2002, p.174 (60), illus., pl. 30
Collection: National Library of Ireland, Dublin (PD 2009 TX 60)
This is probably the view from Mackintosh's bedroom in the Pensione Laurent.

69. Tomb of Carlo Marsuppini, Santa Croce, inscribed upper left 'TOMB OF CARLO MARSUPPINI/SANTA CROCE, FLORENCE' signed and dated lower right 'Chas R McIntosh./May 1891.', pencil and watercolour
385 x 280 mm
Provenance: Dr. Thomas Howarth by 1943; his sale Christie's London, Thursday 17th February 1994 (30), illus., p.30
Exhibited: University of Toronto School of Architecture, Toronto, 1967 (117); Art Gallery of Ontario, Toronto, 1978 (38)
Literature: Billcliffe, 1978 (23)
Collection: Unknown
Mackintosh visited Santa Croce on 20th May and returned to make sketches on 21st and 22nd May.

70. Sculpture from the tomb of Michelangelo, Santa Croce, inscribed 'Sculpture From Tomb of Michael Angelo, S. Croce, Florence', signed lower right 'CRM', dated 'May 1891', pencil
340 x 253 mm
Provenance: Dr. Thomas Howarth by 1943
Collection: Untraced
Mackintosh visited Santa Croce on 20th May and returned to make sketches on 21st and 22nd May.

71. Studies of ceiling decoration, San Miniato al Monte, inscribed centre left 'DECORATION FROM ROOF OF/S. MINIATO FLORENCE', signed and dated lower right 'CRM./MAY 1891.', pencil and watercolour
280 x 389 mm
Provenance: Dr. Thomas Howarth by 1943; his sale Christie's London, Thursday 17th February 1994 (31), illus., p.31
Exhibited: Art Gallery of Ontario, Toronto, 1978 (37)
Literature: Billcliffe, 1978 (23a)
Collection: Unknown
Mackintosh visited San Miniato on 22nd May.

72. Study of pavement in nave, San Miniato al Monte and unidentified font, inscribed lower right 'FLOOR SAN. Miniato/Florence.', pencil
126 x 175 mm
Provenance: As for no. 12
Literature: Grogan, 2002, p.174 (47), illus., pl. 24
Collection: National Library of Ireland, Dublin (PD 2009 TX 47)
Mackintosh visited San Miniato on 22nd May.

73. Doorway of Badia Fiorentina, Via del Proconsolo, at top right of a page of studies from Florence inscribed upper right 'DELLA ROBBIAN/PANEL/DOLPHIN/FREEZE [sic]', and centre right 'S. BADIA FLORENCE', pencil
126 x 175 mm
Provenance: As for no. 12
Literature: Glasgow Museums, 1996 (3) illus., pl. 4; Grogan, 2002, p.174 (61), illus., pl. 31
Collection: National Library of Ireland, Dublin (PD 2009 TX 61)
Mackintosh visited la Badia Fiorentina on 23rd May. The doorway (1495) is by Benedetto da Rovezzano and the enamelled terracotta tympanum, similar to the work of the della Robbia family, is by Benedetto Buglioni.

74. Angel from funeral monument of Count Ugo of Tuscany, Badia Fiorentina, Via del Proconsolo, inscribed lower left 'ANGEL FROM TOMB/S. BADIA, FLORENCE.', signed and dated lower right 'C.R.M./MAY 1891', pencil
341 x 254 mm
Provenance: Dr. Thomas Howarth by 1943; his sale Christie's London, Thursday 17th February 1994 (33), illus., p.32
Exhibited: Art Gallery of Ontario, Toronto, 1978 (89)
Collection: Unknown
Mackintosh visited la Badia Fiorentina on 23rd May

75. Museo Nazionale del Bargello, Via del Proconsolo, on left of a page of studies from Florence and Ravenna, inscribed lower left 'MUSEO NATIONAL [sic]/FLORENCE.', pencil
126 x 175 mm
Provenance: As for no. 12
Literature: Grogan, 2002, p.175 (68), illus., pl. 36
Collection: National Library of Ireland, Dublin (PD 2009 TX 68)
Mackintosh visited the Bargello on 23rd and 25th May.

76. Study of a frieze by Giovanni della Robbia, Museo Nazionale del Bargello, Via del Proconsolo, inscribed at top 'A DELLA ROBBIAN FRIEZE./MUSEO NATIONALE [sic] FLORENCE', signed and dated, lower right 'C.R.M,/MAY 1891.', pencil and watercolour
384 x 280 mm
Provenance: Dr. Thomas Howarth by 1943; his sale Christie's London, Thursday 17th February 1994 (32), illus., p.31
Exhibited: Charles Rennie Mackintosh 1868-1928: a Memorial Exhibition. Art Gallery of Ontario, Toronto, 1978 (36)
Literature: Billcliffe, 1978 (24a)
Collection: Unknown
Mackintosh visited the Bargello on 23rd and 25th May.

77. Study of a fragment of a 16th-century silk brocade, Museo Nazionale del Bargello, Via del Proconsolo, inscribed lower right 'TAPESTRY/FLORENCE/NATIONAL MUSEUM/SILVER GROUND', pencil and watercolour
126 x 175 mm
Provenance: As for no. 12
Literature: Grogan, 2002, p.174 (52), illus., pl. 27
Collection: National Library of Ireland, Dublin (PD 2009 TX 52)
Mackintosh visited the Bargello on 23rd and 25th May.

78. Palazzo Vecchio, Piazza della Signoria, at bottom right of a page of studies from Florence inscribed 'PAL./VECCHIO/FLORENCE.', pencil
126 x 175 mm
Provenance: As for no. 12
Literature: Glasgow Museums, 1996, illus., pl. 4; Grogan, p.174 (61), illus., pl. 31
Collection: National Library of Ireland, Dublin (PD 2009 TX 61)

79. Tower of Palazzo Vecchio, Piazza della Signoria, at bottom left of a page of studies from Florence, pencil
126 x 175 mm
Provenance: As for no. 12
Literature: Grogan, 2002, p.174 (65), illus., pl. 34
Collection: National Library of Ireland, Dublin (PD 2009 TX 65)

80. Palazzo Guadagni, Piazza Santo Spirito, on left of a page of studies from Florence inscribed lower left 'A PALLACE [sic]/FLORENCE', pencil
126 x 175 mm
Provenance: As for no. 12
Literature: Glasgow, 1996, illus., pl. 4; Grogan, 2002, p.174 (61), illus., pl. 31
Collection: National Library of Ireland, Dublin (PD 2009 TX 61)

81. Putti, possibly from ceiling frescoes by Giuseppe Nasini

The Colosseum, Rome

and Giuseppe Tonelli, Palazzo degli Uffizi, inscribed centre left 'UFFITZI [sic]/PALACE/FLORENCE.', pencil
126 x 175 mm
Provenance: As for no. 12
Literature: Grogan, 2002, p.174 (62)
Collection: National Library of Ireland, Dublin (PD 2009 TX 62)
Mackintosh visited the Uffizi on 24th May.

82. Doorway of Palazzo della Zecca, Piazzale degli Uffizi, at top left of a page of studies from Florence, inscribed upper left 'FLORENCE', pencil
126 x 175 mm
Provenance: As for no. 12
Literature: Grogan, 2002, p.174 (64), illus., pl. 33
Collection: National Library of Ireland, Dublin (PD 2009 TX 64)

83. Unidentified rusticated doorway and jamb profile, at top right of a page of studies from Florence, inscribed at top right 'DOOR.', pencil
126 x 175 mm
Provenance: As for no. 12
Literature: Grogan, 2002, p.174 (64), illus., pl. 33
Collection: National Library of Ireland, Dublin (PD 2009 TX 64)
Grogan identifies this as the doorway of Palazzo Bianca Capello on Via Maggio, the next street to Mackintosh's pensione. However, there are subtle differences and the jamb has a different profile.

84. Palazzo Bartolini-Salimbeni, and study of one of its first floor windows, Via delle Terme, at bottom of a page of studies from Florence, inscribed lower left 'PALLACE [sic]', and lower right 'WINDOW', pencil
126 x 175 mm
Provenance: As for no. 12
Literature: Grogan, 2002, p.174 (64), illus., pl. 33
Collection: National Library of Ireland, Dublin (PD 2009 TX 64)

85. Palazzo Antinori, Via de' Tornabuoni, at top of a page of studies from Florence, pencil
126 x 175 mm
Provenance: As for no. 12
Literature: Grogan, 2002, p.174 (65), illus., pl. 34
Collection: National Library of Ireland, Dublin (PD 2009 TX 65)

86. Palazzo Gianfigliazzi, Via de' Tornabuoni, inscribed lower left 'FLORENCE', pencil
126 x 175 mm
Provenance: As for no. 12
Literature: Grogan, 2002, p.174 (63), illus., pl. 32
Collection: National Library of Ireland, Dublin (PD 2009 TX 63)

87. Studies from Palazzo Strozzi, Via de' Tornabuoni, inscribed 'STRINGS', 'CORNICE', 'WINDOW JAMB', pencil
126 x 175 mm
Provenance: As for no. 12
Literature: Grogan, 2002, p.174 (66), illus., pl. 35
Collection: National Library of Ireland, Dublin (PD 2009 TX 66)

88. Studies from Palazzo Strozzi, Via de' Tornabuoni, inscribed lower left 'STROZZI/ PALLACE [sic]/FLORENCE', pencil
126 x 175 mm
Provenance: As for no. 12
Literature: Grogan, 2002, p.175 (67)
Collection: National Library of Ireland, Dublin (PD 2009 TX 67)

89. Cornice brackets, Loggia del Bigallo, Piazza San Giovanni, inscribed at bottom 'WOODEN Eaves Brackets/Loggia del Bigallo/ Florence', pencil
126 x 175 mm
Provenance: As for no. 12
Literature: Grogan, 2002, p.174 (53)
Collection: National Library of Ireland, Dublin (PD 2009 TX 53)

90. Unidentified palazzo and tower, signed with initials and dated 'C.R.M./MAY 1891.', inscribed upper right 'A FLORENTINE/ PALLACE [sic]' and lower left 'A/ FLORENTINE/ TOWER.', pencil
273 x 178 mm
Provenance: Dr. Thomas Howarth by 1943, who presented it to the Charles Rennie Mackintosh Society, 1973
Exhibited: Edinburgh Festival Society, Edinburgh, 1968 (14); *Charles Rennie Mackintosh*, Glasgow Museums, Glasgow, 1996 (4)
Literature: Robertson, 1990, illus., pl. 30
Collection: Charles Rennie Mackintosh Society
The two buildings may have been amongst those destroyed or damaged by the retreating German army in August 1944. The tower, which incorporates a della Robbia panel above its entrance, strongly resembles the Torre dei Marsili (dating from 1260), Borgo San Jacopo 17-19. This was only partly destroyed and subsequently restored 1981-5. The palazzo fairly closely accords with a description of the no-longer extant 13th-century Torre dei Girolami, Via Por Santa Maria.

91. Unidentified doorway, at lower right of a page of studies from Rome and Florence, inscribed on right 'FLORENCE', pencil
126 x 175 mm
Provenance: As for no. 12
Literature: Grogan, 2002, p.174 (54) and pl. 28
Collection: National Library of Ireland, Dublin (PD 2009 TX 54)
This is similar to windows and doorways in Michelangelo's Laurentian Library.

92. Unidentified doorway, at lower left of a page of studies from Rome and Florence, inscribed on right 'MOSAIC./DOOR/ FLORENCE', pencil
126 x 175 mm
Provenance: As for no. 12
Literature: Grogan, 2002, p.174 (55), illus., pl. 29
Collection: National Library of Ireland, Dublin (PD 2009 TX 55)

93. Ponte Vecchio, watercolour
Literature: Billcliffe, 1978 (24)
Collection: Unknown
Mackintosh recorded making this drawing on 25th and 26th May.

94. Unidentified altar cloth, inscribed centre right 'ALTER [sic] CLOTH. FLORENCE', pencil
126 x 175 mm
Provenance: As for no. 12
Literature: Grogan, 2002, p.174 (42)
Collection: National Library of Ireland, Dublin, (PD 2009 TX 42)

EMPOLI

95. Torre di Sant'Agostino, at top left of a page of studies from Florence and Empoli, inscribed top left 'EMPOLI.', pencil
126 x 175 mm
Provenance: As for no. 12
Literature: Grogan, 2002, p.174 (60), illus., pl. 30
Collection: National Library of Ireland, Dublin (PD 2009 TX 60)

PISA

96. Study of a bay and a window, Palazzo Agostini, Lungarno Pacinotti, at top of a page of studies from Pisa and Pistoia, inscribed upper left 'PISA./PAL. AGOSTINA [sic]', pencil
126 x 175 mm
Provenance: As for no. 12
Literature: Grogan, 2002, p.175 (69), illus., pl. 37
Collection: National Library of Ireland, Dublin (PD 2009 TX 69)

97. Porta di San Ranieri, Pisa Cathedral, at top of a page of studies from Pisa and Ravenna, inscribed upper right 'DOOR/PISA CATHEDRAL', pencil
126 x 175 mm
Provenance: As for no. 12

C. R. Mackintosh, San Vitale,
Ravenna, 1891

Literature: Grogan, 2002, p.175 (73), illus., pl. 39
Collection: National Library of Ireland, Dublin (PD 2009 TX 73)
98. Tomb of Archbishop Pietro Ricci, by Andrea Guardi (c.1455), Campo Santo (now in Museo dell'Opera del Duomo), on a page of studies from Pisa, inscribed centre right 'TOMB CAMPO SANTO. PISA.', pencil
126 x 175 mm
Provenance: As for no. 12
Literature: Grogan, 2002, p.175 (70), illus., p.55, fig. 8
Collection: National Library of Ireland, Dublin (PD 2009 TX 70)
99. Tomb, Campo Santo (possibly destroyed in July 1944), at bottom of a page of studies inscribed centre right 'TOMB. PISA./CAMPO SANTO.' pencil
126 x 175 mm
Provenance: As for no. 12
Literature: Grogan, 2002, p.175 (71)
Collection: National Library of Ireland, Dublin (PD 2009 TX 71)
The ornamental detail at the top of this page may or may not relate to the tomb.
100. Capital, Campo Santo, at top of a page of studies from Pisa, inscribed upper right, 'CAP.', pencil
126 x 175 mm
Provenance: As for no. 12
Literature: Grogan, 2002, p.175 (70), illus., p.55, fig. 8
Collection: National Library of Ireland, Dublin (PD 2009 TX 70)
101. Capital, Campo Santo, at bottom of a page of studies from Pisa, inscribed lower left 'CAP.', pencil
126 x 175 mm
Provenance: As for no. 12
Literature: Grogan, 2002, p.175 (72), illus., pl. 38
Collection: National Library of Ireland, Dublin (PD 2009 TX 72)
102. Mosaic fragment, Campo Santo, (now in Museo dell'Opera del Duomo), at top of a page of studies from Pisa inscribed 'MOSAIC PATERN. [sic] CAMPO SANTO PISA.', pencil
126 x 175 mm
Provenance: As for no. 12
Literature: Grogan, 2002, p.175 (72), illus., pl. 38
Collection: National Library of Ireland, Dublin (PD 2009 TX 72)
When in Glasgow, Mackintosh had previously copied William James Anderson's drawing of this same fragment onto the title page of an earlier sketchbook. See Anderson, *Architectural Studies in Italy* (1890), pl. IV and National Library of Ireland, Dublin (PD 2011 TX 1).

PISTOIA

103. Campanile, San Paolo, inscribed 'PISTOJA [sic]', at bottom left of a page of studies from Pisa and Pistoia, pencil
126 x 175 mm
Provenance: As for no. 12
Literature: Grogan, 2002, p.175 (69), illus., pl. 37
Collection: National Library of Ireland, Dublin (PD 2009 TX 69)
104. Exterior bay, San Giovanni Fuorcivitas, at left of a page of studies from Pistoia and Ravenna, inscribed top left 'PISTOJA./SAN LORENZO [sic]', pencil
126 x 175 mm
Provenance: As for no. 12
Literature: Grogan, 2002, p.175 (75), illus., pl. 41
Collection: National Library of Ireland, Dublin (PD 2009 TX 75)
105. Palazzo del Comune, (previously Palazzo degli Anziani), Piazza del Duomo, on a page of studies inscribed on left 'PAL./COMUNE./PISTOJA [sic]', pencil
126 x 175 mm
Provenance: As for no. 12
Literature: Grogan, 2002, p.175 (74), illus., pl. 40
Collection: National Library of Ireland, Dublin, (PD 2009 TX 74)
106. Campanile, Pistoia Cathedral, inscribed centre right 'CAMPANILE/PISTOJA [sic]/CATHEDRAL.', signed and dated lower right 'CRM/MAY 1891', pencil
263 x 179 mm
Provenance: Dr. Thomas Howarth by 1943; his sale Christie's London, Thursday 17th February 1994 (36), illus., p.33
Exhibited: Art Gallery of Ontario, Toronto, 1978 (44)
Collection: Unknown

BOLOGNA

107. Campanile, Cattedrale di San Pietro, on left of a page of studies from Bologna and Ravenna, inscribed centre left 'DUOMO/BOLOGNA. [sic]', pencil
126 x 175 mm
Provenance: As for no. 12
Literature: Grogan, 2002, p.175 (76), illus., pl. 42
Collection: National Library of Ireland, Dublin (PD 2009 TX 76)
108. Torre degli Asinelli, inscribed on right 'CAMPANILE [sic]/BOLOGNA.', signed and dated lower right 'C.R.M./MAY 1891', pencil
250 x 169 mm
Provenance: Dr. Thomas Howarth by 1943; his sale Christie's London, Thursday 17th February 1994 (34), illus., p.31

Exhibited: Art Gallery of Ontario, Toronto 1978 (43)
Collection: Unknown
This is one of Bologna's two famous leaning towers. It dates from 1109-19, is 97.5 m high and 1.23 m out of the perpendicular. It is thought to have been built by the Asinelli family. The drawing shows the view of the tower from the Palazzo Bolognini, Via Santo Stefano.

109. Two studies of Corinthian capitals, inscribed upper right 'CAPS FROM/BOLOGNA', pencil
335 x 221 mm
Provenance: Dr. Thomas Howarth by 1943; his sale Christie's London, Thursday 17th February 1994 (35), illus., p.32
Exhibited: Art Gallery of Ontario, Toronto, 1978 (42)
Collection: Unknown
The capital at the top is from Palazzo Bolognini, Via Santo Stefano 9-11. That at the bottom is unidentified.

RAVENNA

110. Detail of mosaic frieze, south wall, Sant'Apollinare Nuovo, pencil and watercolour
432 x 342 mm
Provenance: Mackintosh Estate
Exhibited: Edinburgh Festival Society, Edinburgh, 1968 (15), illus., pl. 3; Hunterian Art Gallery, Glasgow, 1990 (56); National Galleries of Scotland, Edinburgh, 2005 (10)
Literature: Billcliffe, 1978 (25); Robertson, 1990, illus., pl. 26; Macaulay, 2010, illus., pl. 79
Collection: Hunterian Art Gallery, University of Glasgow (GLAHA 41433)

111. Sant'Apollinare in Classe, inscribed lower right 'S.APOLLINAIRE [sic] IN CLASSE./RAVENNA.', pencil
126 x 175 mm
Provenance: As for no. 12
Literature: Grogan, 2002, p.175 (81), illus., pl. 46
Collection: National Library of Ireland, Dublin, (PD 2009 TX 81)

112. Apse mosaic, Sant'Apollinare in Classe, inscribed lower left 'Mosaic Decoration/St Apollinaris [sic] in Classe/Ravenna', signed lower right 'Chas R Mackintosh', pencil and watercolour
472 x 330 mm
Provenance: Mackintosh Estate
Literature: Billcliffe, 1978 (26)
Collection: Hunterian Art Gallery, University of Glasgow (GLAHA 41432).

113. Doorway from Classe Monastery and details, Museo Nazionale, at bottom of a page of studies from Pisa and Ravenna, inscribed lower right 'DOORWAY RAVENNA.', pencil
126 x 175 mm
Provenance: As for no. 12
Literature: Grogan, 2002, p.175 (73), illus., pl. 39
Collection: National Library of Ireland, Dublin (PD 2009 TX 73)

114. Doorway from Classe Monastery, Museo Nazionale, at bottom right of a page of studies from Pistoia and Ravenna, inscribed 'DOOR/RAVENNA', pencil
126 x 175 mm
Provenance: As for no. 12
Literature: Grogan, 2002, p.175 (75), illus., pl. 41
Collection: National Library of Ireland, Dublin (PD 2009 TX 75)

115. Campanile, San Giovanni Evangelista, on right of a page of studies from Bologna and Ravenna, inscribed lower right 'RAVENNA', pencil
126 x 175 mm
Provenance: As for no. 12
Literature: Grogan, 2002, p.175 (76), illus., pl. 42
Collection: National Library of Ireland, Dublin (PD 2009 TX 76)

116. Neonian Baptistery, on right of a page of studies from Florence and Ravenna, inscribed upper right 'BAPTISTRY. RAV.', pencil
126 x 175 mm
Provenance: As for no. 12
Literature: Grogan, 2002, p.175 (68), illus., pl. 36
Collection: National Library of Ireland, Dublin (PD 2009 TX 68)

117. Detail of mosaic, Neonian Baptistery, inscribed lower right 'Mosaic Decoration, Baptistry, Ravenna', pencil and watercolour
280 x 370 mm
Provenance: Dr Thomas Howarth by 1943
Collection: Private collection

118. Studies of marble transennae, Museo Arcivescovile, inscribed lower left 'NOTES FROM/DUOMO/RAVENNA./Marble Frets.', pencil
126 x 175 mm
Provenance: As for no. 12
Literature: Grogan, 2002, p.175 (78), illus., pl. 44
Collection: National Library of Ireland, Dublin (PD 2009 TX 78)

119. San Vitale, inscribed upper right 'S. VITALE RAVENNA.', pencil and watercolour
126 x 175 mm
Provenance: As for no. 12
Literature: Grogan, 2002, p.175 (80), illus., pl. 45
Collection: National Library of Ireland, Dublin (PD 2009 TX 80)

120. Wrought iron grating, Via Mario Gordini 80, inscribed upper left 'Window guard./Wrot [sic] Iron./RAVENNA', pencil
126 x 175 mm
Provenance: As for no. 12
Literature: Grogan, 2002, p.175 (79), illus., p.57, fig. 10
Collection: National Library of Ireland, Dublin (PD 2009 TX 79)

FERRARA

121. Castello Estense, inscribed lower right 'CASTELLO DUCHI [sic]/FERRARA.', pencil
126 x 175 mm
Provenance: As for no. 12
Literature: Grogan, 2002, p.175 (83), illus., pl. 48
Collection: National Library of Ireland, Dublin (PD 2009 TX 83)

122. Entrance doorway and details, Palazzo Schifanoia, inscribed lower right 'PAL. SCHIFANTO [sic]/FERRARA.', pencil
126 x 175 mm
Provenance: As for no. 12
Literature: Grogan, 2002, p.175 (77), illus., pl. 43
Collection: National Library of Ireland, Dublin (PD 2009 TX 77)

123. Window, garden front, Palazzo Schifanoia, at top left of a page of studies from Ferrara, inscribed 'WINDOW', pencil
126 x 175 mm
Provenance: As for no. 12
Literature: Grogan, 2002, p.175 (82), illus., pl. 47
Collection: National Library of Ireland, Dublin (PD 2009 TX 82)

124. Doorway, Largo Castello 20, and detail, at top of a page of studies from Ferrara and Venice, inscribed upper right 'DOORWAY/FERRARA/SAME ROUND/DOOR.', pencil
126 x 175 mm
Provenance: As for no. 12
Literature: Grogan, 2002, p.175 (84), illus., pl. 49
Collection: National Library of Ireland, Dublin (PD 2009 TX 84)

125. Doorway, Via Volta Paletto 9, and detail, at top right of a page of studies from Ferrara inscribed 'DOOR.', pencil
126 x 175 mm
Provenance: As for no. 12
Literature: Grogan, 2002, p.175 (82), illus., pl. 47
Collection: National Library of Ireland, Dublin (PD 2009 TX 82)

126. Unidentified well head, at centre right of a page of studies

The Forum, Rome

from Ferrara, inscribed lower right 'WELL HEAD.', pencil
126 x 175 mm
Provenance: As for no. 12
Literature: Grogan, 2002, p.175 (82), illus., pl. 47
Collection: National Library of Ireland, Dublin (PD 2009 TX 82)
127. Unidentified campanile, at lower left of a page of studies from Ferrara, inscribed lower left 'FERRARA', pencil
126 x 175 mm
Provenance: As for no. 12
Literature: Grogan, 2002, p.175 (82), illus., pl. 47
Collection: National Library of Ireland, Dublin (PD 2009 TX 82)
128. Campanile, San Benedetto, at lower left of a page of studies from Ferrara and Venice, pencil
126 x 175 mm
Provenance: As for no. 12
Literature: Grogan, 2002, p.175(84), illus., pl. 49.
Collection: National Library of Ireland, Dublin (PD 2009 TX 84).
129. Façade and details of an unidentified courtyard, inscribed upper left 'COURTYARD FERRARA./ PAL.', pencil
335 x 246 mm
Provenance: Dr. Thomas Howarth by 1943; his sale Christie's London, Thursday 17th February 1994 (37), illus., p.33
Exhibited: Art Gallery of Ontario, Toronto, 1978 (45)
Collection: Unknown

VENICE
130. Campanile, San Marco, inscribed centre right 'CAMPANILE/S.MARKS/VENICE', signed and dated lower rght 'C.RM/JUNE 1891', pencil
250 x 169 mm
Provenance: Dr. Thomas Howarth by 1943; his sale Christie's London, Thursday 17th February 1994 (38), illus. p.33
Exhibited: Art Gallery of Ontario, Toronto, 1978 (57)
Collection: Unknown
131. Venice from the Lido, watercolour,
117 x 343 mm
Provenance: Miss Nancy Mackintosh, on whose death passed to her sister Mrs Ellen Gibb, from whose estate purchased in 1966
Exhibited: MacLellan Galleries, Glasgow, 1933 (115); Edinburgh Festival Society, Edinburgh, 1968 (17)
Literature: Edinburgh, 1968 (17), illus., pl. 3; Billcliffe, 1978 (28), illus., pp.56-57; Kaplan, 1996, illus., pl. 204; Robertson, 2005, illus., p.17, fig. 15
Collection: Hunterian Art Gallery, University of Glasgow (GLAHA 41955)
The watercolour would have been produced on the afternoon of 3rd June when Mackintosh visited the Lido.
132. Altarpiece, Capella di San Tarasio, San Zaccaria, inscribed upper right 'Alter piece [sic]/S. Zaccaria/Venice', signed and dated lower right 'CRM June 1891', pencil
273 x 178 mm
Provenance: Dr. Thomas Howarth by 1943, who presented it to the Charles Rennie Mackintosh Society in 1992
Exhibited: Edinburgh Festival Society, Edinburgh, 1968 (16)
Collection: Charles Rennie Mackintosh Society
The altarpiece depicting the Virgin and Child and Saints, (1443) is by Stefano di Sant'Agnese, Antonio Vivarini and Giovanni d'Alemagna.
133. Chimney piece, Sala Grimani, Doge's Palace, inscribed centre right 'CHIMNEY PIECE/DOGES PALLACE [sic]/VENICE.', signed and dated lower right 'CRM/JUNE 1891', pencil
345 x 262 mm
Provenance: Dr. Thomas Howarth by 1943; his sale Christie's London, Thursday 17th February 1994 (39), illus., p.34
Exhibited: Art Gallery of Ontario, Toronto, 1978 (58)
Literature: Robertson, 1990, illus., pl. 34; Grogan, 2006, illus., p.11
Collection: Catherine S. Wright
Mackintosh noted the Chimney pieces in the Doge's Palace on his visit on 4th June. The Chimney piece (c.1486-1501) is by Tullio and Antonio Lombardo. It had previously been sketched by William James Anderson. See Anderson, *Architectural Studies in Italy* (1890).
134. South transept window, Santi Giovanni e Paolo, inscribed upper left 'GLASS WINDOW/S. GIOV. E PAOLO/VENICE', signed and dated lower right 'C.R.M./JUNE 1891', pencil and watercolour
387 x 284 mm
Provenance: Dr. Thomas Howarth by 1943, who presented it to the Hunterian Art Gallery, 2000
Collection: Hunterian Art Gallery, University of Glasgow (GLAHA 53094).
Mackintosh visited the church on 4th June but could have made the drawing on 6th or 7th June when he recorded making sketches.
135. Well head, Campo San Zanipolo, inscribed upper left 'WELL HEAD/VENICE.', signed and dated 'C.RM/JUNE 6th 1891', pencil
251 x 335 mm
Provenance: Dr. Thomas Howarth by 1943; his sale Christie's London, Thursday 17th February 1994 (40), illus., p.34
Exhibited: Art Gallery of Ontario, Toronto, 1978 (52)
Literature: Crawford, 1995, illus., pl. 8; Grogan, 2006, illus., p.12
Collection: Unknown
136. Decorated pilaster, Santa Maria dei Miracoli, inscribed upper right 'CARVED PILASTERS./S MIRACOLI/VENICE.', signed and dated lower right 'CRM /JUNE 1891', pencil
373 x 275 mm
Provenance: Dr. Thomas Howarth by 1943; his sale Christie's London, Thursday 17th February 1994 (41), illus., p.35
Exhibited: Art Gallery of Ontario, Toronto, 1978 (53), illus., p.20
Collection: Unknown
Mackintosh visited Santa Maria dei Miracoli on 4th June and recorded sketching there on 8th and 9th June. The drawings are from the northern pilaster in the chancel.
137. Pulpit, Santa Maria dei Miracoli, inscribed lower left 'PULPIT S. MARIA DEL [sic] MIRACOLI/VENICE.', signed and dated lower right 'C.R.M./JUNE 1891.', pencil
343 x 252 mm
Provenance: Dr. Thomas Howarth by 1943; his sale Christie's London, Thursday 17th February 1994 (42), illus., p.35
Exhibited: Art Gallery of Ontario, Toronto, 1978 (36)
Collection: Unknown
The drawing is a study of the northernmost of two pulpits.
138. Chancel and subsidiary studies, Santa Maria dei Miracoli, inscribed 'S. Miracoli Venice/Chancel', signed and dated lower right 'CRM/June 1891', pencil
Provenance: Dr. Thomas Howarth by 1943; his sale Christie's London, Thursday 17th February 1994 (43), illus., p.35
Exhibited: Art Gallery of Ontario, Toronto, 1978 (55)
Collection: Unknown
139. Altar screen and detail, Santa Maria dei Miracoli, inscribed lower left 'S. MARIA DEL [sic] MIRACOLI/ALTER [sic] SCREEN', signed and dated lower right 'CRM/June 1891', pencil
279 x 375 mm
Provenance: Dr. Thomas Howarth by 1943; his sale Christie's London, Thursday 17th February 1994 (44), illus., p.36
Exhibited: Art Gallery of Ontario, Toronto, 1978 (54)
Literature: Robertson, 1990, illus., pl. 33
Collection: Unknown
140. Frieze and capitals, Santa Maria dei Miracoli, inscribed lower right 'S. MIRACOLI./VENICE', signed and dated bottom right 'C.R.M./June 1891' pencil
255 x 355 mm

Provenance: Dr. Thomas Howarth by 1943, who presented it to the University of Stirling, 1981
Collection: University of Stirling Art Collection (1981.3)

141. Ca' d'Oro, watercolour
Provenance: Miss Nancy Mackintosh 1933
Exhibited: Glasgow Institute of Fine Arts, Glasgow, 1892 (775); MacLellan Galleries, Glasgow, 1933 (164)
Literature: Billcliffe, 1978 (27), illus., p.53
Collection: Private collection

142. Venetian Palace, watercolour?
Exhibited: Glasgow Institute of Fine Arts, Glasgow, 1892 (796)
Literature: Billcliffe, 1978 (29)
Collection: Unknown

143. Dogana da Mar, on a page of studies from Venice, inscribed centre left 'VENICE', pencil
126 x 175 mm
Provenance: As for no. 12
Literature: Grogan, 2002, p.175 (86), illus., pl. 50; Grogan, 2006, illus., p.13
Collection: National Library of Ireland, Dublin (PD 2009 TX 86)

144. Benedictine Abbey of San Gregorio, on a page of studies from Venice, inscribed centre left 'VENICE', pencil
126 x 175 mm
Provenance: As for no. 12
Literature: Grogan, 2002, p.175 (86), illus., pl. 50; Grogan, 2006, illus., p.13
Collection: National Library of Ireland, Dublin (PD 2009 TX 86)

145. View from quay of the Zecca, on a page of studies from Venice, inscribed centre left 'VENICE', pencil
126 x 175 mm
Provenance: As for no. 12
Literature: Grogan, 2002, p.175 (86), illlus., pl. 50; Grogan, 2006, illus., p.13
Collection: National Library of Ireland, Dublin (PD 2009 TX 86)

146. Gondola head, on a page of studies from Ferrara and Venice, inscribed lower right 'GONDOLA/HEAD.', pencil
126 x 175 mm
Provenance: As for no. 12
Literature: Grogan, 2002, p.175 (84), illus., pl. 49
Collection: National Library of Ireland, Dublin (PD 2009 TX 84)

147. Plan and internal elevation of San Giovanni Crisostomo, inscribed upper right 'A Venetian Ch' with other notes, pencil
126 x 175 mm
Provenance: As for no. 12
Literature: Grogan, 2002, p.175 (85); Grogan, 2006, illus., p.14
Collection: National Library of Ireland, Dublin (PD 2009 TX 85)

VICENZA

148. Casa Cogollo known as 'Casa di Palladio', Corso Andrea Palladio 165-167, inscribed lower right 'CASA DI PALLADIO/ VICENZA.', signed and dated 'C.RM./JUNE 1891', pencil
272 x 183 mm
Provenance: Dr. Thomas Howarth by 1943; his sale Christie's London, Thursday 17th February 1994 (46), illus., p.36
Exhibited: Art Gallery of Ontario, Toronto, 1978 (47)
Collection: Unknown
Once attributed to Palladio, the façade dates from 1559-62 and is possibly by Giovanni Antonio Fasolo (1530-72).

149. Architectural details and studies of wrought-iron work, inscribed upper right 'NOTES FROM/ VICENZA.', and at bottom 'SOME WROT [sic] IRON WORK.', pencil
273 x 183 mm
Provenance: Dr Thomas Howarth by 1943; his sale Christie's London, Thursday 17th February 1994 (45), illus., p.36
Exhibited: Art Gallery of Ontario, Toronto, 1978 (46)
Collection: Untraced
There is a balcony similar to that on Mackintosh's drawing on Corso Andrea Palladio. The examples of wrought-iron work are untraced.

150. Palazzo Thiene [?], Contra Porti 12, pencil
230 x 160 mm
Provenance: Keppie Henderson architects Glasgow, from whom purchased by Professor William J. Smith in 1930; donated by him to the Glasgow School of Art in 1959
Collection: The Glasgow School of Art Archives and Collections: Charles Rennie Mackintosh, *North Italian Sketchbook, 1891* (MC: G 57 p.4)
This sketch of an unidentified building closely resembles the Palazzo Thiene which is attributed to Giulio Romano and Palladio. If it has been correctly identified, it is the earliest drawing in the sketchbook which Mackintosh used during the remainder of his journey.

VERONA

151. Castel Vecchio and part of Ponte di Castel Vecchio, two chimneys and a balcony, inscribed left centre 'Notes from Verona', pencil
230 x 160 mm
Provenance: As for no. 150
Collection: The Glasgow School of Art Archives and Collections: Charles Rennie Mackintosh, *North Italian Sketchbook, 1891* (MC: G 57 p.1)

152. San Zeno Maggiore, sheet of studies from stalls, inscribed upper right 'S. Zenone Verona /Carving from Stalls', pencil
230 x 160 mm
Provenance: As for no. 150
Collection: The Glasgow School of Art Archives and Collections: Charles Rennie Mackintosh, *North Italian Sketchbook, 1891* (MC: G 57 p.2)

153. Campanile, San Zeno Maggiore, inscribed on right 'Campanile/S. Zenone/Verona', pencil
230 x 160 mm
Provenance: As for no. 150
Collection: The Glasgow School of Art Archives and Collections: Charles Rennie Mackintosh, *North Italian Sketchbook, 1891* (MC: G 57 p.3)

154. Bay of nave and studies of interior, San Zeno Maggiore, inscribed lower right 'Bay of Nave/S. Zenone Verona', pencil
230 x 160 mm
Provenance: As for no. 150
Literature: Billcliffe, 1977, ilus., p.20
Collection: The Glasgow School of Art Archives and Collections: Charles Rennie Mackintosh, *North Italian Sketchbook, 1891* (MC: G 57 p.5)

155. West front and detail of arcading, Church of San Zeno Maggiore, inscribed lower right 'Front/S. Zenone/Verona.', pencil
230 x 160 mm
Provenance: As for no. 150
Collection: The Glasgow School of Art Archives and Collections: Charles Rennie Mackintosh, *North Italian Sketchbook, 1891* (MC: G 57 p.6)

156. Measured study of stalls, San Zeno Maggiore, inscribed lower left 'S. Zenone Verona/Wood Stalls', dated lower right 'June 1891', pencil
230 x 160 mm
Provenance: As for no. 150
Collection: The Glasgow School of Art Archives and Collections: Charles Rennie Mackintosh, *North Italian Sketchbook, 1891* (MC: G 57 p.7)

The Arch of Titus, Rome

157. Measured study of a chair, San Zeno Maggiore, inscribed lower right 'Chair/S. Zenone Verona', pencil
230 x 160 mm
Provenance: As for no. 150
Collection: The Glasgow School of Art Archives and Collections: Charles Rennie Mackintosh, *North Italian Sketchbook, 1891*
(MC: G 57 p.8)

158. Three heraldic bas-reliefs on Prefettura and Tribunali, Piazza dei Signori, inscribed upper right 'Verona', pencil
230 x 160 mm
Provenance: As for no. 150
Collection: The Glasgow School of Art Archives and Collections: Charles Rennie Mackintosh, *North Italian Sketchbook, 1891*
(MC: G 57 p.9)

159. Palazzo della Ragione and four details, Piazza dei Signori, inscribed upper right 'Pal. del. Ragione/Piazza dei Signori/Verona', pencil
230 x 160 mm
Provenance: As for no. 150
Collection: The Glasgow School of Art Archives and Collections: Charles Rennie Mackintosh, *North Italian Sketchbook, 1891*
(MC: G 57 p.10)

160. Torre dei Lamberti, inscribed centre left 'Campanile/Pal. del [sic] Ragione/Verona', pencil
230 x 160 mm
Provenance: As for no. 150
Literature: Robertson, 1999, illus., pl. 6
Collection: The Glasgow School of Art Archives and Collections: Charles Rennie Mackintosh, *North Italian Sketchbook, 1891*
(MC: G 57 p.19).

161. West portal, Sant'Anastasia, inscribed lower right, 'Doorway. S. Anistasia [sic]/Verona', pencil
230 x 160mm
Provenance: As for no. 150.
Collection: The Glasgow School of Art Archives and Collections: Charles Rennie Mackintosh, *North Italian Sketchbook, 1891*
(MC: G 57 p.12).

162. Interior bay, Sant'Anastasia, inscribed lower right 'S. Anistasia [sic]/Verona', pencil
230 x 160 mm
Provenance: As for no. 150
Collection: The Glasgow School of Art Archives and Collections: Charles Rennie Mackintosh, *North Italian Sketchbook, 1891*
(MC: G 57 p.17)

163. Studies of unidentified intarsia work, dated 'June 12th 1891', inscribed at lower left 'Column' and at lower right 'Intersia [sic] Panel', dated 'June 12th 1891', pencil
230 x 160 mm
Provenance: As for no. 150
Collection: The Glasgow School of Art Archives and Collections: Charles Rennie Mackintosh, *North Italian Sketchbook, 1891*
(MC: G 57 p.13)
The drawing might have been made in Santa Maria in Organo which he visited on 12th June.

164. Campanile, Santa Maria in Organo, inscribed lower right 'S. Maria in Organo/Verona', pencil
230 x 160 mm
Provenance: As for no. 150
Collection: The Glasgow School of Art Archives and Collections: Charles Rennie Mackintosh, *North Italian Sketchbook, 1891* (MC: G 57 p.18)

165. Stalls, Santa Maria in Organo, inscribed upper left 'Stalls./ S. Maria in Organo/Verona', dated lower right '12th June 1891', pencil
230 x 160 mm

Provenance: As for no. 150
Literature: Billcliffe, 1977, illus., p.20; Robertson, 1999, illus., pl. 1
Collection: The Glasgow School of Art Archives and Collections: Charles Rennie Mackintosh, *North Italian Sketchbook, 1891*
(MC: G 57 p.15)

166. Measured studies of unidentified wooden screen, Santa Maria in Organo, inscribed upper right 'S. Maria in Organo/Wooden Screen', pencil
230 x 160 mm
Provenance: As for no. 150
Collection: The Glasgow School of Art Archives and Collections: Charles Rennie Mackintosh, *North Italian Sketchbook, 1891*
(MC: G 57 p.16)

167. Doorway, Verona Cathedral
Collection: Unknown
Mackintosh recorded that he rose at 5 a.m. on 14th June to make this sketch.

MANTUA

168. Sheet of studies of three unidentified architectural details, one study inscribed 'Mantua', pencil
230 x 160 mm
Provenance: As for no. 150
Collection: The Glasgow School of Art Archives and Collections: Charles Rennie Mackintosh, *North Italian Sketchbook, 1891*
(MC: G 57 p.11)

CREMONA

169. West front, Cremona Cathedral, inscribed lower right ` 'A Caution/Cremona Cathedral.', with other notes, pencil
230 x 160 mm
Provenance: As for no. 150
Literature: Robertson, 1999, illus., pl. 2
Collection: The Glasgow School of Art Archives and Collections: Charles Rennie Mackintosh, *North Italian Sketchbook, 1891*
(MC: G 57 p.38)

170. Arcade over porch, Cremona Cathedral, inscribed lower right 'ARCADE OVER PORCH/CREMONA CATHEDRAL.', signed and dated 'C.R.M/ June 1891.', pencil
311 x 249 mm
Provenance: Mackintosh Estate
Collection: Hunterian Art Gallery, University of Glasgow
(GLAHA 41431)

171. Studies of a column from a pulpit and a frame, Cremona Cathedral, inscribed on right 'Pulpit/Cremona' and 'A Frame/Cremona Duomo', pencil
230 x 160 mm
Provenance: As for no. 150
Collection: The Glasgow School of Art Archives and Collections: Charles Rennie Mackintosh, *North Italian Sketchbook, 1891*
(MC: G 57 p.22)
The frame is from the monument to Nicolaus Ala, dated 1652, in the north transept.

172. Capitals from pulpit, Cremona Cathedral, on a sheet of studies from Cremona and Milan inscribed and dated upper right'CAPS FROM PULPIT/CREMONA CATHEDRAL/ JUNE 1891', pencil
318 x 495 mm
Provenance: Dr Thomas Howarth by 1943
Exhibited: Art Gallery of Ontario, Toronto, 1978 (48)
Literature: Finucci, 1981, vol. 1, illus., p.80
Collection: Unknown

The Arch of Constantine, Rome

173. Exterior bay of Cathedral Baptistery and subsidiary studies, inscribed upper right 'Batisterio [sic] Cremona/Exterior', pencil
230 x 160 mm
Provenance: As for no. 150
Collection: The Glasgow School of Art Archives and Collections: Charles Rennie Mackintosh, *North Italian Sketchbook*, 1891
(MC: G 57 p.20)

174. Interior bay of Cathedral Baptistery and subsidiary studies, inscribed upper right 'Batisterio [sic] Cremona/Interior', pencil
230 x 160 mm
Provenance: As for no. 150
Collection: The Glasgow School of Art Archives and Collections: Charles Rennie Mackintosh, *North Italian Sketchbook*, 1891
(MC: G 57 p.21)

175. Apse, San Michele and subsidiary studies, inscribed lower left 'S. Michele Cremona.', dated lower right '15 June 1891', pencil
230 x 160 mm
Provenance: As for no. 150
Collection: The Glasgow School of Art Archives and Collections: Charles Rennie Mackintosh, *North Italian Sketchbook*, 1891
(MC: G 57 p.37)

176. Unidentified palazzo with details, inscribed lower right 'Brick House Cremona' and dated '15th June 1891', pencil
230 x 160 mm
Provenance: As for no. 150
Collection: The Glasgow School of Art Archives and Collections: Charles Rennie Mackintosh, *North Italian Sketchbook*, 1891
(MC: G 57 p.35)

BRESCIA

177. Torre del Popolo, unidentified building – possibly the Broletto, and detail of an arch, inscribed on left 'The Broletto/Brescia/(12 Cent)', pencil
230 x 160 mm
Provenance: As for no. 150
Collection: The Glasgow School of Art Archives and Collections: Charles Rennie Mackintosh, *North Italian Sketchbook*, 1891
(MC: G 57 p.27)

178. Sant'Agostino, Vicolo Sant'Agostino, inscribed upper left 'A Brick House/ Brescia', dated lower right '16th June 1891', pencil
Two sheets: each 230 x 160 mm
Provenance: As for no. 150
Literature: Robertson, 1990, illus., pl. 25; Robertson, 1999, illus., pl. 3
Collection: The Glasgow School of Art Archives and Collections: Charles Rennie Mackintosh, *North Italian Sketchbook*, 1891
(MC: G 57 pp.28-29)

179. Sarcophagus, Duomo Nuovo, inscribed lower right 'Sarcophagus/Brescia Cathedral.', dated '16 June 1891' pencil
230 x 160 mm
Provenance: As for no. 150
Collection: The Glasgow School of Art Archives and Collections: Charles Rennie Mackintosh, *North Italian Sketchbook*, 1891
(MC: G 57 p.36)
This is from the third altar on the south. The sarcophagus (circa 1500) contains the bodies of 'D. D. Apolonii et Philastri'; it was transferred in 1674 from the crypt of Old Cathedral.

180. The Castle, inscribed at bottom 'The Castle Brescia', pencil
230 x 160 mm
Provenance: As for no. 150
Literature: Robertson, 1999, illus., pl. 4
Collection: The Glasgow School of Art Archives and Collections: Charles Rennie Mackintosh, *North Italian Sketchbook*, 1891
(MC: G 57 p.14)

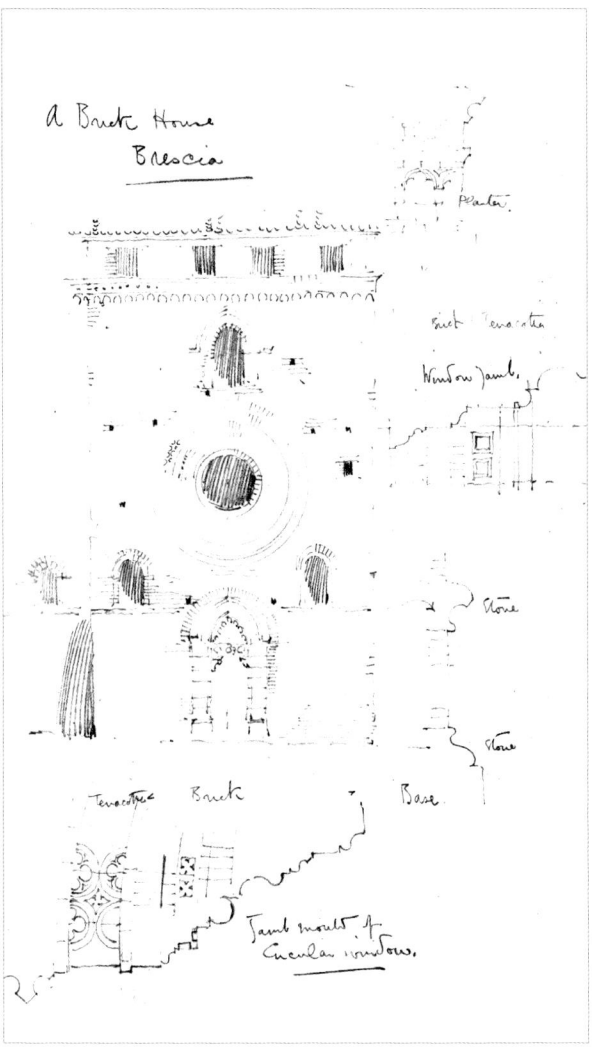

C. R. Mackintosh, Sant'Agostino, Brescia, 1891

BERGAMO

181. The Broletto and details, inscribed and dated upper left 'THe [sic] Biblioteca Bergamo/17th June 1891', pencil
230 x 160 mm
Provenance: As for no. 150
Collection: The Glasgow School of Art Archives and Collections: Charles Rennie Mackintosh, *North Italian Sketchbook*, 1891
(MC: G 57 p.30)

182. Santa Maria Maggiore, inscribed lower left 'S. Maria/Maggiore/Bergamo.', pencil
230 x 160 mm
Provenance: As for no. 150
Literature: Robertson, 1999, illus., pl. 5
Collection: The Glasgow School of Art Archives and Collections: Charles Rennie Mackintosh, *North Italian Sketchbook*, 1891
(MC: G 57 p.31)

APPENDIX 1

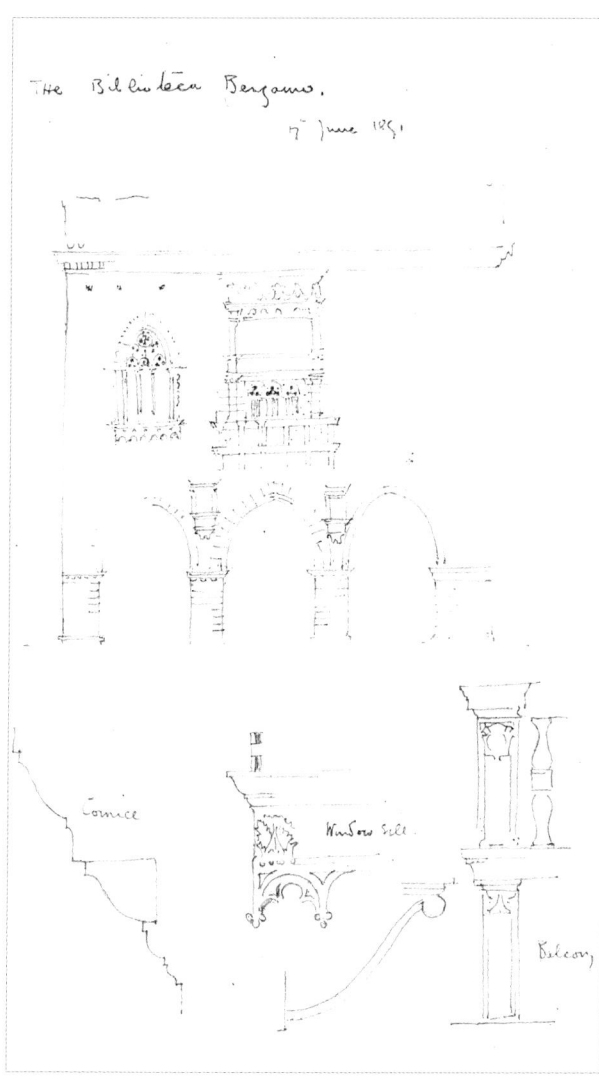

C. R. Mackintosh, Broletto, Bergamo, 1891

183. Façade of Casa dell'Arciprete and details, Via Gaetano Donizetti, inscribed upper left 'A Marble House/Bergamo.', pencil
Two sheets: each 230 x 160 mm
Provenance: As for no. 150
Collection: The Glasgow School of Art Archives and Collections: Charles Rennie Mackintosh, *North Italian Sketchbook, 1891*
(MC: G 57 pp.32-33)

184. Sant'Agostino, inscribed at bottom 'Quartieri S. Agostino/ Bergamo.', pencil
230 x 160 mm
Provenance: As for no. 150
Literature: Macleod, 1968, illus., pl. 7; Billcliffe, 1977, illus., p.18
Collection: The Glasgow School of Art Archives and Collections: Charles Rennie Mackintosh, *North Italian Sketchbook, 1891*
(MC: G 57 p.34)

LAKE COMO

185. Study of boats and a building at Lecco, inscribed and dated upper left 'On Lago Como, 18th June 1891.' and upper right 'LECCO', pencil
230 x 160 mm
Provenance: As for no. 150
Collection: The Glasgow School of Art Archives and Collections: Charles Rennie Mackintosh, *North Italian Sketchbook, 1891*
(MC: G 57 p.25)

186. Lake Como, studies of boats and view of Varenna, from the west side of the Lake, inscribed upper right 'Baleggio [sic]' and centre left 'Varenna', pencil
230 x 160 mm
Provenance: As for no. 150
Collection: The Glasgow School of Art Archives and Collections: Charles Rennie Mackintosh, *North Italian Sketchbook, 1891*
(MC: G 57 p.23)

187. Churches and landscape and a boat, inscribed upper left 'Bellano', centre right 'Gravedona' and centre left 'The shadow of a cloud.', pencil
230 x 160 mm
Provenance: As for no. 150
Collection: The Glasgow School of Art Archives and Collections: Charles Rennie Mackintosh, *North Italian Sketchbook, 1891*
(MC: G 57 p.24).
At top right is the Church of Sant'Andrea in the hamlet of Bonzeno, at centre and right the campanili of Santa Maria delle Grazie and Santa Maria del Tiglio, both at Gravedona.

188. Landscape study with boats on Lake Como, pencil
230 x 160 mm
Provenance: As for no. 150
Collection: The Glasgow School of Art Archives and Collections: Charles Rennie Mackintosh, North Italian Sketchbook, 1891
(MC: G 57 p.26)

189. Gates, Villa del Balbionello, Campo, inscribed on left 'Iron Gates/CAMPO./L. Como', pencil
230 x 160mm
Provenance: As for no. 150
Collection: The Glasgow School of Art Archives and Collections: Charles Rennie Mackintosh, *North Italian Sketchbook, 1891*
(MC: G 57 p.39)

COMO

190. Transept interior and details, Como Cathedral, inscribed lower left 'Como Cathedral/Trancept [sic] Interior', pencil
230 x 160 mm
Provenance: As for no. 150
Collection: The Glasgow School of Art Archives and Collections: Charles Rennie Mackintosh, *North Italian Sketchbook, 1891*
(MC: G 57 p.41)

191. North transept exterior and details, Como Cathedral, inscribed lower right 'Como Cathedral/Exterior of Trancept. [sic]', pencil
230 x 160 mm
Provenance: As for no. 150
Collection: The Glasgow School of Art Archives and Collections: Charles Rennie Mackintosh, *North Italian Sketchbook, 1891*
(MC: G 57 p.42)

192. South door and two finials, Como Cathedral, inscribed on right 'Como/Cathedral', pencil
230 x 160 mm
Provenance: As for no. 150
Literature: Billcliffe, 1977, illus., p.29
Collection: The Glasgow School of Art Archives and Collections: Charles Rennie Mackintosh, *North Italian Sketchbook, 1891*(MC: G 57 p.57)

The Pantheon, Rome

193. Sant'Abbondio from east, pencil, inscribed lower left 'S. Abondio[sic]/Como', signed and dated lower right 'CRM/ JUNE 1891', pencil
350 x 257 mm
Provenance: Dr. Thomas Howarth by 1943; his sale Christie's London, Thursday 17th February 1994 (47), illus., p.37
Exhibited: Art Gallery of Ontario, Toronto, 1978 (49), illus., p.19
Literature: Robertson, 1990, illus., pl. 38; Macaulay, 2010, illus., pl. 84
Collection: Toyota Municipal Museum of Art

194. Studies of west and part of south façade, with plan, Sant'Abbondio, inscribed on right, 'S.Abbondio/Como', pencil
230 x 160 mm
Provenance: As for no. 150
Collection: The Glasgow School of Art Archives and Collections: Charles Rennie Mackintosh, *North Italian Sketchbook, 1891* (MC: G 57 p.45)

195. Studies of exterior of apse, San Fedele, inscribed lower right 'S. Fedele/Como', pencil
230 x 160 mm
Provenance: As for no. 150
Collection: The Glasgow School of Art Archives and Collections: Charles Rennie Mackintosh, *North Italian Sketchbook, 1891* (MC: G 57 p.46)

196. The Broletto, inscribed lower right 'The Broletto Como', pencil
230 x 160 mm
Provenance: As for no. 150
Collection: The Glasgow School of Art Archives and Collections: Charles Rennie Mackintosh, *North Italian Sketchbook, 1891* (MC: G 57 p.58)

MILAN

197. Statue of Moses, Milan Cathedral, inscribed centre right 'MOSES/MILAN/CATHEDRAL', signed and dated lower right 'CRM/ JUNE 1891', pencil and blue wash
305 x 223 mm
Provenance: Dr. Thomas Howarth by 1943
Exhibited: Art Gallery of Ontario, Toronto, 1978 (51)
Collection: Unknown
The statue is on the exterior south face of the south transept adjacent to the doorway.

198. Statue of St. Jerome, Milan Cathedral (recto of 196), inscribed centre right 'S. GEROLAMO/MILAN/CATHEDRAL.', signed and dated lower right 'CRM/JUNE 1891', pencil and watercolour
355 x 255 mm
Provenance: Dr. Thomas Howarth by 1943; his sale Christie's London, Thursday 17th February 1994 (51), illus., p.39
Exhibited: University of Toronto School of Architecture, Toronto, 1967 (115); Edinburgh Festival Society, Edinburgh, 1968 (18)
Literature: Billcliffe, 1978 (30)
Collection: Private collection
The statue is on the exterior west face of the south transept.

199. Top of a nave pier, Milan Cathedral, (verso of 195), pencil
355 x 255 mm
Provenance: Dr. Thomas Howarth by 1943; his sale Christie's London, Thursday 17th February 1994 (51)
Collection: Private collection

200. Detail of a buttress, north façade of nave, Milan Cathedral, inscribed centre left 'A BUTTRESS/MILAN/CATHEDRAL.', signed with initials and dated lower right 'C.R.M./JUNE 1891', pencil and blue wash
335 x 235 mm (approx.)
Provenance: Dr. Thomas Howarth by 1943
Exhibited: University of Toronto School of Architecture, Toronto,

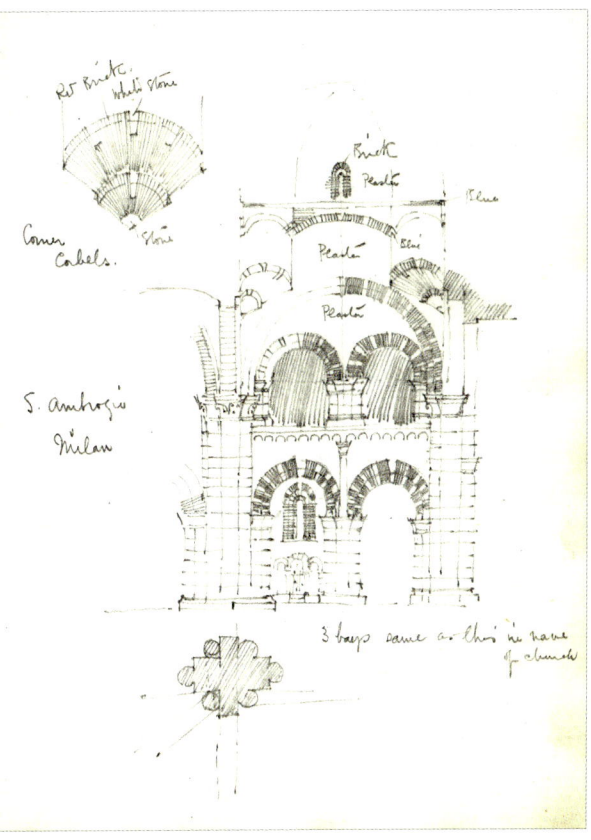

C. R. Mackintosh, Interior bay, Sant'Ambrogio, Milan, 1891

1967 (120); Art Gallery of Ontario, Toronto, 1978 (50)
Literature: Billcliffe, 1978 (31)
Collection: Unknown

201. Studies of tomb of Marco Carelli (d.1394), Milan Cathedral, inscribed lower right 'Tomb/Milan Cath', pencil
230 x 160 mm
Provenance: As for no. 150
Collection: The Glasgow School of Art Archives and Collections: Charles Rennie Mackintosh, *North Italian Sketchbook, 1891* (MC: G 57 p.43)
The tomb is located in the south aisle.

202. Studiolo Dantesco, Museo Poldi Pezzoli, inscribed upper right 'large flower' and centre left 'Tree of life', pencil
230 x 160 mm
Provenance: As for no. 150
Collection: The Glasgow School of Art Archives and Collections: Charles Rennie Mackintosh, *North Italian Sketchbook, 1891* (MC: G 57 p.44)

203. Studies of ornament, Studiolo Dantesco, Museo Poldi Pezzoli, inscribed with colour notes, pencil
230 x 160 mm
Provenance: As for no. 150
Collection: The Glasgow School of Art Archives and Collections: Charles Rennie Mackintosh, *North Italian Sketchbook, 1891* (MC: G 57 p.59)

204. Studies of Palazzo della Ragione, inscribed lower right 'Pal. Della Ragione/Milan', pencil
230 x 160 mm
Provenance: As for no. 150
Collection: The Glasgow School of Art Archives and Collections: Charles Rennie Mackintosh, *North Italian Sketchbook, 1891* (MC: G 57 p.47)

205. Plan of Sant'Alessandro, inscribed lower left 'Plan/S. Allesandro [sic]/Milan', pencil
230 x 160 mm
Provenance: As for no. 150
Collection: The Glasgow School of Art Archives and Collections: Charles Rennie Mackintosh, *North Italian Sketchbook, 1891* (MC: G 57 p.48)

206. Plan of Sant'Alessandro, pencil
160 x 95 mm
Provenance: As for no. 150
Collection: The Glasgow School of Art Archives and Collections: Charles Rennie Mackintosh, *North Italian Sketchbook, 1891* (MC: G 57 p.63a)

207. Southern bay at crossing, with details, Sant'Ambrogio, inscribed on left 'S. Ambrogio/Milan', pencil
230 x 160 mm
Provenance: As for no. 150
Literature: Billcliffe, 1977, illus., p.20
Collection: The Glasgow School of Art Archives and Collections: Charles Rennie Mackintosh, *North Italian Sketchbook, 1891* (MC: G 57 p.49)

208. Main west doorway with plan, Sant'Ambrogio, inscribed lower right 'Doorway./S. Ambrogio/ Milan', pencil
230 x 160 mm
Provenance: As for no. 150
Collection: The Glasgow School of Art Archives and Collections: Charles Rennie Mackintosh, *North Italian Sketchbook, 1891* (MC: G 57 p.50)

209. West façade, north west door and three capitals, Sant'Ambrogio, inscribed lower right 'S. Ambrosio [sic]/Milan', pencil
230 x 160 mm
Provenance: As for no. 150
Collection: The Glasgow School of Art Archives and Collections: Charles Rennie Mackintosh, *North Italian Sketchbook, 1891* (MC: G 57 p.51)
Capitals, from top clockwise, are from the southern side of nave (another example is on the north side of the atrium, displayed as a museum object by 2004); in the north aisle near the crossing; on the north side of the atrium displayed by 2004 as a museum object.

210. Plan and section and other details, San Lorenzo Maggiore, dated 'July 1891' and inscribed lower right 'S. Lorenzo/Milan', pencil
230 x 160 mm
Provenance: As for no. 150
Literature: Robertson, 1990, illus., pl. 36
Collection: The Glasgow School of Art Archives and Collections: Charles Rennie Mackintosh, *North Italian Sketchbook, 1891* (MC: G 57 p.52)

211. Interior bay, Sant'Eustorgio, inscribed lower right 'S. Eustorgio/Milan', pencil
230 x 160 mm
Provenance: As for no. 150
Literature: Macleod, 1968, illus., pl. 6; Billcliffe, 1977, illus., p.20.
Collection: The Glasgow School of Art Archives and Collections: Charles Rennie Mackintosh, *North Italian Sketchbook, 1891* (MC: G 57 p.53)

212. Monument to Saint Peter Martyr, Capella Portinari, Sant'Eustorgio, inscribed upper left 'Monument/S. Eustorgio./Milan', pencil
230 x 160 mm
Provenance: As for no. 150
Collection: The Glasgow School of Art Archives and Collections: Charles Rennie Mackintosh, *North Italian Sketchbook, 1891* (MC: G 57 p.69)

213. Tomb, Sant'Eustorgio, inscribed on right 'Tomb./S.Eustorgio/Milan', pencil
230 x 160 mm
Provenance: As for no. 150
Collection: The Glasgow School of Art Archives and Collections: Charles Rennie Mackintosh, *North Italian Sketchbook, 1891* (MC: G 57 p.54)
The Tomb, dated 1600, is in the fifth bay from the west in the north aisle.

214. Capitals from south transept, Sant'Eustorgio, on a sheet of studies from Cremona and Milan inscribed on left 'MILAN.' and on right 'S. EUSTORGIO.'
318 x 495 mm
Provenance: Dr. Thomas Howarth by 1943
Exhibited: Art Gallery of Ontario, Toronto, 1978 (48)
Literature: Finucci, 1981, vol. 1, illus., p.80
Collection: Unknown

215. West doorway, Santa Maria delle Grazie, inscribed upper left 'Doorway/S. Maria Del [sic] Grazie/Milan', pencil
230 x 160 mm
Provenance: As for no. 150
Literature: Billcliffe, 1977, illus., p.9
Collection: The Glasgow School of Art Archives and Collections: Charles Rennie Mackintosh, *North Italian Sketchbook, 1891* (MC: G 57 p.56)

216. Tomb in Santa Maria delle Grazie, inscribed lower right 'Tomb/S. Maria Del [sic]/Grazie/Milan', pencil
230 x 160 mm
Provenance: As for no. 150
Collection: The Glasgow School of Art Archives and Collections: Charles Rennie Mackintosh, *North Italian Sketchbook, 1891* (MC: G 57 p.54)
The monument to Della Torre (1483) by Tommaso Cazzaniga (fl. 1481-1504) is in the first chapel from the west in the south aisle.

217. Studies of ornament, Museo Archeologico, inscribed upper right 'Notes from the Arch. Museo/Milan', pencil
180 x 110 mm
Provenance: As for no. 150
Collection: The Glasgow School of Art Archives and Collections: Charles Rennie Mackintosh, *North Italian Sketchbook, 1891* (MC: G 57 p.61)
The sources for these drawings have not been located.

218. Monument of Bishop Battista Bagaroto, Museo Archeologico, inscribed at top 'Monument.', pencil
180 x 55 mm
Provenance: As for no. 150
Collection: The Glasgow School of Art Archives and Collections: Charles Rennie Mackintosh, *North Italian Sketchbook, 1891* (MC: G 57 p.62.1)
The monument (1519) is the work of Andrea Fusina.

219. Chimney piece, Museo Archeologico, inscribed at top 'Fireplace', pencil
180 x 55 mm
Provenance: As for no. 150
Collection: The Glasgow School of Art Archives and Collections:

Loggia di Lanzi, Florence

CHARLES RENNIE MACKINTOSH'S ITALY

Above: C. R. Mackintosh, Intarsia work on choir stalls, Certosa di Pavia, 1891
Right: C. R. Mackintosh, West front, San Michele, Pavia, 1891;

Charles Rennie Mackintosh, *North Italian Sketchbook*, 1891
(MC: G 57 p.62.2)
The chimney piece has not been identified.
220. Three marble panels, Museo Archeologico, inscribed at bottom 'Marble Panel', pencil
180 x 55 mm
Provenance: As for no. 150
Collection: The Glasgow School of Art Archives and Collections: Charles Rennie Mackintosh, *North Italian Sketchbook*, 1891
(MC: G 57 p.62.3)
The panels are by Agostino Busti.
221. Doorway of Palazzo Bentivoglio, Museo Archeologico, inscribed lower right 'Arch. Museo/Milan/Entrance Door', pencil
158 x 93 mm
Provenance: As for no. 150
Collection: The Glasgow School of Art Archives and Collections: Charles Rennie Mackintosh, *North Italian Sketchbook*, 1891
(MC: G 57 p.63)
The doorway dates from the early 16th century.
222. Palazzo Fontana-Silvestri, Corso Venezia 10, inscribed lower left 'Milan' and lower right 'Doorway.', pencil
230 x 160 mm
Provenance: As for no. 150
Collection: The Glasgow School of Art Archives and Collections: Charles Rennie Mackintosh, *North Italian Sketchbook*, 1891
(MC: G 57 p.66)
223. Studies of Ospedale Maggiore, inscribed lower right 'Ospedale/Maggiore/Milan', pencil
230 x 160 mm
Provenance: As for no. 150
Collection: The Glasgow School of Art Archives and Collections: Charles Rennie Mackintosh, *North Italian Sketchbook*, 1891
(MC: G 57 p.70)

CERTOSA DI PAVIA
224. Domestic building, window and balcony, pencil
230 x 160 mm
Provenance: As for no. 150
Collection: The Glasgow School of Art Archives and Collections: Charles Rennie Mackintosh, *North Italian Sketchbook*, 1891
(MC: G 57 p.55)
The building resembles the Hotel-Ristorante Milano at the Certosa di Pavia where Mackintosh stayed. The window and balcony have not been identified.
225. Entrance Gateway, inscribed at bottom 'ENTRANCE GATEWAY./CERTOSA DI PAVIA.', pencil and watercolour
376 x 267 mm
Provenance: Dr. Thomas Howarth by 1943; his sale Christie's London, Thursday 17th February 1994 (58), illus., p.42
Exhibited: Art Gallery of Ontario, Toronto 1978 (64)
Literature: Billcliffe, 1978 (32a)
Collection: Unknown
226. Entrance Gateway: details, inscribed upper right 'Details of Entrance Gateway/Certosa di Pavia', pencil
Provenance: Dr. Thomas Howarth by 1943; his sale Christie's London, Thursday 17th February 1994 (59), illus., p.42
Exhibited: Art Gallery of Ontario, Toronto, 1978 (74)
Collection: Unknown
227. Blind window, West front, inscribed lower left 'CERTOSA DI PAVIA', signed and dated on mount, lower right 'CRM JULY 1891', pencil and watercolour
675 x 378 mm
Provenance: Glasgow School of Art by 1968
Exhibited: Edinburgh Festival Society, Edinburgh, 1968 (20); Hunterian Art Gallery, Glasgow, 1990 (55); Glasgow Museums, Glasgow, 1996 (5); National Galleries of Scotland, Edinburgh, 2005 (9)
Literature: Billcliffe, 1978 (32); Robertson, 1990, illus., pl. 32; Hunterian, 1990, illus., p.19

Collection: The Glasgow School of Art Archives and Collections (MC: G 1)
The blind window is the work of Giovanni Antonio Amadeo, the bas reliefs and medalions below are attributed to Antonio and Cristoforo Mantegazza.

228. Carved Angel, West Front, inscribed lower right, 'Certosa di Pavia', pencil and watercolour
384 x 272 mm
Provenance: Dr. Thomas Howarth by 1943; his sale Christie's London, Thursday 17th February 1994 (54), illus., p.40
Exhibited: Art Gallery of Ontario, Toronto, 1978 (63)
Literature: Billcliffe, 1978 (32c)
Collection: Unknown
The angel, attributed to Cristoforo and Antonio Mantegazza, is located to the immediate north of the west doorway.

229. Ceiling decoration, Nave, inscribed lower right 'Ceiling Decoration/Certosa di Pavia', pencil and watercolour
363 x 275 mm
Provenance: Dr. Thomas Howarth by 1943; his sale Christie's London, Thursday 17th February 1994 (55), illus., p.40
Exhibited: University of Toronto, School of Architecture, Toronto, 1967 (118); Art Gallery of Ontario, Toronto, 1978 (71)
Literature: Billcliffe, 1978 (33)
Collection: Unknown

230. Details of screen of side chapel, Nave, inscribed upper right 'ALTER [sic] SCREENS/ CERTOSA DI PAVIA.', signed and dated lower right 'C.R.M./JULY 1891', pencil
229 x 332 mm
Provenance: Dr Thomas Howarth by 1943
Collection: Private collection
The Baroque screens were installed across the entrances to all the side chapels in the 17th to 18th centuries.

231. Lavabo, first chapel from west in north aisle, inscribed lower right 'CERTOSA DI PAVIA.', signed and dated 'C.R.M/JULY 1891.', pencil and watercolour
382 x 272 mm
Provenance: Dr. Thomas Howarth by 1943; his sale Christie's London, Thursday 17th February 1994 (53), illus., p.40
Exhibited: Art Gallery of Ontario, Toronto, 1978 (67)
Collection: Unknown
The lavabo, constructed in coloured marbles, c.1475-97 has been attributed to Cristoforo and Antonio Mantegazza, both of whom had worked on the west front.

232. Crossing: interior of dome, inscribed on right 'Dome/Pavia', pencil
230 x 160 mm
Provenance: As for no. 150
Collection: The Glasgow School of Art Archives and Collections: Charles Rennie Mackintosh, *North Italian Sketchbook, 1891* (MC: G 57 p.71)

233. Detail of a bronze candelabra, inscribed bottom right 'BRONZE CANDELEBRA[sic]/CERTOSA DI PAVIA.', signed and dated bottom left 'C.R.M JULY 1891.', pencil
344 x 255 mm
Provenance: Dr Thomas Howarth by 1943, who presented it to the Hunterian Art Gallery, 2000
Exhibited: Art Gallery of Ontario, Toronto, 1978 (78)
Collection: Hunterian Art Gallery, University of Glasgow (GLAHA 53126)
The candelabra is one of two by Annibale Fontana located in the north transept.

234. Details of stalls, inscribed lower right 'NOTES FROM STALLS/ CERTOSA DI PAVIA.', signed and dated C.R.M./JULY 1891, pencil
356 x 260 mm
Provenance: Dr. Thomas Howarth by 1943; his sale Christie's London, Thursday 17th February 1994 (67), illus., p.45
Exhibited: Art Gallery of Ontario, Toronto, 1978 (75), illus., p.21
Literature: Robertson, 1990, illus., pl. 29
Collection: Unknown

235. Study of intarsia panel from stalls, inscribed lower left 'INTERSIA [sic] PANEL/ CERTOSA DI PAVIA.', pencil and watercolour
280 x 375 mm or smaller
Provenance: Dr. Thomas Howarth by 1943; his sale Christie's London, Thursday 17th February 1994 (56)
Exhibited: Art Gallery of Ontario, Toronto, 1978 (60)
Literature: Billcliffe, 1978 (33c, 33d or 33e)
Collection: Unknown

236. Study of intarsia panel from stalls, inscribed at centre 'INTERSIA [sic] PANEL/ CERTOSA DI/ PAVIA.', pencil and watercolour
280 x 375 mm or smaller
Provenance: Dr. Thomas Howarth by 1943; his sale Christie's London, Thursday 17th February 1994 (56), illus., p.41
Exhibited: Art Gallery of Ontario, Toronto, 1978 (61)
Literature: Billcliffe, 1978 (33c, 33d or 33e)
Collection: Unknown

237. Study of intarsia panel from stalls, inscribed lower left 'INTERSIA [sic] PANEL/ CERTOSA DI/ PAVIA.', pencil and watercolour
280 x 375 mm or smaller
Provenance: Dr. Thomas Howarth by 1943; his sale Christie's London, Thursday 17th February 1994 (56), illus., p.41
Exhibited: Art Gallery of Ontario, Toronto, 1978 (62)
Literature: Billcliffe, 1978 (33c, 33d or 33e)
Collection: Unknown

238. Study of intarsia panel from stalls, inscribed lower right 'INTERSIA [sic] PANEL. /CERTOSA DI PAVIA./1/2 FULL SIZE.', pencil and watercolour
247 x 335mm
Provenance: Dr. Thomas Howarth by 1943; his sale Christie's London, Thursday 17th February 1994 (57)
Exhibited: Art Gallery of Ontario, Toronto, 1978 (69)
Literature: Billcliffe, 1978 (33a or 33b)
Collection: Unknown

239. Study of intarsia panel from stalls, inscribed upper right 'INTERSIA [sic] PALEL [sic]/CERTOSA DI/ PAVIA.', pencil and watercolour
272 x 374 mm
Provenance: Dr. Thomas Howarth by 1943; his sale Christie's London, Thursday 17th February 1994 (57), illus., p.41
Exhibited: Art Gallery of Ontario, Toronto, 1978 (70)
Literature: Billcliffe, 1978 (33a or 33b)
Collection: Unknown

240. Study of intarsia panel from stalls, inscribed lower right 'INTERSIA[sic] PANEL, CERTOSA DI/PAVIA.', pencil and watercolour
247 x 336 mm
Provenance: Dr. Thomas Howarth by 1943, who presented it to the Hunterian Art Gallery, 2000
Collection: Hunterian Art Gallery, University of Glasgow (GLAHA 53123)

241. Study of intarsia panel from stalls, inscribed lower right 'INTERSIA[sic] PANEL/ CERTOSA DI PAVIA.', pencil and watercolour
247 x 336 mm
Provenance: Dr. Thomas Howarth by 1943, who presented it

to the Hunterian Art Gallery, 2000
Collection: Hunterian Art Gallery, University of Glasgow (GLAHA 53124)

242. Study of intarsia panel from stalls, inscribed upper left 'INTEIRSIA[sic] PANEL/CERTOSA DI PAVIA', pencil and watercolour
248 x 337 mm
Provenance: Dr. Thomas Howarth by 1943, who presented it to the Hunterian Art Gallery, 2000
Collection: Hunterian Art Gallery, University of Glasgow (GLAHA 53125)

243. Studies of fountain in Lavatorium, inscribed top left, 'FOUNTAIN IN LAVATORY/CERTOSA DI PAVIA./DETAILS 1-4. F.S.', pencil
336 x 249 mm
Provenance: Dr. Thomas Howarth by 1943; his sale Christie's London, Thursday 17th February 1994 (64), illus., p.44
Exhibited: Art Gallery of Ontario, Toronto, 1978 (72)
Collection: Unknown
The lower part is by Alberto Maffioli, the upper part by Antonio and Cristoforo Mantegazza.

244. Details and decorative elements from the fountain in Lavatorium, inscribed lower right 'Details of/Fountain in Lavatory./Certosa di Pavia, pencil and grey wash
380 x 265 mm
Provenance: Dr. Thomas Howarth by 1943; his sale Christie's London, Thursday 17th February 1994 (60), illus., p.42
Exhibited: Art Gallery of Ontario, Toronto, 1978 (65)
Collection: Unknown

245. Decorative details from fountain in Lavatorium, inscribed top right 'Details of Fountain/in Lavatory/Certosa di Pavia/Quarter Full Size.', pencil
336 x 249 mm
Provenance: Dr. Thomas Howarth by 1943; his sale Christie's London, Thursday 17th February 1994 (63), illus., p.43
Collection: Unknown

246. Plan of well in Lavatorium, inscribed centre left 'Plan of Well/in Lavatory/Certosa di Pavia', pencil
271 x 182 mm
Provenance: Dr. Thomas Howarth by 1943; his sale Christie's London, Thursday 17th February 1994 (61), illus., p.43
Exhibited: Art Gallery of Ontario, Toronto, 1978 (77)
Collection: Unknown
The well has been attributed to Giovanni Antonio Amadeo.

247. Bronze outlets in Lavatorium, inscribed at bottom 'Sketch of Bronze Outlets/in Lavatory/Certosa di Pavia' with subsidiary notes, pencil
272 x 182 mm
Provenance: Dr. Thomas Howarth by 1943; his sale Christie's London, Thursday 17th February 1994 (62), illus., p.43
Exhibited: Art Gallery of Ontario, Toronto, 1978 (73)
Collection: Unknown

248. Doorway to Small Cloister in South Transept, inscribed lower right 'Doorway/CERTOSA DI PAVIA', signed and dated 'C.R.M./July 1891.', pencil and watercolour
346 x 264 mm
Provenance: Dr. Thomas Howarth by 1943; his sale Christie's London, Thursday 17th February 1994 (52), illus., p.39
Literature: Billcliffe, 1978 (32b)
Collection: Unknown
The doorway is the work of Antonio and Cristoforo Mantegazza. See also no. 250.

249. Doorway in Small Cloister, inscribed lower right 'Doorway in Small Cloister/Certosa di Pavia/Detail quarter full size.', signed and dated 'Chas. R. McIntosh.July 1891', pencil
335 x 250 mm
Provenance: Dr. Thomas Howarth by 1943; his sale Christie's London, Thursday 17th February 1994 (65), illus., p.44
Exhibited: Art Gallery of Ontario, Toronto, 1978 (66)
Collection: Unknown
The doorway is the work of Antonio and Cristoforo Mantegazza.

250. Doorway in Small Cloister, inscribed top right 'DOORWAY IN SMALL/CLOISTER/CERTOSA', signed with monogram and dated lower left 'JULY 1891', pencil, pen and black ink on tracing paper
500 x 354 mm
Provenance: Dr. Thomas Howarth by 1943; his sale Christie's London, Thursday 17th February 1994 (66), illus., p.44
Exhibited: Art Gallery of Ontario, Toronto, 1978 (68)
Collection: Unknown
The study shows two doorways: that at the top is the one in the Small Cloister, the one beneath it is the other side of the same doorway in the south transept which gives access to the Small Cloister. See also no. 248.

251. Panel in Refectory and study of two corbels, inscribed upper right 'NOTES FROM/CERTOSA DI/PAVIA.', centre left 'PANEL IN REFECTORY.' and lower centre left 'CORBELS.', signed and dated bottom right 'C.R.M./JULY 1891', pencil
320 x 225 mm (sight)
Provenance: Dr. Thomas Howarth by 1943, who presented it to the Gamble House, Pasadena, 1990
Literature: Finucci, 1981, vol. 1, illus., p.124
Collection: Gamble House, Pasadena, California

PAVIA

252. West front of San Michele, inscribed top left S. Michele/Pavia, pencil
131 x 182 mm
Provenance: University of Strathclyde School of Architecture before 1968; deposited in the University of Strathclyde Archives in 1983 by Dr. Frank Walker of the University's Department of Architecture and Building Science
Exhibited: Edinburgh Festival Society, Edinburgh, 1968 (19)
Collection: Strathclyde University Archives (F11/7)

253. Five studies of mouldings from south doorway, San Michele, inscribed lower right 'S. Michele/Pavia', dated '21st July 1891', pencil
230 x 160mm
Provenance: As for no. 150
Collection: The Glasgow School of Art Archives and Collections: Charles Rennie Mackintosh, *North Italian Sketchbook*, 1891 (MC: G 57 p.73)

254. Study of capital in interior and plan, San Michele, inscribed centre 'S. Michele./Pavia' and lower right 'Plan S. Michele', pencil
230 x 160 mm
Provenance: As for no. 150
Collection: The Glasgow School of Art Archives and Collections: Charles Rennie Mackintosh, *North Italian Sketchbook*, 1891 (MC: G 57 p.74)

Baptistery doors, Florence

CHARLES RENNIE MACKINTOSH'S ITALY

Above: C. R. Mackintosh, Unidentified Church Tower, 1891
Opposite: Portion of nave, Monreale Cathedral. Fergusson, *A History of Architecture in all Countries*, vol. 2, p.402

UNIDENTIFIED DRAWINGS

255. A frieze and two campanili, pencil
126 x 175 mm
Provenance: As for no. 12
Literature: Grogan, 2002, p.174 (58), illus., p.52, fig. 7
Collection: National Library of Ireland, Dublin (2009 TX 58)
The drawings occupy the same page as no. 55, the campanile of Santa Maria dei Servi which is captioned 'Orvieto'. They have not, however, been identified as being located in Orvieto.

256. Study of a font, inscribed at top, 'Font', pencil
126 x 175 mm
Provenance: As for no. 12
Literature: Grogan, 2002, p.174 (47), illus., pl. 24
Collection: National Library of Ireland, Dublin (2009 TX 47)
Captioned by Mackintosh as a font this might alternatively be a holy water stoup. The drawing is on the same page as a sketch from San Miniato in Florence (see no. 72) but has not been identified as being located there.

257. North Italian building and chimney, pencil
126 x 175 mm
Provenance: As for no. 12
Literature: Grogan, 2002, p.175 (69), illus., pl. 37
Collection: National Library of Ireland, Dublin (2009 TX 69)
The drawing is on the same page as sketches from Pistoia and Pisa (nos. 103 and 96).

258. Vernacular building, pencil
230 x 160 mm
Provenance: As for no. 150
Collection: The Glasgow School of Art Archives and Collections: Charles Rennie Mackintosh, *North Italian Sketchbook, 1891* (MC: G 57 p.40)

259. Vernacular building, pencil
126 x 175 mm
Provenance: As for no. 12
Literature: Grogan, 2002, p.175 (75), illus., pl. 41
Collection: National Library of Ireland, Dublin (PD 2009 TX 75)
The drawing is on the same page as nos. 104 and 114.

260. Church tower, watercolour,
365 x 171 mm
Provenance: Miss Nancy Mackintosh, 1933: by family descent
Exhibited: MacLellan Galleries, Glasgow, 1933 (129); Edinburgh Festival Society, Edinburgh, 1968 (21)
Literature: Billcliffe, 1978 (36), illus., p.53
Collection: Private collection
The tower resembles, but is not identical with, the campaniles of San Lorenzo and San Fermo Maggiore in Verona, both of which also stand next to a river. Similar towers are encountered across much of Northern Italy.

261. Sheet of studies of three unidentified architectural details, one study inscribed 'MANTUA', pencil
230 x 160 mm
Provenance: As for no. 150
Collection: The Glasgow School of Art Archives and Collections: Charles Rennie Mackintosh, *North Italian Sketchbook, 1891* (MC: G 57 p.11). See also no. 168.

262. Study of an image of a child, inscribed lower right 'THE CHILD' pencil
230 x 160 mm
Provenance: As for no. 150
Collection: The Glasgow School of Art Archives and Collections: Charles Rennie Mackintosh, *North Italian Sketchbook, 1891* (MC: G 57 p.60)
From its position in Mackintosh's sketchbook it is fairly reasonable to assume that the drawing relates to Milan.

263. Studies of two pieces of ornament, pencil
230 x 160 mm
Provenance: As for no. 150
Collection: The Glasgow School of Art Archives and Collections:
Charles Rennie Mackintosh, *North Italian Sketchbook*, 1891
(MC: G 57 p.67)
From their position in Mackintosh's sketchbook it is fairly reasonable to assume that these drawings relate to Milan.

264. Studies of three pieces of ornament, pencil and watercolour
230 x 160 mm
Provenance: As for no. 150
Collection: The Glasgow School of Art Archives and Collections:
Charles Rennie Mackintosh, *North Italian Sketchbook*, 1891
(MC: G 57 p.68)
From their position in Mackintosh's sketchbook it is fairly reasonable to assume that these drawings relate to Milan.

265. Sketch of an unidentified church interior, pencil
230 x 160 mm
Provenance: As for no. 150
Collection: The Glasgow School of Art Archives and Collections:
Charles Rennie Mackintosh, *North Italian Sketchbook*, 1891
(MC: G 57 p.72)
This may relate to San Michele in Pavia.

266. Study of an Acanthus Scroll, pencil
335 x 246 mm
Provenance: Dr. Thomas Howarth by 1943; his sale Christie's London, Thursday 17th February 1994 (50), illus., p.38
Exhibited: Art Gallery of Ontario, Toronto 1978 (40)
Collection: Unknown
This drawing might originate from Italy but there is no clear supporting evidence.

267. Study of a Church Interior, pencil
342 x 254 mm
Provenance: Dr. Thomas Howarth by 1943; his sale Christie's London, Thursday 17th February 1994 (49), illus., p.38
Exhibited: Art Gallery of Ontario, Toronto 1978 (41)
Collection: Unknown
This drawing has always been included among the Italian sketches, but there is no evidence that it should belong with them. It has been conjectured that it represents a staircase (Toronto 1978), but it is more likely a study of a Gothic choir stall and is possibly English.

268. Working sheet of sketches, inscribed with measurements and calculations, pencil
246 x 335 mm
Provenance: Dr. Thomas Howarth by 1943; his sale Christie's London, Thursday 17th February 1994 (48), illus., p.38
Exhibited: Art Gallery of Ontario, Toronto 1978 (1)
Collection: Unknown
This drawing has always been included among the Italian sketches, but there is no evidence for this. It has been identified as a study of elevations (Howarth Sale) but might more reasonably be taken to be a plan of part of a building with elaborate Gothic mouldings.

The Bargello, Florence

APPENDIX 2
1892 LECTURE ILLUSTRATIONS

Illustrations used by Mackintosh in his lecture 'A Tour in Italy', given to the Glasgow Architectural Association, 6th September 1892 and to the Architectural Section of the Philosophical Society of Glasgow, 28th November 1892.

Catalogue numbers are given where they relate to known drawings. Illustrations without catalogue numbers are either missing drawings or photographs which Mackintosh collected on his tour.

Naples: Naples Museum, bronze tabernacle (9)
Naples: Trinità Maggiore, doorway (10)
Naples: Santa Maria del Carmine, tower (13)
Naples: Porta Capuana (11)
Naples: Certosa, well (14)
Palermo: Cathedral, exterior (16)
Palermo: Capella Palatina, interior
Rome: Vatican Museum.
Rome: Sistine Chapel
Rome: Triumphal arch (30 or 32)
Orvieto: Cathedral (48)
Siena: Cathedral, campanile (57)
Siena: Cathedral, baptistery (63)
Siena: Torch bearers (67)
Venice: Pedestals of standards, Piazza di San Marco
Venice: Doge's Palace, bronze well heads
Venice: Doge's Palace, interior
Venice: San Marco, apse
Venice: San Marco, great door, or mosaic of the Fall and Deluge
Venice: Scuola Grande di San Rocco, bronze doors
Venice: Ca'd'Oro (141)
Venice: Venetian Palace (Palazzo Continari, or Foscari, or Pisani, or Spinelli, or Grimani) (142)
Venice: Church: (San Giorgio dei Greci, or San Zaccaria, or Santi Giovanni e Paolo)
Padua: Sant'Antonio, alto relievos in arcade of sanctuary
Padua: Town Hall
Milan: Cathedral, capital (199)

APPENDIX 3
STUDENT REFERENCE BOOKS

Books relating to Italian and Classical Architecture recommended on the architectural courses at the Glasgow School of Art taken by Mackintosh as a student.

The nearest editions in time to Mackintosh's period as a student are listed. They are not necessarily the editions he would have used.

Chambers, William, *A Treatise on Civil Architecture* (London: Lockwood & Co., 1862)
Fergusson, James, *A History of Architecture in all Countries*, 4 vols. (London: John Murray, 1874)
Fergusson, James, *An Illustrated Handbook of Architecture* (London: John Murray, 1859)
Gwilt, Joseph, *An Encyclopaedia of Architecture* (London: Longmans, Green & Co., 1876)
Leeds, William Henry, *Rudimentary Architecture for the Use of Beginners and Students: The Orders and their Aesthetic Principles* (*Weale's Rudimentary Series*) (London: Crosby Lockwood & Co., 1886)
Normand, Charles Pierre Joseph, *A Parallel of the Orders of Architecture*
Penrose, Francis Cranmer, *An Investigation into the Principles of Athenian Architecture* (Macmillan, 1888)
Rosengarten, Albert, *A Handbook of Architectural Styles* (London: Chatto and Windus, 1878), awarded to Mackintosh as a prize in 1887
Smith, T. Roger, *Architecture: Classic and Early Christian* (London: Sampson Low Marston, Searle & Rivington, 1882), awarded to Mackintosh as a prize in 1888
Smith, T. Roger, *Architecture: Gothic and Renaissance* (London: Sampson Low, 1880), awarded to Mackintosh as a prize in 1887

Bibliography

Alexander Thomson Memorial, *Minute Book* (Glasgow Institute of Architects)
Anderson, William James, *Architectural Studies in Italy* (Glasgow: Maclure, Macdonald, 1890)
Anderson, William James, *The Architecture of the Renaissance in Italy: a general view for the use of students and others*, 3rd edition (London: B. T. Batsford, 1901)
The Architect (1891)
Art Gallery of Ontario, *Charles Rennie Mackintosh 1868-1928: a memorial exhibition* (Toronto: Art Gallery of Ontario, 1978)
Baedeker, Karl, *Belgium and Holland: Handbook for Travellers* (Leipsic: Karl Baedeker, 1891)
Baedeker, Karl, *Italy: Handbook for Travellers: first part: Northern Italy*, 11th remodelled edition (Leipsic: Karl Baedeker, 1899)
Baedeker, Karl, *Italy: Handbook for Travellers: second part: Central Italy and Rome*, 10th revised edition (Leipsic: Karl Baedeker, 1890)
Baedeker, Karl, *Italy: Handbook for Travellers: third part: Southern Italy and Sicily*, 13th revised edition (Leipsic: Karl Baedeker, 1900)
Billcliffe, Roger, *Architectural Sketches & Flower Drawings by Charles Rennie Mackintosh* (London: Academy Editions, 1977)
Billcliffe, Roger, *Charles Rennie Mackintosh: the Complete Furniture, Furniture Drawings & Interior Designs* (London: Lutterworth Press, 1979)
Billcliffe, Roger, *Mackintosh Watercolours* (London: John Murray, 1978)
British Architect, 34-38 (1890-2)
Burkhauser, Jude, 'Sala M'Arte Decorativa Scozzese: Charles Rennie Mackintosh and the Glasgow Group at the Venice Biennale Exhibition of 1899', *Charles Rennie Mackintosh Society Newsletter*, 58, Spring 1992, pp.9-13
Christie's, *The Dr. Thomas Howarth Collection: Important Works by Charles Rennie Mackintosh, Margaret and Frances Macdonald and Herbert MacNair* (London: Christie's, 1994)
Clark, Aylwin, *The McKenzie Sisters* (Duns: Black Ace Books, 1996)
Crawford, Alan, *Charles Rennie Mackintosh* (London: Thames and Hudson, 1995)
Department of Science and Art, *Directories*, 1884-1894 (London: H.M.S.O., 1884-1889)
Dickens, Charles, *Pictures from Italy* (1846)
Dictionary of Scottish Architects, www.scottish architects.org.uk
Edinburgh Festival Society, *Charles Rennie Mackintosh (1868-1928): Architecture, Design and Painting* (Edinburgh: Edinburgh Festival Society, 1968)
Fergusson, James, *A History of Architecture in all Countries from the Earliest Times to the Present Day*, 4 vols. (London: John Murray, 1874)
Fergusson, James, *An Illustrated Handbook of Architecture* (London: John Murray, 1859)
Fergusson, James, *History of the Modern Styles of Architecture*, 2nd edition (London: John Murray, 1873)
Finucci, Maria Cristina, *L'influenza del viaggio in Italia sulla formazione del linguaggio architettonico di Charles Rennie Mackintosh*, Università degli Studi di Firenze: Facoltà' di Architettura: Istituto di storia dell' Architettura e Restauro: Unpublished Thesis, 1980-81
Glasgow Herald (1889)
Glasgow Museums, *Charles Rennie Mackintosh* (London: Abbeville Press, 1996)
Glasgow School of Art, *Annual Reports 1884-1894* (The Glasgow School of Art Archives and Collections, GSAA/GOV/1/2)
Glasgow School of Art, Correspondence to Department of Science and Art, 1882-9 (The Glasgow School of Art Archives and Collections, GSAA/SEC/3)
Glasgow School of Art, *Syllabus of Lectures*, Session 1888-89 (University of Strathclyde Archives)
Glendinning, Miles, MacInnes, Ranald and MacKechnie, Angus, *A History of Scottish Architecture from the Renaissance to the Present Day* (Edinburgh: Edinburgh University Press, 1996)
Grogan, Elaine, *Beginnings: Charles Rennie Mackintosh's Early Sketches*, (Oxford: Architectural Press in Association with National Library of Ireland, Dublin 2002)
Grogan, Elaine, 'Charles Rennie Mackintosh's Antwerp Sketches', *Charles Rennie Mackintosh Society Journal*, 85, Winter 2003, pp.12-16
Grogan, Elaine, 'The Paris Sketches of Charles Rennie Mackintosh', *Charles Rennie Mackintosh Society Journal*, 88, Spring 2005, pp.7-11
Grogan, Elaine, 'Young Mackintosh in Venice', *Charles Rennie Mackintosh Society Journal*, 91, Winter 2006, pp.10-15
Howarth, Thomas, *Charles Rennie Mackintosh and the Modern Movement*, 2nd edition (London: Routledge & Kegan Paul, 1977)
Hunterian Art Gallery, C. R. Mackintosh Architectural Drawings (Glasgow: Hunterian Art Gallery, 1990)
L'Exposition Internationale des Arts Décoratifs Moderne à Turin, 1902 (Darmstadt: Alexander Koch, 1902)
Macaulay, James, *Charles Rennie Mackintosh* (New York: Norton, 2010)
Mackintosh, Charles Rennie, 'Architecture (1893)' in **Robertson, Pamela**, editor, *Charles Rennie Mackintosh: the Architectural Papers* (Oxford: White Cockade in association with the Hunterian Art Gallery, 1990), pp.201-211
Mackintosh, Charles Rennie, 'A Tour in Italy (1892)' in **Robertson, Pamela**, editor, *Charles Rennie Mackintosh: the Architectural Papers* (Oxford: White Cockade in association with Hunterian Art Gallery, 1990), pp.109-125
Mackintosh, Charles Rennie, 'Correspondence relating to the Italian Tour', in **Robertson, Pamela**, editor, *Charles Rennie Mackintosh: the Architectural Papers* (Oxford: White Cockade in association with the Hunterian Art Gallery, 1990) pp.226-234
Mackintosh, Charles Rennie, 'Diary of a Tour in Italy (1891)',

BIBLIOGRAPHY

in **Robertson, Pamela**, editor, *Charles Rennie Mackintosh: the Architectural Papers* (Oxford: White Cockade in association with the Hunterian Art Gallery, 1990), pp.89-107

Mackintosh, Charles Rennie, 'Elizabethan Architecture (c.1892)', in **Robertson, Pamela**, editor, *Charles Rennie Mackintosh: the Architectural Papers* (Oxford: White Cockade in association with the Hunterian Art Gallery, 1990), pp.141-151

Mackintosh, Charles Rennie, *Italian Sketchbook* (National Library of Ireland, Dublin, 2009 TX)

Mackintosh, Charles Rennie, *North Italian Sketchbook*, 1891 (The Glasgow School of Art Archives and Collections, MC: G 57)

Mackintosh, Charles Rennie, 'Scotch Baronial Architecture (1891)', in **Robertson, Pamela**, editor, *Charles Rennie Mackintosh: the Architectural Papers* (Oxford: White Cockade in association with the Hunterian Art Gallery, 1990), pp.49-63

Mackintosh, Charles Rennie, *Scottish Sketchbook* (National Library of Ireland, Dublin, 2011 TX)

Mackintosh, Charles Rennie, 'Seemliness (1902)', in **Robertson, Pamela**, editor, *Charles Rennie Mackintosh: the Architectural Papers* (Oxford: White Cockade in association with the Hunterian Art Gallery, 1990), pp.213-225

Mackintosh, Charles Rennie, 'Memoir on the Italian Tour', in **Robertson, Pamela**, editor, *Charles Rennie Mackintosh: the Architectural Papers* (Oxford: White Cockade in association with the Hunterian Art Gallery, 1990), pp.235-236

MacLellan Galleries, *Charles Rennie Mackintosh, Margaret Macdonald Mackintosh: memorial exhibition* (Glasgow: MacLellan Galleries, 1933)

Macleod, Robert, *Charles Rennie Mackintosh* (London: Country Life, 1968)

National Galleries of Scotland, *Charles Rennie Mackintosh in France* (Edinburgh: National Galleries of Scotland, 2005)

Neat, Timothy and McDermot, Gillian, *Closing the Circle: Thomas Howarth, Mackintosh and the Modern Movement: a Biography* (Aberdour: iynx, 2002)

Robertson, Pamela, editor, *Charles Rennie Mackintosh: the Architectural Papers* (Oxford: White Cockade in association with the Hunterian Art Gallery, 1990)

Robertson, Pamela, editor, *Charles Rennie Mackintosh: Architectural Studies* (Glasgow: Hunterian Art Gallery, 1999)

Rosengarten, Albert, *A Handbook of Architectural Styles* (London: Chatto and Windus, 1878)

Rubis, Kati, 'Charles Rennie Mackintosh and the Porta Capuana' (Richmond, Virginia: Department of Art History, Virginia Commonwealth University, 2005)

Ruskin, John, *The Seven Lamps of Architecture* (The Works of John Ruskin, Vol. 8), edited by E. T. Cook and Alexander Wedderburn (London: George Allen, 1903)

Ruskin, John, *The Stones of Venice*, Vol, 2: *The Sea-Stories* (The Works of John Ruskin, Vol. 10), edited by E. T. Cook and Alexander Wedderburn (London: George Allen, 1904)

Ruskin, John, *The Stones of Venice*, Vol, 3: *The Fall* (The Works of John Ruskin, Vol. 11), edited by E. T. Cook and Alexander Wedderburn (London: George Allen, 1904)

Shapiro, Harold I., editor, *Ruskin in Italy: Letters to his Parents 1845* (Oxford: Clarendon Press, 1972)

Smith, T. Roger, *Architecture: Classic and Early Christian* (London: Sampson Low Marston, Searle & Rivington, 1882)

Smith, T. Roger, *Architecture: Gothic and Renaissance* (London: Sampson Low, 1880)

Street, George Edmund, *Notes of a Tour in Northern Italy* (Artists Abroad) (London: Waterstone, 1986), reprint of 2nd edition, first published in 1855

University of Toronto School of Architecture, *Exhibition of Work by Charles Rennie Mackintosh 1868-1928: Architect, Designer & Watercolourist* (Toronto: 1967)

Walker, David, 'The Glasgow Years', Wendy Kaplan, editor, *Charles Rennie Mackintosh* (New York: Abbeville Press in association with Glasgow Museums, 1996), pp.115-151

Young, Andrew McLaren, 'Mackintosh and Italy', in Alison, Filippo, *Charles Rennie Mackintosh as a Designer of Chairs* (Warehouse, 1973)

Index

A

Adriatic 52
Aegean 58
Agostino di Giovanni (1285-c.1347) 48
Aitchison, George (1825-1910) 86
Ala, Nicolaus (d.1652) 102
Alberti, Leon Battista (1404-72) 44
Albornoz (Cardinal, 1310-67) 48
Alfonso (King of Aragon, Sicily and Naples, 1396-1458) 22
Amadeo, Giovanni Antonio (1447-1522) 67, 75, 108, 109
Ambrose of Milan, Saint (c.340-970) 70
Ammannati, Bartolomeo (1511-92) 49
Anderson, William James (1863-1900) 11, 14, 16, 17, 33, 43, 59, 60, 65, 77, 98, 100
Angelico, Fra. (Guido di Pietro; c.1400-55) 46, 48
Antiochenos, Georgios (d.1151) 25
Antoninus Pius (Roman Emperor, 86-161) 33, 39
Antwerp 74, 75, 80, 87, 89, 113
Apollonius of Brescia, Saint (2nd century) 64
Arnolfo di Cambio (c.1245-1302) 41, 47, 48, 49, 94
Augustus (Roman Emperor, 63 B.C.- A.D. 14) 39
Austria 58, 62, 69

B

Baccio d'Agnolo (1462-1543) 48
Baedeker guide books 20, 29, 36, 38, 45, 48, 51, 66, 75, 113
Bagaroto, Battista, Bishop (d. c.1519) 106
Balearic Islands 51
Bassi, Martino (1541-91) 70
Bastianino, Sebastiano (c.1532-1602) 55
Bellagio 65
Bellano 65
Bellini, Gentile (c.1429-1507) 75
Bellini, Giovanni (c.1435-1516) 75
Benci di Cione (d.1388) 48
Benedetto da Maiano (1442-97) 75
Benedetto da Rovezzano (1474-1552) 96
Benedictine Order 26, 46, 101
Benone, Giuseppe (1618-84) 67
Benvenuto da Imola, Fra. (13th century) 67
Bergamo 8, 64, 65, 66, 71, 77, 80, 103: Casa dell'Arciprete 65, 104; Citta Alta 64; Citta Bassa 64; Broletto (Biblioteca) 64; Capella Colleoni 65; funicular railway 64; Hotel Capella d'Oro 64; Piazza Mercato delle Scarpe 64; Piazza Vecchia 64; Sant'Agostino 64; Santa Maria Maggiore 65; Torre Civica 64; Via Gaetano Donizetti 104; Viale Giovanni XXIII (Viale della Stazione) 64
Bergognone, Ambrogio (1455?-1524?) 73, 75
Bernini, Giovanni Lorenzo (1589-1680) 35, 36, 39
Bertini, Giovanni Battista (1799-1849) 75
Bertini, Giuseppe (1825-98) 72
Black Sea 58
Blackie, John Stuart (1809-95) 36, 39
Blow, Detmar (1867-1939) 87
Bologna 52, 98: Cattedrale di San Pietro 98; Duomo (Cathedral); Palazzo Bolognini 99; Piazza del Nettuno 52; Piazza Maggiore 52; Piazza VittorioEmanuele 52; San Petronio 52; SantiVitale e Agricola 52; Torre degli Asinelli 99; Via dell'Indipendenza 52; Via Santo Stefano 99
Borromini, Francesco (1599-1667) 35, 36, 39
Bramante, Donato (1444-1514) 33, 70, 72
Brancaccio, Rinaldo (Cardinal, d.1427) 23
Bregno, Andrea (1421-1506) 35, 37, 39, 48, 93
Brenta Canal 57
Brescia 8, 64, 103: Albergo Capello 64; Broletto 64; Castle 103; Corso Martiri della Liberta (CorsoVittorio Emanuele) 64; Duomo Nuovo 64; Duomo Vecchio 64; Municipio (Loggia) 64; Piazza Paolo VI (Piazza del Duomo) 64; Sant'Agostino 64; Santa Maria dei Miracoli 64; Santa Maria del Carmine 67; Torre del Popolo 64; Vicolo Sant'Agostino 103
British Architect 13, 17, 77, 78, 81, 87
Brunelleschi, Filippo (1377-1446) 44, 45, 46, 48, 49
Brussels 74
Buglioni, Benedetto (1461-1521) 49, 96
Burne-Jones, Sir Edward Coley (1833-1898) 78, 87
Buscheto (fl. 11th century) 55
Busti, Agostino (1480/3-1548) 107

C

Cadenabbia: Hotel Belle Ile 65
Callander 69
Campbell Douglas & Sellars (architectural practice) 12
Campi, Giulio (c.1502-72) 75
Campo: Villa del Balbiano 65
Candelabra 21, 78, 108
Cangrande II della Scala 67
Caravaggio (Michelangelo Merisi, 1571-1610) 35
Carelli, Marco (d.1394) 75, 105
Carthusian Order 23, 37, 73
Cazzaniga, Tommaso (fl. 1481-1504) 106
Certosa di Pavia: Hotel-Ristorante Milano 72, 107
Chalmers, James (1858-1927) 16, 86
Charles V (Holy Roman Emperor, 1500-58) 29
Château d'Écouen 74
Chimney piece 16, 59, 60, 72, 74, 100, 107
Civita Vecchia 51
Classis 52
Clement VII (Pope, 1478-1534) 38, 39
Clifford, Henry Edward (1852-1932) 87
Codussi, Domenico (fl. 16th century) 67
Codussi, Mauro (c.1440-1504) 67
Colico 65
Colleoni, Bartolomeo (1400-75) 59
Como 65: Broletto 66; Duomo (Cathedral); Piazza del Mercato 66; San Fedele 66; Sant'Abbondio 66; Via Vittorio Emanuaele II 66
Como, Lake 65
Conservazione dei Monumenti di Sicilia 25
Constantine I (Roman Emperor, 324-37) 35
Cook, Thomas: see Thomas Cook
Corenzio, Belisario (c.1560-1640) 29
Corinthian 33, 36, 37, 39, 90, 99
Corsica 51
Costa, Lorenzo (1460-1535) 63
Cotswolds 84
Cozzarelli, Giacomo (1453-1515) 48
Cremona 63, 67, 77, 87, 102, 103, 106: Albergo Italia e Capello 63; Baptistery 63; Corso Campi 63; Duomo (Cathedral) 64; San Michele 63
Cronaca (Simone del Pollaiolo, 1454-1508) 48
Cumae 21
Cuzco (Steam Ship) 20, 21
Cyprus 58

INDEX

D
Dante Alighieri (1266-1321) 72
Della Robbia, Giovanni (1469-1529) 47, 52, 96
Della Robbia, Luca (1399/1400-1482) 45
Department of Science and Art 78
Desiderio da Settignano (c.1428-64) 46
Dickens, Charles (1812-70) 54, 55
Diotisalvi (fl. 12th century) 55
Dods, Robin (Robert) Smith (1868-1920) 42, 48, 62
Domenico da Venezia (1445-80) 61
Domenico di Niccolo dei Cori (c.1362-before 1453) 48
Dominican Order 59, 62,47
Donatello (c.1386-1466) 23, 43, 47, 49
Donzelli , Giuseppe (Fra. Nuvolo, d.1637) 29
Dorset 84
Dossi, Dosso (1480-1542) 54, 55, 75
Dreghorn, Allan (1706-65) 23

E
Edinburgh 42
Emilia 52
Empoli: San Stefano degli Agostiniani 51
Erecheum 16
Este, Dukes of Ferrara 54
Este, Borso d', Duke of Ferrara (1413-71) 54
Exarch of the Eastern Roman Empire 53

F
Fabris, Emilio de (1808-83) 48
Fanzago, Cosimo (c.1591-1678) 23
Farmer, Dr. Henry George (1882-1965) 89
Farnese collection 21
Fasolo, Giovanni Antonio (1530-72) 67
Federighi, Antonio (c.1420-90) 48, 94
Fergusson, James (1808-86) 24, 25, 26, 29, 33, 36, 39, 48, 64, 67, 74, 75, 110, 112, 113
Ferrara 5, 8, 54, 99, 101: Castello Estense 99; Duomo (Cathedral); Largo Castello 99; Palazzo Schifanoia 54; railway station 54; San Benedetto 54; Via Volta Paletto 99; Viale Cavour 54
Filarete, Antonio (c.1400-69) 71
Filippi, Camillo (1500-74) 55
Filippi, Cesare (1536-1604) 55
Filippi, Sebastiano (Bastianino, c.1532-1602) 55
Filippino degli Organi (fl. 1400-50) 75
Florence 44, 80, 84, 96, 97, 99:
  Badia Fiorentina 46; Bargello 46; Borgo San Jacopo 97; Cascine; Loggia dei Lanzi 45; Loggia del Bigallo 97; Palazzo Antinori 84, 97; Palazzo Bartolini-Salimbeni 97; Palazzo Bianca Capello 97; Palazzo degli Uffizi 97; Palazzo della Zecca 97; Palazzo Gianfigliazzi 97; Palazzo Guadagni 96; Palazzo Medici-Riccardi 48, 49; Palazzo Pitti 47, 48; Palazzo Spini-Feroni; Palazzo Strozzi 48, 49, 97; Palazzo Vecchio 45, 46, 47, 96; Pensione Laurent 96; Piazza della Signoria 96, 45, 46; Piazza Santo Spirito 96; Piazzale degli Uffizi 97; Piazza San Giovanni 36, 48, 93, 97; Ponte Vecchio 45, 48, 51, 97; railway station; River Arno 44, 51; San Lorenzo 80; San Marco 46; San Miniato al Monte 46, 96; Santa Croce 45, 46, 96; Santa Maria Novella 38, 44, 46; Santo Spirito 44, 46, 96; Santa Trinità Bridge 44, 45, 48; Via Cavour 46; Torre dei Girolami 97; Torre dei Marsili 97; Via de' Tornabuoni 97; Via del Presto 44, 48; Via del Proconsolo 46, 47, 96; Via delle Terme 97; Via Maggio 48; Via Por Santa Maria 97
Fontana, Annibale (1540-87) 108
Fontana, Carlo (1634-1714) 35
Fontana, Domenico (1543-1607) 36, 39
Fontana, Giovanni (1540-1614) 39
Foppa, Vincenzo (fl. 1427-1515) 75
Francesco del Borgo di Santo Sepolcro (before 1441-68) 39
Francesco del Cossa (c.1438-c.1481) 54
Francia, Francesco (c.1450-1517) 75
Franciscan Order 60
Fuga, Ferdinando (1699-1781) 29
Fusina, Andrea (before 1495-1526) 57, 107

G
Gagliardi, Filippo (d.1659) 36
Galilei, Alessandro (1691-1736) 33, 35, 39,
Genoa 14, 69, 73, 75
Genovese, Gaetano (1795-1860) 29
Genuino, Giuseppe (fl. 18th century) 29
Georgios Antiochenos (fl. 1132-43) 25
Ghiberti, Lorenzo (1378-1455) 43, 49
Ghirlandaio, Domenico(1449-1494) 49
Giacomo della Porta (1539-1602) 39
Giambologna (Giovanni Bologna, 1529-1608) 45, 48, 49
Gibraltar 19
Gildard, Robert James 16
Giotto di Bondone (1266/7-1337) 75
Giovanni d'Alemagna (fl. 1440-1450) 100
Giovanni da Verona, Fra. (c.1457-1525) 67
Giovanni degli Eremitani, Fra. (fl. 1255 1320) 61
Giovanni di Balduccio (c.1290-after 1339) 75
Giovanni di Cecco (14th century) 48
Giovanni di Simone (fl. 13th century) 55
Giugni, Bernardo (1396-1466) 49
Giuliano da Maiano (c.1432-1490) 22, 55, 84
Glasgow: Buchanan Street 85; Corporation Galleries 12; Firpark Terrace 77; Glasgow Architectural Association 77, 94, 95, 112; Glasgow Art Galleries 67, 78; Glasgow Herald 16, 29, 80, 82, 113; Glasgow Institute of Architects 5, 16, 85, 113; Glasgow Philosophical Society 112; Glasgow School of Art 4; Glasgow Style 9, 80, 85; Religious Institution Rooms 77; St. Andrew's Halls 12, 13; St. Andrew's in the Square 23; Scotland Street School 85; Wylie Hill Department Store 12
Gonzaga, Dukes of Mantua 62, 63
Gordon, John (c.1835-1912) 16
Gozzoli, Benozzo (1420-97) 48
Gravedona: Santa Maria del Tiglio 65;
Santa Maria delle Grazie 104
Gregorini, Domenico (c.1700-77) 36
Guercio, Gaspare (1611-79) 29

H
Hadrian (Roman Emperor, 76-138) 37, 39
Helena, Saint (c.250-c.330) 36
Herculaneum 20
Hercules 90
Hill, George Smith (1868-1944) 16
Honeyman, John(1831-1914) 78
Howarth, Thomas (1914-2000) 5, 9, 16, 89 ,90, 91, 92, 93, 94, 95, 96, 97, 98, 99, 100, 101, 103, 105, 106, 107, 108, 109, 111, 113, 114
Hutchison, John (c.1841-1908) 12, 42

I
Innocent VIII (Pope, 1432-92) 35

J
Jackson, Thomas Graham (1835-1924) 87
Jacopino da Tradate (fl. 1401-40) 75
Jacopo della Quercia (1371/4-1438) 48
Jerusalem 51
Julius II (Pope, 1443-1513) 33, 37, 39, 43
Justinian I (Eastern Roman Emperor, c.482-565) 53

K
Keppie , John (1862-1945) 9, 12, 14, 19, 74, 78, 80, 87, 89, 101

L
La Spezia 51
Lake Como 65, 104,
Lecco 65, 104
Leiper, William (1839-1916) 14, 16, 87
Leo X (Pope, 1475-1521) 38
Leonardo da Vinci (1452-1519) 73
Leone (Steam Ship) 24
Leopardi, Alessandro (fl. 1400-1521) 67
Levis, Eustache de (Archbishop of Arles, d.1489) 92
Levis, Philippe de (Cardinal, 1435-1475) 92
Lombardo, Antonio (1458-1516) 100
Lombardo, Cristoforo (fl. 16th century) 75
Lombardo, Pietro (c.1438-1515) 59
Lombardo, Tullio (1455-1532) 100
Lombardy 62
Lonati, Bernardino 39, 93
London 42, 74
Longhena, Baldassare (1604-82) 67
Lorenzo di Mariano (1476-1534) 48
Lucca 42, 51, 54, 87
Luini, Bernardino (c.1485-1532) 73

M
McKenzie, George (1866-1913) 14, 19, 73, 74
Maderno, Carlo (1556-1629) 32, 39
Maffioli, Alberto (fl. 15th century) 109
Maitani, Lorenzo (1270/75-1330) 48
Manchester Municipal Technical Schools 80, 82

Mantegazza, Antonio (d.1493) 108, 109
Mantegazza, Cristoforo (d.1482) 108, 109
Mantegna, Andrea (1431-1506) 60, 63
Mantua 62: Ducal Palace; Palazzo del Tè 63; Ponte dei Molini 62; San Sebastiano 63; Sant'Andrea 63
Marsuppini, Carlo (1399-1453) 46, 96,
Matas, Niccolo (1798-c.1872) 49
Matroneum 70
Medici, Cosimo I de' (Grand Duke of Tuscany, 1519-74) 47
Medici, Cosimo de' (Cosimo il Vecchio, 1389-1464) 49
Medici, Francesco I de' (Grand Duke of Tuscany, 1541-1587) 48
Memmi, Lippo (fl. 1317-47) 48
Mengoni, Giuseppe (1829-1877) 75
Michelangelo (Michelangelo Buonarotti, 1475-1564) 35, 37, 38, 39, 43, 46, 48, 49
Michelozzo (Michelozzo Michelozzi, 1396-1472) 23, 46, 47, 49, 96, 97
Milan 69, 105: Castello Sforzesco 71; Corso Magenta 70; Corso di Porta Ticinese 70; Corso Venezia 71; Duomo (Cathedral); Galleria Vittorio Emanuele II 69; Hotel Biscione e Bellevue 66, 75; Museo Archeologico 72; Museo Poldi Pezzoli 72; Ospedale Maggiore 71, 104; Palazzo della Ragione 71; Palazzo Fontana-Silvestri 71; Piazza de' Mercanti 71; Piazza del Duomo 71; Piazza Fontana 69; Pinacoteca di Brera; San Lorenzo Maggiore 70; Sant'Alessandro 71; Sant'Ambrogio 80; Sant'Eustorgio 70, 106; Santa Maria alla Porta 71; Santa Maria delle Grazie 71; Stazione Ferrovio Nord 69; Via Moroni
Mino da Fiesole (1431-85) 39, 49
Mocetto, Gerolamo (c.1470-after 1531) 67
Monreale: Duomo (Cathedral)
Montacute House, Somerset 84
Monte Cassino 31

N
Nanni di Baccio Bigio (d. c.1568) 35
Naples 20, 90: British Consulate 24; Castel Sant'Elmo 24; Castel Nuovo 20; Castello dell' Ovo 20; Certosa di San Martino 23, 91; Dogana 20; Duomo (Cathedral) 22; Galleria Umberto Primo 20; Hôtel du Vésuve 20; Monte di Dio 21; Museo Nazionale 21; Opera San Carlo 21; Palazzo Reale 21, 24, 25, 27; Palazzo Reale di Capodimonte 21; Piazza Acquaverde; Piazza del Carmine 91; Piazza dei Martiri; Piazza del Plebiscito 20, 21; Piazza Gesù Nuovo 22; Piazza Mercato 22; Porta Capuana 22; Post Office 22; railway station; San Domenico Maggiore 23; San Francesco di Paola 20; Sant'Angelo a Nilo 23; Sant'Anna dei Lombardi 23; Santa Chiara; Santa Maria del Carmine 23; Santa Trinità Maggiore (Gesù Nuovo) 23; Strada Monte Oliveto 22; Strada Nuova 90; University 21; Vesuvius 20; Via Partenope 20; Via Toledo 21; Villa Nazionale 21; Vomero 23
Napoleon Bonaparte (1769-1821) 58, 59, 69
Nasini, Giuseppe (1657-1736) 97
Nasmith, Mungo (1730-70) 23
National Course of Instruction
Navigazione Generale Italiana 24
Neon (Bishop of Ravenna, c.450-75) 53
Nero (Roman Emperor, 37-68) 34
Neroni, Bartolomeo (c.1505-71) 48
New Zealand 42
Nicolo da Imola, Fra. (fl. 13th century) 67
Nobili, Agostino (///) 49

O
Odoacer the Hurian, King of Italy (443-93) 52
Olivetan order 67
Olivieri, Maffeo (1484-1543/4) 67
Olivieri, Pier Paolo (1515-99) 39
Onoforio di Giordano (fl. 1436-55) 29
Orcagna, Andrea (di Cione, fl. 1344-68) 48
Orient Steam Navigation Company 19
Orvieto 41: Corso Cavour 41; Duomo (Cathedral); Fortezza 48; funicular railway 41; Hotel Aquila Bianca 41; Palazzo Communale 41; Piazza del Commune 41; Piazza della Repubblica 41; Piazza Santa Maria 41; railway station 41; Santa Maria dei Servi 42; Via Belesario 42; Via del Duomo 41; Via Garibaldi 41

P
Padua 60: Arena Chapel (Scrovegni Chapel) 60; Eremitani 60; Palazzo della Ragione 61; San Lorenzo 60; Sant'Antonio 60; Santa Giustina 60
Paestum 20, 24, 67, 87
Palermo 24: Albergo Trinacria 24; Archiepiscopal Palace 28, 91; British Consulate 24; Capella Palatina 25; Corso Vittorio Emanuele 24; Dogana 24; Duomo (Cathedral); Hôtel de France 24; Hotel Rebecchino 25; La Martorana (Santa Maria dell'Ammiraglio) 25; Monte Catalfano 24; Monte Pellegrino 24; Museo Nazionale 24; Palazzo Reale 25; Piazza Maritima; Porta Nuova 28; San Francesco d'Assisi 25; San Giovanni degli Eremiti 25; Sant'Antonio 29; Santa Maria della Catena 28; Via Butera 24; Via Macqueda 24
Palladio, Andrea (1508-80) 58
Papal Curia 31
Paris 74
Paschal I (Pope, 817-824) 35
Passalacqua, Pietro (c.1690-1748) 36
Pavia 74: Corso Garibaldi 74; San Michele 74
Paterson, Oscar (1863-1934) 90
Paxton, James (c.1864-?) 42
Pedro de Toledo (1484-1553) 21
Perugino (Pietro Vannucci, 1446-1523) 75
Peruzzi, Baldassarre (1481-1537) 48
Peter Martyr, Saint (1206-52) 70
Petrie, Alexander (d.1905) 87
Picchiatti, Francesco Antonio (1617-1694) 29
Piccolomini, Francesco (Cardinal, 1439-1503) 48; see also Pius III (Pope)
Pinturicchio (Bernardino di Betto, 1454-1513) 35, 37
Pisa 51: Baptistery; Caffè dell'Ussero; Campanile; Campo dei Miracoli; Campo Santo; Duomo (Cathedral); Lungarno Pacinotti 97; Museo dell'Opera del Duomo 55, 98; Palazzo Agostini 51, 52, 97; Ponte di Mezzo 51
Pisano, Andrea (c.1270-1348/9) 49
Pisano, Giovanni (1245-1320) 48, 55
Pisano, Nicola (c.1200- after 1278) 43, 48
Pistoia 51, 52: Baptistery; Ospedale del Ceppo; Palazzo del Comune 52; Piazza del Duomo 51; Piazza Gavinana (Piazza Cino) 51; San Giovanni Fuorcivitas 52; San Paolo 52; Via Cavour 51
Pius II (Pope, 1405-1464) 33, 92
Pius III (Pope, 1439-1503) 33, 39; see also Piccolomini, Francesco (Cardinal)
Plymouth 19
Poldi Pezzoli, Gian Giacomo (1822-79) 71, 72, 105
Pompeii 20, 21, 22, 24, 34, 89, 90: Forum 21, 89; House of Cornelius Rufus 22, 90; Museum 21; Porta Ercolano 21; Porta 20; Street of Tombs 21; Temple of Vespasian 21; tomb of Naevoleia Tyche 21
Pontelli, Baccio (1450-92) 39
Ponzio, Flaminio (1560-1613) 39
Poynter, Ambrose Macdonald (1867-1923) 16
Primaticcio, Francesco (1504-70) 63
Pugin Travelling Scholarship 77

Q
Quadrilateral 62

R
Rainaldo (fl. 12th century) 51
Rainaldi, Carlo (1611-91) 39
Raphael (Raffaello Sanzio; 1483-1520) 33, 34, 35, 38, 39, 48
Ravenna 52: Archbishop's Palace 53; Duomo (Cathedral); Monastery of Classe 54; Municipal Museum 54; Museo Arcivescovile 99; Museo Nazionale 99; Neonian Baptistery 53; San Giovanni Evangelista 53; San Vitale 53; Sant'Apollinare in Classe 53; Sant'Apollinare Nuovo 53; Via Mario Gordini 99
Ribera, Giuseppe (1591-1652) 29
Ricci, Pietro (Archbishop of Pisa, 1411-17) 51
Risorgimento 51
Rocco, Emanuele (1852-1922) 29
Roger II (Count and King of Sicily, 1095-1154) 25
Romano, Giovanni Cristoforo (1456-1512) 93
Romano, Giulio (1499-1546) 67, 101
Romano, Marco (fl. 14th century) 67
Rome 31-39, 92: Arch of Constantine 34; Arch of Titus 34, Baths of Diocletian 37;

British Consulate 21; Campo dei Fiori 33; Campo Vaccino 32; Capitoline Hill 37; Capitoline Museum 37; Colosseum 32,92; Corso Vittorio Emanuele II 92; Dogana di Terra 33; Domus Aurea 34; Esquiline Hill 37; Fort Monteverde 34; Forum of 16; Forum Romanum 32; Hôtel Europa 31; Lateran 36; Mamertine Prison 37; Museo delle Terme 37; Museo Lateranese 36; Palazzo della Cancelleria 38; Palazzo di Venezia 33, 93; Palazzo Massimo alle Terme 39; Palazzo Ruspoli 92; Pantheon 20, 33, 38, 92; Pensione Michel 39; Piazza Cancelleria 33; Piazza dei Cinquecento 39; Piazza del Popolo 31, 93; Piazza della Repubblica 37; Piazza delle Terme 37; Piazza di San Silvestro in Capite 31; Piazza di Santa Maria Maggiore 35, 92; Piazza di Spagna 31; Piazza Navona 38; Piazza San Claudio 31; Piazza San Giovanni in Laterano 36; Piazzale Flaminio 93; Pincio 38; Porta del Popolo 35, 93; Porta Pia 35; Porta Pinciana 35; Porta Portese 34; Post Office 34; St. Peter's 32, 35, 37; Presbyterian Church 36; San Carlo alle Quattro Fontane 36; San Francesco 93; San Giovanni in Laterano 33, 35, 36, 93; San Lorenzo in Damaso 38; San Lorenzo fuori le Mura 37, 93; San Martino ai Monti 36; San Pietro in Carcere 37; San Pietro in Vincoli 37; Sant'Adriano 37; Sant'Agnese in 38; Sant'Andrea della Valle 33, 92; Santa Croce in Gerusalemme 36; Santa Maria dei Miracoli 31; Santa Maria degli Angeli 37; Santa Maria del Popolo 37, 93; Santa Maria della Vittoria 36, 39; Santa Maria in Aracoeli 37; Santa Maria in Montesanto 31; Santa Maria Maggiore 35, 92; Santa Maria Nova; Santa Maria sopra Minerva 38; Santa Prassede 35, 37, 92; Santa Pudenziana 35; Senate House 37; Temple of Antoninus and Faustina; Temple of Neptune 39; Trinità dei Monti 35, 92; Vatican 31, 32, 34, 38, 92; Vatican Museums 32, 38, 92 ; Via del Corso 92; Via del Pellegrino 33; Via della Vite 31; Via delle Sette Sale 36; Via di Pietra 33; Via Sistina 32, 35; Via Urbana 35; Via Venti Settembre 36; Villa Borghese 38; Villa Medici 35
Rosa, Salvator (1615-73) 75
Rosengarten, Albrecht (1809-93) 21, 22, 29, 45, 46, 48, 49, 112, 114
Rovere, Cristoforo delle (d.1477) 39
Rovere, Domenico delle (d.1501)
Royal Institute of British Architects 67, 77
Ruskin, John (1819-1900) 14, 15, 17, 51, 58, 59, 60, 62, 65, 67, 73, 75, 114

S
Salmon, William Forrest (1843-1911) 16
Sanmicheli, Michele (1484-1559) 67
Sansovino, Jacopo (1486-1570) 67
Scaligeri, overlords of Verona 62

Scamozzi, Vincenzo (1552-1616) 67
Scrosati, Luigi (1815-69) 71, 72
Segaloni, Matteo (fl. 1627) 46
Sellars, James (1843-1888) 12, 13, 21
Seville Cathedral 69
Sforza, Dukes of Milan 69
Sforza, Francesco (Duke of Milan, 1401-66) 71
Sforza, Ludovico Maria (Duke of Milan, 1452-1508) 73
Shields, John (1821-1912) 16, 63, 67, 69, 73, 75, 77, 86
Siciliano, Jacopo (Giacomo del Duca, 1520-c.1601) 21
Sicily 24
Siena 42: Campo; Duomo (Cathedral) 42; Palazzo del Magnifico 48; Palazzo Pollini 43, 84, 95; Palazzo Pubblico 43; Pensione Chiusarelli 42; Piazza San Giovanni 48; Torre del Mangia 48; Via Baldassarre Peruzzi 43; Via San Domenico 42
Sienese School of painting 48
Signorelli, Lucca (c.1441-1523) 42, 48
Sixtus IV (Pope, 1414-84) 39
Sixtus V (Pope, 1521-90) 39
Skirving, Alexander (c.1849-1919) 16
Smith, William James (1893-1979) 89
Soane Medallion Competition 67, 77
Solari, Guiniforte (1429-81) 71
Sommer, Giorgio (1834-1914) 5
Sophia (Queen of Sweden, 1836-1913) 20
Soria, Giovanni Battista (1581-1651) 39
South Kensington Museum 78
Southern Railway stations, London 29
Stabiae 21
Stanzione, Massimo (1585-1656) 29
Stark, Malcolm Jnr. (1854-c.1935) 16
Stefano di Sant'Agnese (fl. late 14th century) 100
Stevenson, John James (1831-1908) 87
Street, George Edmund (1824-81) 62, 64, 67
Strozzi, Filippo (1428-91) 49
Swanston, John Daniel (1868-1956) 16

T
Talenti, Francesco (14th century) 48, 49
Talenti, Simone (14th century) 48
Tedesco, Lapo (13th-14th century)
Theodoric the Ostrogoth (454-526) 53
Thomas Cook (travel firm) 19
Thomson, Alexander (1817-75) 5, 11, 16, 33, 77: Travelling studentship 11, 13; Trustees 9
Tilbury 19
Tintoretto, Jacopo (1519-94) 58, 59, 75
Titian (Tiziano Vecellio, c.1485-1576) 48, 54, 55, 58, 59, 60, 63, 75
Tivoli: Cascades 37; Hadrian's Villa 37; Porta Santa Croce 37; Temple of the Sybil; Temple of Vesta; Villa d'Este 38
Tombs 11, 23, 33, 35, 37, 45, 46, 49, 59, 62, 70, 80, 90,
Tonelli, Giuseppe (1668-1732) 97
Torre Annunziata 20
Triburtine Sybil 39

Trivulzio Candelabrum 69, 78
Tuscany 14, 42, 46,

U
Ugo, Margrave of Tuscany (950-1001) 46
Umbria 41

V
Valadier, Giuseppe (1762-1839) 39
Vanvitelli, Luigi (1700-1773) 37
Varenna 65, 104
Vasari, Giorgio (1511/12-74) 46, 47, 49
Vases 21, 86,
Vassalletto, Iacopo (13th century) 39
Vassalletto, Pietro (13th century) 39
Vatican: see Rome: Vatican
Veneto
Venice 57-60: Accademia di Belle Arte 59; Ca'd'Oro 58, 60; Calle Traghetto 58; Campo San Zanipolo 100; Dogana da Mar 67, 101; Doge's Palace 16, 58, 59, 67, 101; Fondamenti Nuovi 60; Giudecca 58; Grand Canal 57, 58; Hôtel Milan et Pensione Anglaise 57; Lagoon 57, 59; Lido 59, 100; Murano 57, 60, 67; Palazzo Contarini 58; Palazzo Foscari 58; Palazzo Grimani 58; Palazzo Pisani 58; Palazzo Spinelli 58; Piazza di San Marco 112; Piazzetta 60; Procuratie Nuove 58; Redentore 58; Rialto 57, 60; St. Mark's 58, 63; San Donato 60; San Giorgio dei Greci 60, 67, 112; San Giorgio in Alga 57; San Giorgio Maggiore 58; San Giovanni Crisostomo 60, 101; San Gregorio 60, 67, 101; San Michele 63; San Zaccaria 60, 100, 112; Santa Fosca 60; Santa Maria dei Frari 60; Santa Maria dei Miracoli 59, 60, 100, 101; Santa Maria del Carmine 60, 67; Santa Maria della Salute 58; Santi Giovanni e Paolo 59, 100, 112; Scuola di San Rocco 59, 60; Torcello 60; Zecca 101
Verona 62: Castelvecchio 62; Duomo (Cathedral) 62; Palazzo della Ragione 62; Piazza dei Signori 62, 102; Ponte di Castelvecchio 62; Prefettura 102; River Adige 62; San Zeno Maggiore 62; Sant'Anastasia 62; Santa Maria in Organo 62; Torre dei Lamberti 62; Tribunali 102
Veronese, Il (Paolo Calliari, 1528-88) 58, 60, 67
Verrocchio, Andrea del (c.1435-88) 59, 67
Vespasian (Roman Emperor, A.D. 17-79) 21, 39, 90
Vespignani, Virginio (1808-82) 48
Vicenza 62: Casa Cogollo ('Casa di Palladio') 67, 101; Contra Porti 101; Corso Andrea Palladio (Corso Principe Umberto) 62, 67, 101; Palazzo della Ragione ('Basilica') 62; Palazzo Thiene 62, 101; Teatro Olimpico 62, 67
Visconti, Dukes of Milan 64, 69
Visconti, Gian Galeazzo (1351-1402) 69, 73
Vivarini, Antonio (c.1415-76/84) 100
Vivarini, Bartolomeo (fl. 1450-99) 67

W
Walker, Dr. Frank (1938-) 109
Watson, Thomas Lennox (1850-1920) 16
Webb, Aston (1849-1930) 78
Wilde, Oscar (1854-1900) 20
Willa, (widow of Uberto, Margrave of Tuscany, 10th century) 46
William II (King of Sicily) (1155-89) 26

Giotto's Campanile, Florence Cathedral